The Colonial Era

A Documentary Reader

Edited by
Paul G. E. Clemens

D0188229

Blackwell
Publishing

Editorial material and organization © 2008 by Paul G. E. Clemens

BLACKWELL PUBLISHING
350 Main Street, Malden, MA 02148-5020, USA
9600 Garsington Road, Oxford OX4 2DQ, UK
550 Swanston Street, Carlton, Victoria 3053, Australia

The right of Paul G. E. Clemens to be identified as the Author of the Editorial Material in this Work
has been asserted in accordance with the UK Copyright, Designs, and Patents Act 1988.

First published 2008 by Blackwell Publishing Ltd

1   2008

Library of Congress Cataloging-in-Publication Data

The Colonial Era : a documentary reader / [compiled by] Paul G.E. Clemens.
    p. cm. — (Uncovering the past : documentary readers in American history)
    Includes bibliographical references and index.
    ISBN 978-1-4051-5661-5 (hardcover : alk. paper) — ISBN 978-1-4051-5662-2 (pbk. : alk. paper)
1. United States—History—Colonial period, ca. 1600–1775—Sources. I. Clemens, Paul G. E., 1947-
E187.C67 2008
973.2–dc22

2007012824

A catalogue record for this title is available from the British Library.

Set in 10/12.5pt Sabon
by SPi Publisher Services, Pondicherry, India
Printed and bound in Singapore
by Utopia Press Pte Ltd

For further information on
Blackwell Publishing, visit our website:
www.blackwellpublishing.com

The Colonial Era

Uncovering the Past: Documentary Readers in American History
Series Editors: Steven Lawson and Nancy Hewitt

The books in this series introduce students in American history courses to two important dimensions of historical analysis. They enable students to engage actively in historical interpretation, and they further students' understanding of the interplay between social and political forces in historical developments.

Consisting of primary sources and an introductory essay, these readers are aimed at the major courses in the American history curriculum, as outlined further below. Each book in the series will be approximately 225–50 pages, including a 25–30-page introduction addressing key issues and questions about the subject under consideration, a discussion of sources and methodology, and a bibliography of suggested secondary readings.

Published

Stanley Harrold
The Civil War and Reconstruction: A Documentary Reader

Paul G. E. Clemens
The Colonial Era: A Documentary Reader

In preparation

Camilla Townsend
American Indian History: A Documentary Reader

Brian Ward
The 1960s: A Documentary Reader

Robert Ingalls and David Johnson
The United States Since 1945: A Documentary Reader

Sean Adams
The Early American Republic: A Documentary Reader

for
Jesse
and
Sarah-Elizabeth

Contents

Illustrations

Maps

Figures

Tables

Series Editors' Preface

Primary sources have become an essential component in the teaching of history to undergraduates. They engage students in the process of historical interpretation and analysis and help them understand that facts do not speak for themselves. Rather, students see how historians construct narratives that recreate the past. Most students assume that the pursuit of knowledge is a solitary endeavor; yet historians constantly interact with their peers, building upon previous research and arguing among themselves over the interpretation of documents and their larger meaning. The documentary readers in this series highlight the value of this collaborative creative process and encourage students to participate in it.

Each book in the series introduces students in American history courses to two important dimensions of historical analysis. They enable students to engage actively in historical interpretation, and they further students' understanding of the interplay among social, cultural, economic, and political forces in historical developments. In pursuit of these goals, the documents in each text embrace a broad range of sources, including such items as illustrations of material artifacts, letters and diaries, sermons, maps, photographs, song lyrics, selections from fiction and memoirs, legal statutes, court decisions, presidential orders, speeches, and political cartoons.

Each volume in the series is edited by a specialist in the field who is concerned with undergraduate teaching. The goal is not to offer a comprehensive selection of material but to provide items that reflect major themes and debates; that illustrate significant social, cultural, political, and economic dimensions of an era or subject; and that inform, intrigue and inspire undergraduate students. The editor of each volume has written an introduction that discusses the central questions that have occupied historians in this field and the ways historians have used primary sources to answer them. In addition, each introductory essay contains an explanation of the kinds of materials available to investigate a particular subject, the methods by which scholars analyze them, and the considerations that go into interpreting them. Each source selection is introduced by a short headnote that gives students the necessary information and a context for understanding the document. Also, each section of the volume includes questions to guide student reading and stimulate classroom discussion.

Paul G. E. Clemens' *Colonial Era* provides students with an extensive array of well-chosen documents that cover a broad geographic sweep and attend to the diverse range of peoples, issues, and sources in North American history from the seventeenth century through the Great War for Empire in the 1750s and 1760s. Clemens provides as well a lucid introduction to the vast literature on this period and concise but rich headnotes that locate specific documents in this larger context. This volume incorporates the experiences of indigenous peoples and Africans as well as European missionaries, military men, magistrates, and ordinary colonists. The sources stretch across North America – from the West Indies to Massachusetts, Louisiana and California – and illuminate economic, military, political, diplomatic, domestic, social, and cultural developments. The reader combines well-known documents like Olaudah Equiano's memoir, John Smith's tales of Pocahontas, and Eliza Lucas Pinckney's letters with riveting accounts of ongoing conflicts between Indians and Europeans and the more mundane matters traced in wills, inventories, legal codes, and court records. These sources allow students to analyze the lives of politicians, priests, plantation mistresses, merchants, ministers, generals, chiefs, and warriors. They also provide coverage of slaves, servants, traders, farmers, criminals, travelers, and the poor as they grappled with the conquest and settlement of the vast lands of the North American continent.

Steven F. Lawson and Nancy A. Hewitt, Series Editors

Acknowledgments

I wish to thank Herman Bennett for help with Portuguese sources; Trevor Bernard, of the University of Sussex, for providing me with copies of eighteenth-century Jamaican probate inventories; Kristen Bloch for guidance on West Indian sources; Sarah-Elizabeth Clemens for a critical reading of the text; Leslie Doig for help with Massachusetts records; Lydia Edwards for transcribing a Jamaican inventory; Charles Gehring, of the New Netherlands Institute, and Kees Jan Waterman in Leiden for advice about the translation of Dutch terms; Sara Gronim, of CUNY, for information about Jane Colden; Michael Jarvis, at the University of Rochester, for comparing my account of Jeane Gardiner's trial against his copy of the original; Danielle Kovacs, of the University of Massachusetts Library, for help in identifying Francis Brinley; Penny Leveritt, at Historic Deerfield, who located images of eighteenth-century clocks for me; Lane McLaughlin, at the University of Delaware Library, who helped me with the Lawson animal illustrations; Elizabeth Margutti, of the Alderman Library of the University of Virginia, for helping me identify microfilm in the Virginia Colonial Records Project; Marianne Martin, at Colonial Williamsburg, for help with images of eighteenth-century material culture; Elisabeth Oliu for help with the chapter on culture and reading; James Robertson, of the University of the West Indies-Mona, for help with the Jamaican Archives; Laurie Rofini, at the Chester Country Archives, for showing me some uniquely interesting sources; John Vincler, at the Newberry Library, for help with images; and Lorena Walsh for the reference to Joseph Ball. I owe special thanks to Deirdre Ilkson and Janet Moth at Blackwell Publishing for editorial assistance and to Peter Coveney, Nancy Hewitt, and Steven Lawson, my editors, for seeing this project through to completion.

Introduction

Two premises about understanding colonial America shape this book: colonial history is more than just the lives of the rich and powerful; it is equally about the lives of ordinary people. Second, the story of colonial history is one that encompasses the diverse peoples of the Atlantic World. From sources such as wills, court records, diaries, tax lists, muster rolls, archaeological reports, newspapers, town meeting records, letters, and published pamphlets and books scattered in archives not only in the United States, but in Great Britain, the Caribbean, and even Spain and Portugal, one can construct a rich tapestry of experience in a colonial world. That tapestry will help answer questions that historians posed as much as half a century ago about politics and imperial relations; questions that they have posed more recently about social relations and economic arrangements; and questions they are pursuing now about personal identity, sexuality and gender, and intercultural contact.

The history of colonial America, then, is more than a study of the eastern seaboard of North America, more than a story about any one people, and more than a story about the literate elite. Rather, it is a story that encompasses Europe, the western areas of Africa, the Caribbean and Central America, and the lands of the Southwest and the Pacific Coast. Colonial America was part of an Atlantic World, and the Atlantic World, in turn, extended even to the Pacific Ocean, where settlements in what would become Peru and California depended on lifelines back to Europe across the Atlantic. In this vast area, colonial history unfolded as negotiations among diverse peoples, poor and middling as well as rich, and of many cultural backgrounds.

Forty years ago, colonial history was defined primarily as the political, religious, and imperial history of the European peoples who settled English North America, and whose descendants created the United States of America. That definition is today much too narrow. To study the colonies one must have some sense not only of early modern England, but also about life in the coastal societies of Africa; a student must understand the hurdles William Penn faced in securing colonies in West Jersey and Pennsylvania, and also how the English wrestled for a share of the Caribbean; she or he must explore Puritan theology, and also the racial ideas that first rationalized chattel slavery for the British in Barbados. Geographical and cultural breadth is essential to recapturing the colonial past. Even if one's primary interest is the English-speaking settlers in the thirteen colonies that became the new United States, reading documents from early Barbados and eighteenth-century Jamaica will provide telling counterpoints to conditions in the mainland colonies. In the same way, having some sense of the distinctive aspects of French Canada (Jesuit relations with the Hurons, sparse settlement of the St. Lawrence River Valley, Catholic culture) may help students understand early New England more fully. But "breadth" also comes from the way we read sources. The reports that colonial governors sent back to British officials about their colonies are among the most "traditional" sources used by colonial historians. Such a source can be read, as it traditionally was, to discover the factors influencing British colonial policy, but it can also tell us about the class and gender prerogatives of the official, his own sense of himself (his "identity") as a colonial bureaucrat, and about the lives of the people that the official describes in the report.

My Own Path into the Documents

I began my own work as a colonial historian in the 1970s as political and imperial history was giving way to a new-found excitement with social history. But I came to my work, which focused on Maryland's eastern shore, with little sense of exactly what the sources would tell me, and no clear ideas about the questions I might ask. I had a general sense from the new work in social history that was being done in France and Great Britain, and which had influenced historians studying colonial New England, that learning about demography (birth rates, age at death, ratio of women to men, and the like), about how ordinary people made a living (as wage workers, as servants, or as landowners), about family structure and family life (family size, roles of men and women in the household), and about the role of race and class in a society (especially in a society where slave-owning tobacco planters became powerful figures) were key to understanding this region.

But I began with nothing more than that, and an almost inexhaustible enthusiasm for reading voluminous court and probate records (wills and inventories) in the Maryland Archives in Annapolis. Early on I stumbled across a puzzling aspect of the records that became the key to my understanding of the region. In the Maryland court records, in the late 1690s, at many of the sessions of the county courts, there were long lists of English people, boys and girls, as well as young men and women, who were brought before the court as newly arrived servants to have their ages estimated and recorded. Their age, in turn, determined how long they would have to serve as servants. In addition to providing information about how important white servants initially were in a colony that would subsequently rely on slave labor, the age determinations in the court records seemed to follow a pattern. At some court sessions there were few age determinations recorded; at others, there were dozens, even hundreds, suggesting that entire shiploads of servants had recently arrived. The pattern found in one county could often be found in others as well. If the pattern really was general, it would appear too in Virginia records, so I drove with Russell Menard, who was working on similar records from Maryland's western shore counties, to the Virginia State Library in Richmond, and there confirmed that many Virginia counties, in the late 1690s, experienced the same surge in servant immigration. This, in turn, led to a set of broader questions about how conditions in England, and in the Atlantic World, might be shaping the social and economic history of distinct places in Maryland and Virginia in similar ways. In the late 1690s, in particular, a brief pause in the incessant warfare between England and France seemed to have created a trade boom whose effects crescendoed through the Chesapeake region. Counting – something social historians did a great deal of in the 1970s – the recurrence of some very ordinary behavior in local court records thus led to an argument about the relationship of a seventeenth-century Maryland county to the Atlantic World.

Working with Sources

This anecdote, if it has a practical significance, points to two crucial contributions worth remembering when working with sources: First, that their "discovery" and use is generally shaped by the questions being asked by historians in a particular period of time (that is, by the "historiography" of a field) and by the methodologies that are currently fashionable (in this case, counting). Second, that sources that have often been read for one reason can reveal unexpected answers about the past when new questions are asked. The value of the sources in this reader, then, depends in part on understanding the type of questions that historians have asked in the past and are asking today. As suggested above, those questions have changed in the last half-century, in the broadest terms, from political to social to cultural questions, and it is worth considering these changes a little more carefully.

When in 1944 the *William and Mary Quarterly* began a new series of publications on colonial history, one article dealt at length with the work of Charles McLean Andrews, the historian of the British empire in North America, a second article presented a bibliography of Andrews' published work, and a third article was by Andrews himself, "On the Writing of Colonial History." While the *Quarterly* has always been an innovative journal, and its selection of articles has reflected a remarkable diversity in the questions that have concerned historians, the predominant themes in its publication in the middle of the twentieth century concerned British imperial policy and the coming of the American Revolution; the political and literary output of such famous colonists as Thomas Jefferson, William Byrd, and James Madison; and religion in the colonies.

None of these themes disappeared in the mid-1960s (nor have they today), and historians continue to reinvestigate questions about the "Founding Fathers," about Puritan theology, about British policy toward the colonies, and about early American politics. But the articles from this period also suggested the new directions in which historians were going: John Demos published a essay on "Families in Colonial Bristol Rhode Island," with the subtitle, "An Exercise in Historical Demography" (1968); Richard Dunn offered "The Barbados Census of 1680: Profile of the Richest Colony in English America" (1969); and Pauline Maier published, in 1970, "Popular Uprisings and Civil Authority in Eighteenth-Century America." Demos' essay suggested what historians could discover about family life by analyzing, as modern demographers might, the birth, death, and marriage records from colonial churches. He used religious records, but not the sermons that others had analyzed exhaustively, to explore the lives of ordinary people. The general contours of life in seventeenth-century Barbados were well known, but most work before Dunn's was based on official government correspondence or travel narratives. By using the Barbados census, Dunn provided a much more nuanced and complete picture of life on the most exploitive of all of England's New World colonies. Publication of his article in the *Quarterly* also emphasized the fact that the West Indies were every bit as much a part of the English colonial experience as was New England or

Virginia. Maier's article looked at crowd actions, often characterized as "mob violence," to find patterns that might help explain why colonists often took the law into their own hands. Each of these essays – and dozens of other *Quarterly* articles from this period that are equally representative of the trends in colonial history – emphasized the experience of a broad range of colonial peoples and sought to explain their behavior primarily through their social situation. Each used sources that had been used differently or ignored in the past.

Historians in the last decade have ignored neither politics nor social history in writing about colonial America, but they have increasingly asked questions about how people understood themselves and their world, rather than about the "actual" make-up of that world. They have asked, that is, questions about "identity" and meaning as often as questions about behavior. In such work, for example, "race" is no longer merely a category used to count how many people were, for example, "black" and how many "white" in 1680s Barbados, but it is an unstable concept, constructed by specific peoples for specific purposes, and the historian's task is to explore the different ways the concept was defined, applied, and challenged. Equally important, work in the last decade has increasingly placed colonial history in an Atlantic context. And, additionally, much greater attention has been paid to the experiences of women and of Native Americans in colonial America. In all these areas, the *Quarterly* has reflected and often led these trends. Recent special issues of the journal have been devoted to such topics as "Constructing Race" (January 1997); "African and American Atlantic Worlds" (April 1999); and "Sexuality of Early America" (January 2003). The documents that follow in this reader reflect this breadth in defining what colonial history is about without ignoring the crucial questions and sources with which historians were engaged fifty years ago.

Some sense of the innovative use of sources can be obtained by considering three examples, drawn from different eras in the writing of history, that illustrate the historian's craft practiced with skill and imagination.

Charles Sydnor Rethinks Colonial Politics

James Madison's autobiography relates a story that has been retold by countless historians: in the 1777 election to the Virginia legislature, Madison tells us (in the third person) it was "the usage for the candidates to recommend themselves to the voters, not only by personal solicitation, but by the corrupting influence of spirituous liquors, and other treats, having a like tendency. Regarding these as equally inconsistent with the purity of moral and of republican principles...he trusted to the new views of the subject which he hoped would prevail with the people; whilst his competitors adhered to the old practices." He lost. The story serves as one piece of evidence that allowed Charles S. Sydnor, writing in the early 1950s, to recreate the world of eighteenth-century Virginia politics, a political universe quite unlike his own, or ours today. At a time when most writing about politics focused on presidential elections and legislative policy, Sydnor wrote about "political culture." Interested more in how political actors behaved, and the social context in which they sought and exercised power, than in specific political choices they made or in individual political actors (such as Madison), he suggested a strikingly different way of thinking about colonial politics. He was thus writing about a conventional topic, politics, in an unconventional way. And while he drew on all the traditional sources of evidence about colonial politics – personal letters, official accounts written for British officials, legislative reports – he also relied heavily on a play, Robert Munford's *The Candidates*, "a slapstick farce written in 1770," but not published until the end of the century. A new question and a different type of source.

Munford, a Virginia-born, English-educated tobacco planter of considerable wealth, served in numerous appointed political offices in colonial Virginia and had been elected to the House of Burgesses (the "lower house" or assembly of the colony). The play tells the story of a county election for two House seats. Burgess *Worthy* has declined to run for re-election, leaving his friend, *Wou'dbe*, to run alone against a field of hopefuls: *Sir John Toddy*, *Strutabout*, and *Smallhopes*. The play is comic, but Munford, in depicting the vulgar and conniving tactics of *Wou'dbe*'s opponents captures, Sydnor contends, much of the reality of colonial Virginia politics. This was a politic world that turned almost exclusively on the reputation and standing of the rich and the powerful among their lesser neighbors, the "vulgar herd," and in which winning, as Madison ruefully reflected, depended on "swilling the planters with bimbo." In one of many exchanges between a candidate and his neighbors, *Wou'dbe* is told that others have said that he was "the cause of these new taxes." He refuses to deny that he would support new taxes if the legislature found them necessary, to which a voter, *Guzzle* (appropriately drinking at the time), asks bluntly, "And what the devil good do you do then?" Answering modestly, as Madison might have wished, "As much as I have abilities to do," he is again challenged by *Guzzle* as to whether he would help get the price of rum lowered, to which he bluntly responds, "I could not." At the play's end, *Worthy* re-enters the contest, to help his friend, and they together win election to the Burgesses, but along the way the reader has been introduced to a world in which backbiting, influence, alcohol, and false promises are all too capable of defeating political virtue. Sydnor goes to "traditional" historical sources to support his use of *The Candidates*, but, for our purposes, what is most striking about his work is how he used a play to answer questions about politics, and how the theme of the play suggested questions that others had ignored, about how politics operated in eighteenth-century Virginia.[1]

Philip Curtin Asks a New Question about the Slave Trade

Philip Curtin, a historian of western, sub-Saharan Africa and of the impact of the slave trade on the peoples of that region, asked, as he began research on a new project in the 1960s, just how many people were forcibly removed from Africa and brought as slaves to the New World. Curtin was a social historian, and comfortable using quantitative data systematically. The answer, Curtin knew, to his question about the scale of the slave trade that had been given in virtually every study of Africa or of New World slavery was that no one knew or could ever really be sure of its scale, as there were no records. Having asserted that the answer was unknowable, each study then proceeded to provide an answer – a conjecture, an estimate, an informed guess – of somewhere around 15 million people. Curtin first asked, why was this figure repeated so often by scholars who acknowledged they had no real evidentiary basis for the number? What he found was two "genealogies" of citations: a given figure, that cited, as its source, a source that cited another source, that cited yet another source, leading back to an "original" source, that was every bit as speculative as the now widely cited figure of 15 million. To take one of the two examples Curtin outlined: many modern histories of Africa in the 1960s used the figures on slave imports provided by R. R. Kuczynski in 1936 in his study, *Population Movements*. Kuczynski, in turn, had taken his figure (he had come up

[1] Charles S. Sydnor, *American Revolutionaries in the Making: Political Practices on Washington's Virginia* (New York: Free Press, 1965), originally published as *Gentlemen Freeholders* (Chapel Hill: University of North Carolina Press for the Institute of Early American History and Culture, 1952). Madison's story appears on p. 57, but the quote comes from Douglass Adair, ed., "James Madison's Autobiography," *William and Mary Quarterly*, 3rd ser., II (1945), 199–200. The references to "vulgar herd" and "swilling the planters with bimbo" are Sydnor's titles for chapters 3 and 4. The quotes from the play come from Douglass Adair and Jay B. Hubbell, "Robert Munford's 'The Candidates'," *William and Mary Quarterly*, 3rd ser., V (1948), 217 ("slapstick farce"), 243 (dialog). Adair's introduction to these two documents anticipated much of Sydnor's analysis.

with a total of 14,650,000 people who had been imported as slaves in the Americas between the sixteenth and nineteenth centuries) from perhaps the most eminent historian of that era of the African American experience: W. E. B. DuBois. DuBois had estimated in 1911 that 15 million slaves were imported to the Americas. DuBois' statement began with a caution, "[t]he exact number of slaves imported is not known." DuBois, to conclude this brief trip through the sources, had cited the 1861 work of Edward Dunbar, which had provided a chronological breakdown of slave imports from 1500 to 1850 and concluded the total was 13,887,500. Dunbar's essay, published as America was drifting toward civil war, was an anti-slavery statement, and appeared in a journal he edited that dealt with Mexican politics. As Curtin wryly noted, historians might well have "identified the original author [for their own estimate of the slave trade] as 'an obscure American publicist' [Dunbar] rather than 'an eminent student of population statistics' [Kuczynski]," but, of course, they did not. Equally dismaying to Curtin was the fact that standard textbooks of that time could be found that provided estimates ranging from as few as 3.5 million to as many as 25 million.

Curtin's second question, then, was how many slaves were actually brought from Africa, and how many reached the Americas? To a moralist, such a question was not the most important one: one kidnapping, one enslavement, one death in the Middle Passage (the voyage from Africa to the Americas), or one sale was too many. Curtin, of course, condemned slavery too, but he wanted to understand the Atlantic slave trade in ways that others had never bothered to explore. From what regions of Africa did slaves come? To what regions in the New World were they sent? How did the answers to these questions change over time? The answers depend – and this is one way that colonial historians, who almost always work with fragmentary evidence, approach their craft – on piecing together literally thousands of records of exports and imports of human cargoes. Ships stopping at European outposts on the African coast, ships entering the Chesapeake Bay, ships paying duties to a European customs service for every enslaved passenger transported – each became a piece of an enormous puzzle. He worked entirely from published sources, sources that had been sitting in libraries inviting historians to explore such a question systematically, rather than do any fresh digging in the archives. The answers he arrived at opened the door for numerous more specialized studies of the impact of the slave trade on particular regions of Africa and the Americas, and provided a context that allowed other historians of slavery and slave trade to ask entirely new questions about the individual experiences of the women and men caught up in the Atlantic movement of peoples.

John Demos Explores the Boundary between History and Fiction

The focus on the experience of individual people, and on the distinctive perspective that different people have on a particular event, marks much of the current work in colonial history. One particularly imaginative study of this kind is John Demos' *The Unredeemed Captive: A Family Story from Early America*. John Demos tries to tell the story of a family that lived in Deerfield, Massachusetts, when in the winter of 1704 the town was attacked by Indians and their French allies. His protagonists, the Williamses, were not just any family, however, but the family of village minister John Williams and perhaps one of the targets of the attack. When some twenty Mohawk and Abenaki warriors burst into his dwelling house, he unsuccessfully tried to fight them off, then saw his two youngest children and his female slave murdered, while he, his wife, and his five other children were carried away by the invaders. The Williamses faced a long march to a distant land, French Canada, and along the way those who could not keep up, including Eunice Mather Williams, mother of the five surviving children, would be killed.

When Demos began working on this book, he had hoped to recover both the experiences of the Native Americans who attacked Deerfield and then became the masters of the captive Williams family, and of the captives themselves. He was unable to do it – occasionally historians must admit that the sources simply will not yield enough information to answer the questions they ask. The voluminous records left by the French Jesuit missionaries in Canada allowed Demos to put Native Americans fully in the story, but he still "felt incapable of understanding Indians well enough to place them at center-stage." Coming to terms with what it meant to be a captive of the Indians, for the Deerfield survivors, in general, and the, the six surviving Williamses, in particular, became the focus of his work. These European Americans, Demos believed, had "been hard to understand; but after many years of trying, I [thought] I knew them." But even here there was a major problem: Eunice, John's 7-year-old daughter. While her brothers and sisters would be bought (they were essentially slaves) by French settlers, and then eventually ransomed back to New England along with their father, Eunice would remain the "unredeemed captive" of Demos' title. Raised among French Mohawks, she married a Mohawk, and refused not only to return to New England, but, for a long time, even to meet with those who traveled to Canada in hopes of bringing her back to her natal family. When, after her marriage, an intermediary tried to negotiate a meeting between her and her father, she would say nothing, except "No" (and only in French and Mohawk). Demos asks, "What were *her* feelings – held tight, though they were, behind the 'steel in her breast'? Her husband gives us a clue, with his reference to her father's remarriage. And there is, as well a certain logic in her situation. Otherwise we can only speculate – only imagine – but that much, at least, we must try" (pp. xii, 108). Demos quite consciously refuses to step across the blurred line separating history from fiction, but he does try to "imagine" what Eunice may have thought and felt about her experience of captivity. How far will sources let us determine not just "what happened," but, equally importantly, how people experienced their lives?

Asking Questions of the Documents

For a colonial historian, an eighteenth-century clock, a letter from a sixteenth-century explorer to a European patron, a will of a Pennsylvania widow, a newspaper advertisement offering a reward for the return of a runaway Indian slave, a poem about Christian virtues, or an account of an attempted abortion in the court record of a defamation case are all different types of evidence for the writing of stories about early American history. Interpreting this evidence, asking new questions of documents that have been used by other historians, piecing together different types of evidence, re-examining the assumptions that make some types of evidence seemingly more valuable than others – each of these is what makes doing history, in general, and colonial history, in particular, fun.

I have provided a set of questions for each chapter and an introduction for each document that should help the reader understand the document's "significance." These guides are meant to help you to ask your own questions about the sources. As a starting point, it is useful to think about how the questions you find in each chapter relate to the documents. In chapter 1, "English and African Background," for example, I selected four documents that are best read "against" each other: accounts of Europe against accounts of Africa; statistical accounts against descriptive accounts. How can one compare the categories used in Gregory King's statistical account of seventeenth-century English social structure with William Harrison's sixteenth-century description of English social classes? What assumptions did these two writers share about social classes? Why might literate, and politically well-connected men like King and Harrison have considered colonization of North America by English settlers a good thing? One can just as readily compare and contrast the sixteenth-century Portuguese account of Africa with the eighteenth-century African–British account in the same chapter. Or *can* one, given the differences in time and culture between the accounts? Remembering who the author (or engraver) is of each written (or visual) source is important. How does the document reflect her or his situation? What assumptions might influence the way they describe their own experience or that of others? For what audience was the text or representation intended?

Consider, to take a second example, three of the engravings in chapter 2, "Images of the New World." One is a sixteenth-century depiction of a European explorer observing naked "savages" in a New World setting, drawn by an artist who had never been to the Americas and who based his drawing on what may have been a somewhat fictionalized account of a voyage of exploration. Another was drawn in the early seventeenth century by an artist who had actually made several trips to various parts of the Americas and observed numerous Native American people. A third was engraved from a painting done in England for which a Native American woman, Pocahontas (Rebecca), actually sat for the portrait, and may have played a role in determining how she was to be depicted. What do each of these tell us about the way Native Americans looked and acted? What do they tell us about the way Europeans thought Native Americans looked and acted?

Chapter 5, "Founding Colonies," presents a set of "traditional" documents that speak to the institutional arrangements and ideological assumptions that went into creating New World societies. At the very least, they represent the range of distinctive assumptions that colonists brought to the New World. But they also suggest other questions. Are the assumptions of the West Indian servant and slave owners, who wrote draconian codes to control their coerced laborers, incompatible with the social vision expressed in the other two documents? If not, how do you make the fit? If so, how do we explain the existence of slavery and indentured servitude in these colonies? Can we read beyond the formulas in these documents to how people actually behaved? Do slave and servant codes perhaps express fears that have arisen from lived experience in the tobacco and sugar-producing islands of the Caribbean? The questions that conclude the chapter are meant to help you think about some of the meanings of the documents. Other meanings you will hopefully discover for yourself.

In several chapters, I have grouped a set of documents that provide multiple perspectives on a specific experience or event, thus making comparison easier. Thus there are multiple accounts, in chapter 6, "Northern Colonies," of the 1704 Deerfield raid (mentioned above): one dealing with the brutality of the raid itself, one a survival story of the march of the captives to French Canada, and the third an almost scripted account (what we would expect a New England Puritan to say about his stay among

French Catholic missionaries) of captivity. How does living through one experience perhaps affect the memory of another part of the captivity account? What distinction should we make about accounts written immediately after the event and those written years later? Another set of grouped documents, those in chapter 11, "Slavery," focus on newspaper advertisements for runaway laborers in Pennsylvania, Maryland, Virginia, and South Carolina. These advertisements reflect, in the first instance, what slave and servant owners thought about the economic value of their laborers. We suspect, because the owners wanted their laborers back, that the descriptions are as "accurate" as the owners could make them. But granted that, in what ways might they still be shaped by the owners' gender, racial, and class assumptions? What, then, can we learn about the lives of coerced laborers in the colonies from these depictions? What do they suggest about the different worlds of servants and slaves? Of laborers in South Carolina and those in the Chesapeake? Of women and men held in bondage? Half a dozen records is obviously just a sample. A sample such as this can raise questions but not "definitively" answer these questions. How many of these advertisements would one need to look at to begin to draw conclusions safely?

Questions can also be asked across chapters. The topical chapters that structure this reader are not arbitrary; they reflect the categories that historians employ in their study of the field. But these categories are also not fixed, exclusive, or the only possible arrangement of the subject matter. To take two examples: once could rearrange the documents to provide a more geographical focus, and create, alongside the seventeenth-century Northern, Southern, and Borderlands chapters, a chapter exclusively on the British West Indies:

Slave and Servant Codes in the Seventeenth-Century English West Indies
    (Founding Colonies)
Hans Sloane's Observations on Living in Jamaica, 1707 (Southern Colonies)
Inventory of the Slaves of Thomas Beach, Clarendon Parish, Jamaica,
    May 1, 1776 (Everyday Life)

In the same way, although there are numerous documents on gender relations, there is no chapter exclusively on women, yet there are documents that could easily be grouped on the topic:

From the Letterbook of Eliza Lucas Pinckney, 1742 (Family and Gender
    Relations)
The Journal of Esther Edwards Burr: on the Reading of Richardson's
    Pamela, 1755 (Culture)
Phillis Wheatley, *On Virtue*, 1773 (Culture)

One could also create a "chapter" on the ecology of early America, another theme that runs through much of the recent scholarship:

Lawson's History of North Carolina, 1709: Description of Bear and Opossum (Images of the New World)
The Natural Wonders of California: Jose de Gálvez's Expedition, 1769–1770, as Recorded by Father (Franciscan) Juan Crespí (Borderlands)
Cadwallader Colden [Coldengham, New York] to Mr. Peter Collinson [London, England], on Women as Botanists, November 13, 1742 (Culture)

The purpose of this exercise, again, is not to suggest that the categories we use to describe the colonial past are arbitrary, but that the questions we ask determine which documents are important and what their meaning is. As you think about colonial history and formulate your own questions, try to make connections across the chapters as well as within the chapters of this reader.

Several of the conventions employed throughout the reader require a brief comment before one turns to the documents themselves.

Timeframe. The reader contains documents chronologically that stretch from early sixteenth-century comments on fifteenth-century events to documents that come from the late eighteenth century. Most of the documents, however, relate to the period from the sixteenth century to the conclusion in 1763 of the Great War for Empire between France and Great Britain (alternatively called by contemporaries the French and Indian War or the Seven Years War). Where I have strayed beyond 1763, I have done so for a purpose. In the case, for example, of James Ramsay's writings from the 1780s on the British slave trade, I have included the document because Ramsay formulated his ideas in the middle of the eighteenth century, and made the connection between abolition and reorganization of the empire well before others reached the same conclusion, but he did not feel comfortable publishing these ideas until the imperial crisis occasioned by the loss of the American colonies. The ideas in the document, thus, come largely from the last colonial period, while the document itself better relates to the era of the American Revolution.

Through 1752, the official year in the British empire was defined by the Julian calendar, and began on March 25. Typically, a date that fell in January, February, or the first 24 days of March would be expressed as falling in two years, as, for example, February 11, 1731/2 (the date of George Washington's birth using the Julian calendar). But because the Julian calendar had built in an error in its estimate of the solar years, the new calendar that went into effect in 1752 also had to adjust the days as well, so

Washington's birthday became February 22, 1732. Throughout the text I have used the dates given in the documents themselves.

Money. Occasionally the documents include monetary values, expressed either in British pounds sterling or the colonial money of account. The British and colonial pounds were the equivalent of 20 shillings, and each shilling was worth 12 pence (or 240 pence to the pound). A monetary notation of £ 15 6 3, would be read fifteen pounds, six shillings, and three pence. If the notation were for less than a pound, it would be rendered with a slash separating shillings from pence, as in 6/3 (six shillings and three pence), while pence alone were usually written with a "d," as in 3d (three pence). The Bristol port records and the New England farm account in the chapter on "Economy," and the probate inventories in the chapter on "Everyday Life" contain extensive monetary notations. Rather than wonder what the modern "equivalent" of these values might be, it is best to use such values to determine the equivalent worth of dissimilar objects (how does the value of a day's labor by a fieldhand compare to the value of a cow?).

Further exploration. Many of the documents in this reader could lead a reader to one or more internet sites that provide additional information about the topic. Putting "Deerfield" and "1704" into a search engine, for example, will turn up numerous sites that recount the history of the Deerfield raid, including one for *Historic Deerfield*, the primary local organization dedicated to preserving and exploring the history of the community and the raid. Knowing the "author" of a site is a first step in assuring that the material on it is reliable. Many sites change their content repeatedly and they occasionally disappear completely. If you wish to explore some of the questions raised in this reader on the internet, do so, but apply the same close reading to the site itself as you do to the materials on the site.

There are, in addition, a number of databases available either through online subscriptions by university libraries or as standalone CD-ROMs in university libraries that are worth noting, and where relevant they are cited in the text. Such databases have, to note the most crucial example, made everything published in Great Britain and British North America in the eighteenth century available online (if your library has a subscription to *Early American Imprints* and to the *Eighteenth Century Online*).

Spelling. There was no standard way to spell in the colonial period. Moreover, capitalization and the use of contractions did not follow modern rules of grammar. A typical colonial document would replace the "the" we would expect to find with "y^e." I have approached this problem in different ways in different documents. Some documents have been silently modernized, where that does not seem to create a significant change in meaning. If modernizing the text might change the meaning (changing "negroe," for example to "Negro"), I have erred on the side of historical caution and left the original spelling. Other documents have been left completely in the original language. In some cases, this has been to done simply to assure that readers get some of the flavor of colonial prose; in others, it has been to emphasize the distance between us, as readers, and the person who originally wrote the document. The third case involves documents originally written in a language other than English. Here I have drawn on someone else's translation, and that translation, the reader should remember, is in itself a work of scholarship and a major "interpretation" of the meaning of the document.

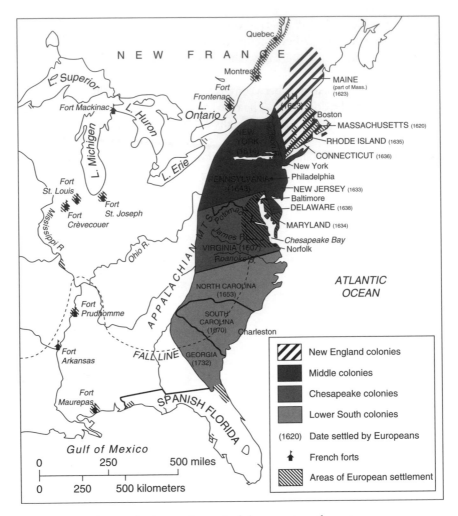

Map 1   American colonies at the end of the seventeenth century
From Mark Newman, *Mapping the American Promise: Historical Geography Workbook*, vol. 1: *To 1877* (Boston: Bedford Books, 1998), p. 27.

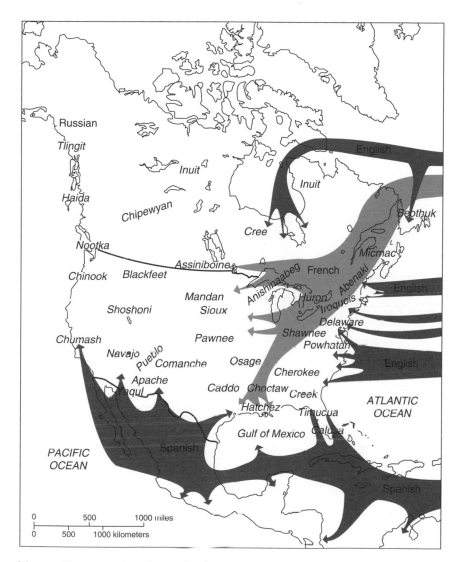

Map 2   European invasions of Indian America
From Colin G. Calloway, *First Peoples: A Documentary Survey of American Indian History*, 2nd edn. (Boston and New York: Bedford/St. Martin's, 2004), p. 65.

Part I   Beginnings

Chapter 1   English and African Background

1. Gregory King's *A Scheme of the Income and Expence of the several Families of England, calculated for the Year 1688*

Gregory King (1648–1712) was a British political economist. Working for various patrons and administrative offices, King developed a mathematical approach to problems the government needed to address – especially financial and demographic questions. His "Natural and political observations upon the state and condition of England, 1696" was produced for a patron and contained his famous "Scheme" (reproduced, in part, below). The "Scheme" was not published until late in the eighteenth century.

The "Scheme" should be read from at least two perspectives: as a description of the social structure of England at the time that colonization of the North Atlantic was progressing rapidly; and as the perception of a well-born, literate Englishman about the "natural" order of his society and the usefulness of particular classes.

Number of Families	Ranks, Degrees, Titles and Qualifications	Heads per Family	Yearly Income per Head		Yearly Expense per Head		
			£	s	£	s	d
160	Temporal Lords	40	80	0	70	0	0
26	Spiritual Lords	20	65	0	45	0	0
800	Baronets	16	55	0	49	0	0
600	Knights	13	50	0	45	0	0
3,000	Esquires	10	45	0	41	0	0
12,000	Gentlemen	8	35	0	32	0	0
5,000	Persons in greater offices and positions	8	30	0	26	0	0
5,000	Persons in lesser offices and positions	6	20	0	17	0	0
2,000	Eminent merchants and traders by sea	8	50	0	37	0	0
8,000	Lesser merchants and trader by sea	6	53	0	27	0	0
10,000	Persons in the law	7	22	0	18	0	0
2,000	Eminent clergymen	6	12	0	10	0	0
8,000	Lesser clergymen	5	10	0	9	4	0
40,000	Freeholders of the better sort	7	13	0	11	15	0
120,000	Freeholders of the lesser sort	5 ½	10	0	9	10	0
150,000	Farmers	5	8	10	8	5	0
15,000	Persons in liberal arts and sciences	5	12	0	11	0	0
50,000	Shopkeepers and tradesmen	4 ½	10	0	9	0	0
60,000	Artisans and handicrafts	4	9	10	9	0	0
5,000	Naval officers	4	20	0	18	0	0
4,000	Military officers	4	15	0	14	0	0
500,586		5 ½	12	18	11	15	4
50,000	Common seamen	3	7	0	7	10	0
364,000	Labouring people and out-servants	3 ½	4	10	4	12	0
400,000	Cottagers and paupers	3 ¼	2	0	2	5	0

(*Continued*)

Table 1.1   (*Continued*)

Number of Families	Ranks, Degrees, Titles and Qualifications	Heads per Family	Yearly Income per Head		Yearly Expense per Head		
			£	s	£	s	d
35,000	Common soldiers	2	7	0	7	10	0
849,000		3 ¼	3	5	3	9	0
[30,000]	Vagrants; as gipsies, thieves, beggars, etc.	1	2	0	4	0	0
500,586	Encreasing the wealth of the kingdom	5 ½	12	18	11	15	4
849,000	Decreasing the wealth of the kingdom	3 ¼	3	3	3	7	6
500,586	Encreasing [total] 3,023,700						
849,000	Decreasing [total] 622,500						
1,349,586	Neat totals 2,401,200						

Source: *The Political and Commercial Works of that celebrated Writer Charles D'Avenant, LL.D., Relating to the Trade and Revenue of England, The Plantation Trade, the East Indian Trade, and African Trade,* 5 vols. (London, 1771), II, 184. King's table had ten columns, of which five have been omitted from this extract; in addition, data from the last three rows of King's table is summarized in the last three rows above.

Study: Peter Laslett, *The World We Have Lost: England Before the Industrial Age* (London: Methuen, 1965, 1984).

2. William Harrison's *Description of England,* 1577

William Harrison was born in London in 1535, and raised and educated in the city; he then served much of his life as a pastor of a rural parish in Essex. His chronicle of England was, in significant measure, a product of his own experiences mixing with the peoples of the realm. In Chapter V of the Description, *"Of Degrees of People in the Commonwealth of England," he divides the English into four social classes: gentlemen, citizens (of towns, including merchants), yeomen (including craftsmen), and laborers (also including craftsmen). The extract below includes his description of merchants, yeomen, and laborers, groups which would, in the next century, supply most of the English New World settlers.*

In this place are also our merchants to be installed, as amongst the citizens (although they often change estate with gentlemen, as gentlemen do with them, by a mutual conversion of the one into the other), whose number is so increased in these our days that their only maintenance is the cause of the exceeding prices of foreign wares, which otherwise, when every nation was permitted to bring in her own commodities, were far better cheap and more plentifully to be had.... I do not deny but that the navy of the land is in part maintained by their traffic, and so are the high prices of wares kept up, now they have gotten the only sale of things, upon pretense of better furtherance of the commonwealth, into their own hands, whereas in times past, when the strange bottoms [foreign vessels] were suffered to come in, we had sugar for 4d. the pound that now, at the writing of this treatise, is worth half-a-crown, raisins or currants for a penny that now are holden at 6d., and sometime at 8d., and 10d. the pound, nutmegs at 2½ d. the ounce, ginger at a penny a ounce, prunes at half penny farthing, great raisins three pound for a penny, cinnamon at 4d. the ounce, cloves at 2d., and pepper at 12d. and 16d. the pound. Whereby we may see the sequel if things not always but very seldom to be such as is pretended in the beginning.

The wares that they carry out of the realm are for the most part broad-cloths and kerseys of all colors, likewise cottons, friezes, rugs, tin, wool, our best beer, baize, bustian, mockadoes tufted and lain, rash, lead, fells, etc. [woolen and cotton goods], which being shipped at sundry ports of our coasts, are borne from thence into all quarters of the world and there are either exchanged for other wares or ready money, to the great gain and commodity of our merchants. And whence in times past their chief trade was into Spain, Portugal, France, Flanders, Dansk [Denmark], Norway, Scotland, and Iceland only, now in these days, as men not contented with these journeys, they have sought out the East and West Indies and made now and then suspicious [promising] voyages, not only unto the Canaries and New Spain, but likewise into Cathay, Moscovia [Russia], Tartary, and the regions thereabout, from whence (as they say) they bring home great commodities. But alas! I see not by all their travel that the prices of things are any whit abated... This only I know, that every function and several vocation striveth with other which of them should have all the water of commodity run into their own cistern.

Yeomen are those which by our law are called *legales homines*, freemen born English, and may dispend of their own free land in yearly revenue to the sum of 40s. sterling, or £6 as money goeth in our times.... The truth is that the word [yeoman] is derived from the Saxon term aeoman, or geoman, which signifieth (as I have read) a settled or staid man, such I mean as, being married and of some years, betaketh himself to stay in the place of his abode for the better maintenance of himself and his family, whereof the single sort have no regard but are likely to be still fleeting, now hither, now thither, which argueth want of stability in determination and resolution of judgment for the execution of things of any importance. This sort of people have a certain pre-eminence and more estimation than laborers and the common sort of artificers, and these commonly live wealthily, keep good houses, and travail to get riches. They are also for the most part farmers to gentlemen... or at the leastwise artificers; and with grazing, frequenting of markets, and keeping of servants (not idle servants as the gentlemen do, but such as get both their own and part of their master's living) do come to great wealth, insomuch that many of them are able and do buy the lands of unthrifty gentlemen, and often, setting their sons to the schools, to the universities, and to the Inns of the Court, or otherwise leaving them sufficient lands whereupon they may live without labor, do make them by those means to become gentlemen; these were they that in times past made all France afraid. And albeit they be not called master as gentlemen are, or sir, as to knights appertaineth, but only John and Thomas, etc., yet have they been found to have done very good service; and the Kings of England in foughten battles were wont to remain among them (who were their footmen) as the French kings did amongst their horsemen, the prince thereby showing where his chief strength did consist.

The fourth and last sort of people in England are day laborers, poor husbandmen, and some retailers (which have no free land), copyholders, and all artificers, as tailors, shoemakers, carpenters, brickmakers, masons, etc. As for slaves and bondmen, we have none; nay, such is the privilege of our country by the especial grace of God and bounty of our princes that if any come hither from other realms, so soon as they set foot on land they become so free of condition as their masters, whereby all note of servile bondage is utterly removed from them, wherein we resemble (not the Germans, who had slaves also, though such as in respect of the slaves of other countries might well be reputed free, but) the old Indians and the Taprobanes [Ceylonese], who supposed it a great injury to Nature to make or suffer them to be bond whom she in her wanted course doth product and bring forth free. This fourth and last sort of people, therefore, have neither voice nor authority in the commonwealth, but are to be ruled and not to rule other; yet they are not altogether neglected, for in cities and corporate towns, for default of yeomen, they are fain to make up their inquests of such manner of people. And in villages they are commonly made churchwardens, sidemen [church official], aleconners [ale inspectors], now and then constables, and many times enjoy the name of headboroughs.

Source: William Harrison, *The Description of England* (1577), ed. Georges Edelen (Ithaca, NY: Cornell University Press, for the Folger Shakespeare Library, 1968), pp. 115–18.

Study: Keith Wrightson, *English Society, 1580–1680* (New Brunswick, NJ: Rutgers University Press, 1982).

3. Gomes Eanes de Zurara's Chronicle of the Initial Portuguese Voyages to Sub-Saharan Africa, 1453

Gomes Eanes de Zurara (1410–73/4) was the chronicler for the Portuguese Crown of the initial fifteenth-century voyages made to western Sub-Saharan Africa (south, geographically, of Cape Bojador). He wrote within the chivalric tradition, and saw these voyages as an extension of the war against Islam in Spain and northern Africa. Unlike later chroniclers of French, Spanish, and English exploits Zurara had little concern with an accurate description of the lands and peoples the Portuguese encountered, unless such a depiction helped him describe the valor of Portuguese soldiers or the greatness of Portuguese rulers (João I, and his third son, Henrique, known as "Henry the Navigator"). His account, Crónica dos feitos de Guiné, *was written in 1453.*

CHAPTER LX. *How those caravels arrived at the river of Nile, and of the Guineas that they took.*

Now these caravels having passed by the land of Sahara . . . came in sight of the two palm trees that Dinis Diaz had met with before, by which they understood that they were at the beginning of the land of the Negroes. And at this sight they were glad indeed, and would have landed at once; but they found the sea so rough upon that coast that by no manner of means could they accomplish their purpose. And some of those who were present said afterwards that it was clear from the smell that came off the land how good must be the fruits of that country, for it was so delicious that from the point they reached, though they were on the sea, it seemed to them that they stood in some gracious fruit garden ordained for the sole end of their delight. And if our men showed on their side a great desire of gaining the land, no less did the natives of it show their eagerness to receive them into it; but of the reception they offered I do not care to speak, for according to the signs they made to our men from the first, they did not intend to abandon the beach without very great loss to one side or the other. Now the people of this green land are wholly black, and hence this is called Land of the

Negroes, or Land of Guinea. Wherefore also, the men and women thereof are called "Guineas," as if one were to say " Black Men." And when the men in the caravels saw the first palms and lofty trees as we have related, they understood right well that they were close to the river of Nile, at the point where it floweth into the western sea, the which river is there called the Senegal. . . .

CHAPTER LXIII: *How the caravels set forth from the river, and of the voyage which they made.*

ALL these secrets and marvels did the genius of our prince bring before the eyes of the people of our kingdom, for although all the matters here spoken of concerning the marvels of the Nile could not be witnessed by his own eyes, for that were impossible, it was a great matter that his ships arrived there, where 'tis not recorded that any other ship of these parts had ever come. And this may truthfully be affirmed according to the matters which at the beginning of this book I have related concerning the passage of Cape Bojador, and also from the astonishment which the natives of that land showed when they saw the first ships, for they went to them imagining they were fish, or some other natural product of the sea. But now returning to our history, after that deed was thus concluded, it was the wish of all the three captains to endeavour to make an honourable booty, adventuring their bodies in whatsoever peril might be necessary.

And because there were so many of those blacks on land that by no means could they disembark either by day or night, Gomez Pirez sought to show that he desired to go among them on peaceful terms, and so placed upon the shore a cake and a mirror and a sheet of paper on which he drew a cross. And the natives when they came there and found those things, broke up the cake and threw it far away, and with their assegais they cast at the mirror, till they had broken it in many pieces, and the paper they tore, showing that they cared not for any of these things.

"Since it is so," said Gomez Pirez to his crossbowmen, "shoot at them with your bows that they may at least understand that we are people who can do them hurt, whenever they will not agree to a friendly understanding." But the blacks seeing the others' intention, began to pay them back, launching at them also their arrows and assegais, some of which our men brought home to this kingdom. And the arrows are so made that they have no feathers, nor a notch for the string to enter, but they are all smooth and short, and made of rushes or reeds, and their iron points are long and some are made of wood fixed in the shafts, which are like the iron spindles with which the women of this country spin. And they use also other little harpoons of iron, the which darts are all equally poisoned with plants. And their assegais are each made with seven or eight harpoon-like prongs, and the plant they use is very venomous.

So all the captains there agreed to make sail, with the intention of entering into the River of Nile, but no one was able to light upon it save Lawrence Diaz... And he, because he was alone, did not dare enter into the river, but he went with the little boat to the place where they took the blacks on the outward voyage; howbeit he turned back without doing anything worthy of mention. And since he did not fall in with the convoy again he came straight to Lagos. And in this wise Gomez Pirez lost the company of the other caravels; and following his course towards Portugal, after taking in water at the isle of Arguim, he came to the Rio do Ouro, and sailed as far up the port where he had been the preceding year with Antam Gonçalvez and Diego Affonso, and there presently the Moors came, and in taking security of them he learnt there were no merchants there. But they sold him a black for a price of five doubloons... [and] he [said] he would return there, when he would find blacks in abundance, and gold, and merchandise by which he might gain much profit.

Source: Gomes Eannes de Azurara, *The Chronicle of the Discovery and Conquest of Guinea*, trans. Charles Raymond Beazley and Edgar Prestage (New York: B. Franklin, 1963). Based on *Crónica dos feitos de Guiné*, the original English edition of which was published by the Hakluyt Society, no. 95. The author's name is most often today listed as Gomes Eanes de Zurara.

Study: Kenneth Baxter Wolf, "The 'Moors' of West Africa and the Beginnings of the Portuguese Slave Trade," *Journal of Medieval and Renaissance Studies*, 14 (1994), 449–69.

4. Olaudah Equiano Recounts his Life in Africa before Being Captured by Slave Traders, 1789

Olaudah Equiano wrote The Interesting Narrative of the Life of Olaudah Equiano *in London in 1789 in part as a protest against the slave trade. Equiano was born in Africa around 1745. He was captured, enslaved in Africa, then sold into the Atlantic slave trade. When no one purchased him in Barbados in 1756, he was taken to Virginia, bought by a planter, and then sold to a ship's captain. There he learned to read (taught by a servant) and to navigate, and he would spend much of the next decade at sea, enslaved but with considerable autonomy. Being allowed to trade on his own account, Equiano would be able to buy his freedom in 1766. He would eventually move to London and become involved in evangelical politics and abolitionism. Equiano's* Narrative *contains some unattributed passages from the accounts of others (standard practice at the time), and as Vincent Carretta's remarkable biography of Equiano demonstrates, Equiano may also have fashioned part of the narrative of his life from the memories of other Africans whom he knew, but this in no way diminishes his telling of his life as, to use Carretta's term, a "self-made man," moving between the worlds of slavery and freedom, Africa and Europe, Old World and New.*

The excerpt below comes from the 1791 American edition of Equiano's Narrative.

Chapter 1. The author's account of his country...That part of Africa, known by the name of Guinea, to which the trade for slaves is carried on, extends along the coast above 3400 miles, from the Senegal to Angola, and includes a variety of kingdoms. Of these the most considerable is the kingdom of Benin, both as to extent and wealth, the richness and cultivation of the soil, the power of its king, and the number and warlike disposition of the inhabitants. It is situated nearly under the line, and extends along the coast about 170 miles, but runs back into the interior part of Africa to a distance hitherto I believe unexplored by any traveller; and seems only terminated at length by the empire of Abyssinia, near 1500 miles from its beginning. This kingdom is divided into many provinces or districts: in one of the most remote and fertile of which , called Eboe, I was born, in the year 1745, in a charming fruitful vale, named Essaka. The distance of this province from the capital of Benin and the sea coast must be very consid erable; for I had never heard of white men or Europeans, nor of the sea: and our subjection to the king of Benin was little more than nominal; for every transaction of the government, as far as my slender observation extended, was conducted by the chiefs or elders of the place....

As our manners are simple, our luxuries are few. The dress of both sexes is nearly the same. It generally consists of a long piece of calico, or muslin, wrapped loosely round the body, somewhat in the form of a highland plaid. This is usually dyed blue, which is our favourite colour. It is extracted from a berry, and is brighter and richer than any I have seen in Europe. Besides this, our women of distinction wear golden ornaments; which they dispose with some profusion on their arms and legs. When our women are not employed with the men in tillage, their usual occupation is spinning and weaving cotton, which they afterwards dye, and make it into garments. They also manufacture earthen vessels, of which we have many kinds. Among the rest tobacco pipes, made after the same fashion, and used in the same manner, as those in Turkey.

Our manner of living is entirely plain; for as yet the natives are unacquainted with those refinements in cookery which debauch the taste: bullocks, goats, and poultry, supply the greatest part of their food. These constitute likewise the principal wealth of the country, and the chief articles of its commerce. The flesh is usually stewed in a pan; to make it savoury we sometimes use also pepper, and other spices, and we have salt made of wood ashes. Our vegetables are mostly plantains, eadas, yams, beans, and Indian corn. The head of the family usually eats alone; his wives and slaves have also their separate tables. Before we taste food we always wash our hands: indeed our cleanliness on all occasions is extreme; but on this it is an indispensable ceremony. After washing, libation is made, by pouring out a small portion of the drink, in a certain place, for the spirits of departed relations, which the natives suppose to preside over their conduct, and guard them from evil. They are totally unacquainted with strong or spirituous liquours; and their principal beverage is palm wine.

As we live in a country where nature is prodigal of her favours, our wants are few and easily supplied; of course we have few manufactures. They consist for the most part of calicoes, earthen ware, ornaments, and instruments of war and husbandry. But these make no part of our commerce, the principal articles of which, as I have observed, are provisions. In such a state money is of little use; however we have some small pieces of coin, if I may call them such. They are made something like an anchor; but I do not remember either their value or denomination. We have also markets, at which I have been frequently with my mother. These are sometimes visited by stout mahogany-coloured men from the south west of us: we call them Oye-Eboe, which term signifies red men living at a distance. They generally bring us fire-arms, gunpowder, hats, beads, and dried fish. The last we esteemed a great rarity, as our waters were only brooks and springs. These articles they barter with us for odoriferous woods and earth, and our salt of wood ashes. They always carry slaves through our land; but the strictest account is exacted of their manner of procuring them before they are suffered to pass. Sometimes indeed we sold slaves to them, but they were only prisoners of war, or such among us as had been convicted of kidnapping, or adultery, and some other crimes, which we esteemed heinous.

Source: Olaudah Equiano, *The Interesting Narrative of the Life of Olaudah Equiano, or Gustavus Vassa, the African, written by himself* (New York, 1791), pp. 3–4, 8–10, 13–14; reprinted from the 1789 London edition.

Study: Vincent Carretta, *Equiano, the African: A Biography of a Self-Made Man* (Athens: University of Georgia Press, 2005).

Further exploration: Vincent Carretta's primary goal in writing a biography of Equiano was not to "prove" that his narrative was an accurate account of his life, but Carretta did try to verify as much of Equiano's account as possible, and, in particular, tried to establish whether the voyages Equiano mentioned in the narrative actually took place (and thus whether he was where he said he was when he said he was). In answering this type of question, historians can use David Eltis et al., *The Trans-Atlantic Slave Trade: Database on CD-ROM* (Cambridge: Cambridge University Press, 1999), which includes records of more than 27,000 trans-Atlantic slave ship voyages made between 1595 and 1866. The interactive format of the database allows users to ask questions about slaving voyages by time and place. Most university libraries have the database.

Discussion Questions

1   In what ways does William Harrison's *Description of England* reinforce or challenge Gregory King's *Scheme. . . . of the Several Families of England*? What conception of "class" do these descriptions suggest literate English people held?
2   Which people from the two authors' descriptions would be most likely to be involved in exploration and colonization efforts?
3   Compare the two descriptions of African society – one by a European and the other by an African. How do they differ? In what ways are they similar?
4   These accounts range chronologically from the sixteenth to the late eighteenth century. In what ways do the documents themselves reveal that they are drawn from different periods of colonial history?
5   Keep these descriptions in mind as you read subsequent documents. How did New World English and African settlements differ from the portraits presented here of Old World society?

Chapter 2   Images of the New World

1. Amerigo Vespucci Discovers America, ca. 1570s

Jan Van der Straet (1525–1605) was a Flemish painter who spent most of his career in Italy, where he often went by the surname Stradanus. He probably drew this picture of Amerigo Vespucci, a Florentine navigator who Europeans wrongly believed to be the first European to have landed on the mainland of America, between 1570 and 1580. Theodor Galle made an engraving from the drawing which circulated widely in the late sixteenth century.

Figure 2.1 Theodor Galle's engraving of Jan Van der Straet's *Amerigo Vespucci Discovers America.*

Source: Jan Van der Straet, *Nova reperta* (Antewerp, ca. 1600), engraved by Theodor Galle, Vault Case Wing fZ 412.85, The Newberry Library, Chicago.

Study: Michael J. Schreffler, "Vespucci Rediscovers America: The Pictorial Rhetoric of Cannibalism in Early Modern Culture," *Art History,* 28 (2005), 295–310.

2. Amerigo Vespucci Describes his First (Third) Voyage to "America," 1505/6

Amerigo Vespucci (1452–1512), a Florentine mariner, sailing under the Portuguese flag, wrote the letter, extracted below, in 1504 (after the last of his three voyages to the "New World"), describing a voyage he purportedly made in 1497 (which, if he actually had made it, would have been the first of four voyages). The letter was printed in 1505–6, about the same time that his Mondus Novus account was also published. The latter would be translated into Latin, French, Dutch, and, in the mid-sixteenth century, English. Both publications would shape the way educated Europeans first imagined America. They probably influenced Jan Van der Straet's drawing of Vespucci's "Awakening" of the New World (as depicted in Theodor Galle's engraving).

For so much as we learned of their manner of life and customs, it was that they go entirely naked, as well the men as the women, without covering any shameful part, not otherwise than as they issued from their mother's womb. They are of medium stature, very well proportioned: their flesh is of a colour that verges into red like a lion's mane, and I believe that if they went clothed, they would be as white as we. They have not any hair upon the body, except the hair of the head which is long and black, and especially in the women, whom it renders handsome. In aspect they are not very good-looking, because they have broad faces, so that they would seem Tartarlike. They let no hair grow on their eyebrows, nor on their eyelids nor elsewhere, except the hair of the head, for they hold hairiness to be a filthy thing. They are very light-footed in walking and in running, as well the men as the women, so that a woman recks nothing of running a league or two, as many times we saw them do, and herein they have a very great advantage over us Christians. They swim beyond all belief, and the women better than the men, for we have many times found and seen them swimming two leagues out at sea without any thing to rest upon. Their arms are bows and arrows very well made, save that they have no iron nor any other kind of hard metal, and instead of iron they put animals' or fishes' teeth, or a spike of tough wood, with the point hardened by fire: they are sure marksmen, for they hit whatever they aim at: and in some places the women use these bows. They have other weapons, such as fire-hardened spears, and also clubs with knobs, beautifully carved. Warfare is used amongst them, against people not of their own language, very cruelly, without granting life to any one, except for greater suffering ...

The manner of their living is very barbarous, for they eat at no certain hours, and as oftentimes as they will. And it does not matter much to them that the will may come rather at midnight than by day, for they eat at all hours. And their repast is made upon the ground without a table-cloth or any other cover, for they have their meats either in earthen basins which they make therefor, or in the halves of pumpkins. They sleep in certain very large nettings made of cotton, suspended in the air. And although this their fashion of sleeping may seem uncomfortable, I say that it is sweet to sleep in those, and we slept better in them than in quilts. They are a people of neat exterior, and clean of body, because of so continually washing themselves as they do. When, saving your reverence, they evacuate the stomach they do their utmost not to be observed, and as much as in this they are cleanly and bashful, so much the more are they filthy and shameless in making water, since, while standing speaking to us, without turning round or shewing any shame, they let go their nastiness, for in this they have no shame.

There is no custom of marriages amongst them. Each man takes as many women as he lists, and when he desires to repudiate them, he repudiates them without any imputation of wrong-doing to him, or of disgrace to the woman, for in this the woman has as much liberty as the man. They are not very jealous and are immoderately libidinous, and the women much more so than the men, so that for decency I omit to tell you the artifice they practice to gratify their inordinate lust. They are very fertile women, and do not shirk any work during their pregnancies, and their travails in childbed are so light that, a single day after parturition, they go abroad everywhere, and especially to wash themselves in the rivers, and are then as sound as fishes....

They eat little flesh except human flesh: for your Magnificence must know that herein they are so inhuman that they outdo every custom even of beasts, for they eat all their enemies whom they kill or capture, as well females as males, with so much savagery, that to relate it appears a horrible thing, how much more so to see it, as, infinite times and in many places, it was my hap to see it. And they wondered to hear us say that we did not eat our enemies, and this your Magnificence may take for certain, that their other barbarous customs are such that expression is too weak for the reality.

Source: Myra Jehlen and Michael Warner, eds., pp. 20–1, 23, from *The English Literatures of America, 1500–1800* (New York: Routledge, 1997). © 1997 by Routledge. Reprinted by permission of Taylor & Francis Inc., LLC.

Study: Louis Montrose, "The Work of Gender in the Discourse of Discovery," *Representations*, 33 (Winter 1991), 1–41.

3. A Native American Warrior, ca. 1590

*John White gained fame for his late sixteenth-century depictions of Native
Americans. White accompanied adventurer Martin Frobisher to Baffin Island
in 1577, and then in 1585 joined the expedition promoted by Walter Raleigh
to Carolina, and was subsequently a leader of the "Virginia" expedition that
settled at Roanoke. Returning to England in 1587, he was not able to make his
way back to Roanoke until 1590, by which time the other colonists had
disappeared. White's watercolors strike historians as accurate depictions of
Inuit and Croatoan Native American peoples, but they are not the images that
Europeans saw. Theodor de Bry reproduced White's paintings as engravings,
altering them, most importantly, by giving White's subjects European features.*

Figure 2.2   John White's Depiction of a Virginia Native American Warrior in
Body Paint, 1624.
Source: © British Museum, London.

4. John Smith, *Of the Naturall Inhabitants of Virginia*, 1624

John Smith (ca. 1580–1631) was born to a middling farm family in England; well educated, and apprenticed as a youth to a merchant, he went on to serve as a soldier in late sixteenth-century wars in Europe, and then traveled widely over the Continent. After being captured in battle and briefly "enslaved," Smith was able to escape and make his way back to England by the winter of 1604–5. Seeking new adventures, in 1607 he became involved with the first English voyage to Virginia, where he served as the de facto *governor for about a year (1608–9) before returning to England.*

Much of Smith's life is known only through his own writings, and historians have long struggled to separate fact from the products of Smith marvelous narrative inventions. The first brief account of his Jamestown experiences was published in 1608 (from a letter he had written, and without his consent), and his own, much longer version appeared in 1612, but it was in his 1624 work, The Generall Historie of Virginia, New-England, and the Summer Isles, *that he told the story most fully. The excerpt below is taken from his description of the Native Americans in the Jamestown region.*

The Land is not populous, for the men be few; their far greater number is of women and children. Within 60 myles of James Towne, there are about some 5000 people, but of men fit for their warres scarce 1500. To nourish so many together they have yet no meanes, because they make so small a benefit of their land, be it never so fertile. Six or seaven hundred have beene the most hath beene seene together, when they gathered themselves to have surprised mee at Pamaunkee, having but fifteene to withstand the worst of their fury. As small as the proportion of ground that hath yet beene discovered, is in comparison of that yet unknowne: the people differ very much in stature, especially in language ... but generally tall and straight, of a comely proportion, and of a colour browne when they are of any age, but they are borne white. Their hayre is generally blacke, but few have any beards. The men weare halfe their heads shaven, the other halfe long; for Barbers they use their women, who with two shels will grate away the hayre, of any fashion they please. The women are cut in many fashions, agreeable to their yeares, but ever some part remaineth long. They are very strong, of an able body and full of agilitie, able to endure to lie in the woods under a tree by the fire, in the worst of winter, or in the weedes and grasse, in Ambuscado in the Sommer. They are inconstant in every thing, but what feare constraineth them to keepe. Craftie, timerous, quicke of apprehension, and very ingenuous. Some are of disposition fearefull, some bold, most cautelous, all Savage. Generally covetous of Copper, Beads, and such like trash. They are soone moved to anger, and so malicious, that they seldome forget an injury: they seldome steale one from another, least their conjurers should reveale it, and so they be pursued and punished. That they are thus feared is certaine, but that any can reveale their offences by conjuration I am doubtfull. Their women are carefull not to be suspected of dishonestie without the leave of their husbands. Each houshold knoweth their owne lands, and gardens, and most live of their owne labours. For their apparell, they are sometime covered with the skinnes of wilde beasts, which in Winter are dressed with the hayre, but in Sommer without. The better sort use large mantels of Deare skins. Not much differing in fashion from the Irish mantels. Some imbrodered with white beads, some with Copper, other painted after their manner. But the common sort have scarce to cover their nakednesse, but with grasse, the leaves of trees, or such like. We have seene some use mantels made of Turky feathers, so prettily wrought and woven with threads that nothing could be discerned but the feathers. That was exceeding warme and very handsome. But the women are alwayes covered about their middles with a skin, and very shamefast to be seene bare. They adorne themselves most with copper beads and paintings. Their women, some have their legs, hands, breasts and face cunningly imbrodered with divers workes, as beasts, serpents, artificially wrought into their flesh with blacke spots. In each eare commonly they have 3 great holes, whereat they hang chaines, bracelets, or copper. Some of their men weare in those holes, a small greene and yellow coloured snake, neare halfe a yard in length, which crawling and lapping her selfe about his necke oftentimes familiarly would kisse his lips. Others weare a dead Rat tyed by the taile. Some on their heads weare the wing of a bird, or some large feather with a Rattell. Those Rattels are somewhat like the chape of a Rapier, but lesse, which they take from the taile of a snake. Many have the whole skinne of a Hawke or some strange foule, stuffed with the wings abroad. Others a broad peece of Copper, and some the hand of their enemy dryed. Their heads and shoulders are painted red with the roote Pocone brayed to powder, mixed with oyle, this they hold in sommer to preserve them from the heate, and in winter from the cold. Many other formes of paintings they use, but he is the most gallant that is the most monstrous to behold.

Source: John Smith, *The Generall Historie of Virginia, New-England, and the Summer Isles ... to this present ... 1624, Second Book* (London, 1624), pp. 29–30.

Study: Karen Ordahl Kupperman, ed., *Captain John Smith: A Select Edition of his Writings* (Chapel Hill: University of North Carolina Press for the Institute of Early American History and Culture, 1988).

5. Pocahontas in England

This engraving, done from a sketch made of Pocahontas in England, dates from about 1616–17, and published in Smith's Generall Historie *in 1624. The original drawing was done by the Dutch-German engraver Simon van de Passe, who also did a portrait of John Smith. Pocahontas was probably about 19 at the time she sat for van de Passe.*

Figure 2.3   Simon van de Passe's Engraving of Pocahontas in England, ca. 1617. Source: From John Smith, *The Generall Historie of Virginia, New-England, and the Summer Isles*. The Newberry Library, Chicago.

6. John Smith on Pocahontas, 1624

John Smith wrote numerous accounts of his now legendary meetings with Pocahontas, one of the daughters of Powhatan, a "chief of chiefs" among the Native Americans in the James River region of the land the English called Virginia. As Smith wrote and rewrote his narratives about his Virginia experiences, he added detail to his stories about Pocahontas. The two extracts below come from his 1624 account. The first describes how Pocahontas "saved" Smith from death after his capture (historians believe that if this scene actually took place, it was part of a ceremony staged purposefully by Powhatan ritually to adopt Smith).

Pocahontas would eventually be kidnapped and taken to Jamestown. There she would convert to Christianity, take the name Rebecca, and marry John Rolfe. The second extract is Smith's account of Pocahontas' marriage.

[Pocahontas saves Smith]
At his [John Smith's] entrance before the King, all the people gaue a great shout. The Queen of *Appamatuck* was appointed to bring him water to wash his hands, and another brought him a bunch of feathers, in stead of a Toewll to dry them: having feated him after their best barbarous manner they could, a long consultation was held, but the conclusion was, two great stones were brought before *Powhatan* : then as many as could layd hands on him, dragged him to them, and thereon laid his head, and being ready with their clubs, to beate out his brianes, *Pocahontas* the Kings dearest daughter, when no intreaty could prevaile, got his head in her armes, and laid out her owne vpon his to saue him from death : whereat the Emperour was contented he should liue to make him hatchets, and her bells, beads, and copper : for they thought him aswell of all occupations as themselues. For the King himselfe will make his owne robes, shooes, bowes, arrowes, pots; plan, hunt, or doe any thing so well as the rest.

[Pocahontas marries John Rolfe]
Long before this [April 1613], Master *Iohn Rolfe,* an honest Gentleman, and of good behaviour, had been in loue with *Pocahontas,* and she with him: which thing at that instant I made knowne to Sir *Thomas Dale* by letter from him, wherein he intreated his aduice, and she acquainted her brother with it, which resolution Sir *Thomas Dale* well approued : the bru[i]te [noise, tidings] of this marriage came soone to the knowledge of *Powhatan,* a thing acceptable to him, as appeared by hius sudden consent, for within ten daies he sent *Opachisco,* an old Vncle of hers, and two of his sons, to see the Manner of the mariage, and to doe in that behalfe what they were requested, for the confirmation thereof, as his deputie; which was accordingly done about the first of Aprill [1614]. An euer since wee haue had friendly trade and commerce, as well with *Powhatan* himselfe, as all his subjects.

Source: John Smith, *The Generall Historie of Virginia, New-England, and the Summer Isles,* 1624, Third Book, p. 49; Fourth Book, p. 113.

Study: Camilla Townsend, *Pocahontas and the Powhatan Dilemma* (New York: Hill & Wang, 2004).

7. Illustration from John Lawson's *A New Voyage to Carolina* (London, 1709)

Figure 2.4   The beasts of Carolina.
Source: Grenville Kane Collection. Rare Books Division. Department of Rare Books and Special Collections. Princeton University Library.

8. John Lawson's *History of North Carolina*, 1709

John Lawson was a well-born Englishman who settled in North Carolina in the early eighteenth century, and resided there about a decade. Soon after arriving, Lawson was sent on an exploration of the Carolina backcountry, which led to the writing of his History of North Carolina *and its publication in London in 1709. The essay was a work of "natural history," describing the plant and animal life of the region and its indigenous inhabitants. He would make subsequent exploratory trips in Carolina, in part to help survey and settle the region, and would die there in 1711, a victim of the Tuscarora War. His death reminds us that ventures such as Lawson's, which seemed heroic, scientific, altruistic, and commercial to his European-American contemporaries, were seen as threatening and invasive by Native American peoples. The extract below from his* History *includes selections from his descriptions of the animals he observed or heard about in North Carolina.*

We will next treat of the Beasts which you shall have an Account of, as they have been discovered.

THE BEASTS OF CAROLINA ARE THE Buffelo, or wild beef. Bear. Panther. Catamount. Wild cat. Wolf. Tier. Polcat. Otter. Bever. Musk-Rat. Possum. Raccoon. Minx. Water-Rat. Rabbet, two sorts. Elks. Stabs. Fallow-Deer. Squirrel, four sorts. Fox. Lion and fackall on the Lake. Rats, two sorts. Mice, two sorts. Moles. Weasel, Dormouse. Bearmouse.

The Buffelo is a wild Beast of America, which has a Bunch on his Back as the Cattle of St. Lawrence are said to have. He seldom appears amongst the English inhabitants, his chief Haunt being in the Land of Mississippi, which is, for the most part, a plain Country; yet I have known some killed on the Hilly Part of Cape-Fear-River, they passing the Ledges of vast Mountains from the said Mississippi, before they can come near us. I have eaten on their Meat, but do not think it so good as our Beef; yet the younger Calves are cried up for excellent Food, as very likely they may be. It is conjectured that these Buffelos, mixt in Breed with our tame Cattle, would much better the Breed for Largeness and Milk, which seems very probable. Of the wild Bull's Skin Buff is made. The Indians cut the Skins into Quarters for the Ease of their Transportation, and make Beds to lie on. They spin the Hair into Garters, Girdles, Sashes, and the like, it being long and curled, and often of a chesnut or red Colour. These Monsters are found to weigh (as I am informed by a Traveler of Credit) from 1600 to 1400 Weight.

The Bears here are very common, though not so large as in Greenland, and the more Northern Countries of Russia. The Flesh of this Beast is very good and nourishing, and not inferior to the best Pork, in Taste. It stands betwixt Beef and Pork, and the young Cubs are a Dish for the greatest Epicure living. I prefer their Flesh before any Beef, Veal, Pork, or Mutton, and they look as well as they eat, their fat being as white as Snow and the sweetest of any Creatures in the World ... This Creature feeds upon all sorts of wild Fruits. When Herrings run, which is in March, the Flesh of such of those Bears as eat thereof, is naught all that Season, and eats filthily. Neither is it good when he feeds on Gum-berries as I intimated before. They are great Devourers of Acorns, and oftentimes meet the Swine in the

Woods, which they kill and eat, especially when they are hungry and can find no other Food. Now and then they get into Fields of Indian Corn or Maiz, where they make a sad Havock, spoiling ten times as much as they eat. The Potatos of this Country are so agreeable to them, that they never fail to sweep them all clean if they chance to come in their way. They are seemingly a very clumsy Creature, yet are very nimble in running up Trees and traversing every limb thereof. When they come down they run Tail foremost. At catching of Herrings, they are most expert Fishers. They sit by the Creek-sides, (which are very narrow) where the Fish run in, and there they take them up as fast as it is possible they can dip their Paws into the Water. There is one thing more to be considered of this Creature, which is, that no Man, either Christian or Indian, has ever killed a She-bear with Young. . . .

The Possum is found no where but in America. He is the Wonder of all the Land-Animals, being the size of a Badger, and near that Colour. The Male's Pizzle is placed retrograde; and in time of coition, they differ from all other Animals, turning tail to tail as dog and bitch when tied. The Female doubtless breeds her young at her Teats; for I have seen them stick fast thereto when they have been no bigger than a small Rasberry, and seemingly inanimate. She has a Paunch, or false Belly, wherein she carries her Young, after they are from those Teats, till they can shift for themselves. Their Food is Roots, poultry or wild Fruits. They have no Hair on their Tails, but a sort of a Scale or hard Crust, as the Bevers have. If a Cat has nine Lives, this Creature surely has nineteen; for if you break every Bone in their Skin, and mash their Skull leaving them for Dead, you may come an hour after, and they will be gone quite away, or perhaps you meet them creeping away. They are a very stupid Creature, utterly neglecting their Safety. They are most like Rats of any thing. I have, for Necessity in the Wilderness, eaten of them. Their Flesh is very white, and well tasted; but their ugly Tails put me out of Conceit with that Fare. They climb Trees as the Raccoons do. Their Fur is not esteemed nor used, save that the Indians spin it into Girdles and Garters.

Source: John Lawson, *Lawson's History of North Carolina, Containing the Exact Description and Natural History of that Country, together with the Present State Thereof and a Journal of a Thousand Miles Traveled through Several Nations of Indians, Giving a Particular Account of Their Customs, Etc. Etc.* (London, 1714), extracts from pp. 118–24.

Study: Susan Scott Parrish, "The Female Opossum and the Nature of the New World," *William and Mary Quarterly*, 3rd ser., LIV (1997), 475–514.

Further exploration: *Eighteenth Century Online* provides full text editions of most English/British publications dating from the century (including many reprinted seventeenth-century works). Search is by keywords, year(s) of publication, and subject area. This is, essentially, the British equivalent of the *Early American Imprints* series.

Discussion Questions

1   Images are important as "representations" of the "New World" as much as records of what explorers or settlers may actually have seen. Begin by considering if the artist was drawing something he actually saw. Then consider the text document in relationship to the visual image. For each of these images, try to think about both what the image tells us about the New World and what it tells us about the way Europeans imagined the New World.

2   In the Amerigo Vespucci representation contrast the images associated with Europe with those associated with America, but also the images in the background with those in the foreground. What does the image suggest about European values and motives in the exploration of the New World? What does it suggest about European attitudes about the peoples of the New World?

3   How does White's depiction of a Croatoan warrior compare with the Native Americans in Jan Van der Straet's work? Does White's image match Smith's characterization? In what way were both of these positive images of Native Americans? It what ways might these images, when consumed by English audiences, have assisted the colonization and settlement project?

4   How is the Pocahontas portrait different from what you would expect of a European depiction of a Native American? What has the artist done to make Pocahontas seem European (and why do you imagine he did this)? In what ways is she still distinctly a Native American? Assuming she sat for this portrait, does the picture itself suggest she had any role in determining its composition?

5   Why were Europeans fascinated about the "natural history" of the New World? What do Lawson's writings and the associated prints suggest about their attitude? What purposes might such investigation have served for Lawson? For his readers?

Chapter 3   Native American Lives

1. The Beginning of the World – Costanoan California Native American Story

Costanoan peoples lived along the southern coast of California (today, between San Francisco and Monterey). In the early twentieth century, Alfred L. Kroeber, who headed the Ethnological and Archaeological Survey of California, interviewed numerous California Native Americans and recorded their "myths." Among those he interviewed were two elderly Costanoans, Jacinta Gonzalez and Maria Viviena Soto, who recounted for him their origins story.

When this world was finished, the eagle, the humming-bird, and Coyote were standing on the top of Pico Blanco. When the water rose to their feet, the eagle, carrying the humming-bird and Coyote, flew to the Sierra de Gabilan. There they stood until the water went down. Then the eagle sent Coyote down the mountain to see if the world were dry. Coyote came back and said: "The whole world is dry." The eagle said to him "Go and look in the river. See what there is there." Coyote came back and said: "There is a beautiful girl." The eagle said: "She will be your wife in order that people may be raised again." He gave Coyote a digging implement of abalone shell and a digging stick. Coyote asked: "How will my children be raised?" The eagle would not say. He wanted to see if Coyote was wise enough to know. Coyote asked him again how these new people were to be raised from the girl. Then he said: "Well, I will make them right here in the knee." The eagle said: "No, that is not good." Then Coyote said: "Well then, here in the elbow." "No, that is not good." "In the eyebrow." "No, that is not good." " In the back of the neck." "No, that is not good either. None of these will be good." Then the humming bird cried: "Yes, my brother, they are not good. This place will be good, here in the belly." Then Coyote was angry. He wanted to kill him. The eagle raised his wings and the humming bird flew in his armpit. Coyote looked for him in vain. Then the girl said: "What shall I do? How will I make my children?" The eagle said to Coyote: "Go and marry her. She will be your wife." Then Coyote went off with this girl. He said to her: "Louse me." Then the girl found a woodtick on him. She was afraid and threw it away. Then Coyote seized her. He said: "Look for it, look for it! Take it! Eat it! Eat my louse!" Then the girl put it into her mouth. "Swallow it, swallow it!" he said. Then she swallowed it and became pregnant. Then she was afraid. She ran away. She ran through thorns. Coyote ran after her. He called to her: "Do not run through that brush." He made a good road for her. But she said: "I do not like this road." Then Coyote made a road with flowers on each side. Perhaps the girl would stop to take a flower. She said: "I am not used to going between flowers." Then Coyote said: "There is no help for it. I cannot stop her." So she ran to the ocean. Coyote was close to her. Just as he was going to take hold of her, she threw herself into the water and the waves came up between them as she turned to a sand flea [or shrimp: *camaron*]. Coyote, diving after her, struck only the sand. He said: "I wanted to clasp my wife but took hold of the sand. My wife is gone."

Source: A. L. Kroeber, *Indian Myths of South Central California*, University of California Publications, American Archaeology and Ethnology, vol. IV, no. 4 (1907), pp. 199–200.

Study: Steven W. Hackel, *Children of Coyote, Missionaries of Saint Francis: Indian–Spanish Relations in Colonial California, 1769–1850* (Chapel Hill: University of North Carolina Press for the Omohundro Institute of Early American History and Culture, 2005).

2. A Dutch View of the Native Americans in the New Netherlands, from a Letter of Isaack de Rasieres to Samuel Blommaert, ca. 1628

Dutch interest in what later became New York can be dated to 1609 when Henry Hudson explored the river that now carries his name; but significant settlement under the auspices of the Dutch West India Company did not begin until the 1620s. The company was primarily interested in profiting from the fur

trade with the Native Americans. Isaack de Rasieres came to the Dutch colony
about 1626 as a commercial agent for the company and stayed little more than
a year. Once back in the Netherlands, he wrote a letter to Samuel Blommaert,
a merchant with interests in Dutch colonial ventures, about the colony.
The extract below is one of the first Dutch accounts of Native American life.

These tribes of savages all have a government. The men in general are rather tall, well proportioned in their limbs, and of an orange color, like the Brazilians; very inveterate against those whom they hate; cruel by nature, and so inclined to freedom that they cannot by any means be brought to work; they support themselves by hunting, and when the spring comes, by fishing. In April, May, and June, they follow the course of these [the fish], which they catch with a drag-net they themselves knit very neatly, of the wild hemp, from which the women and old men spin the thread. The kinds of fish which they principally take at this time are shad, but smaller than those in this country ordinarily are, though quite as fat, and very bony; the largest fish is a sort of white salmon, which is of very good flavor, and quite as large; it has white scales; the heads are so full of fat that in some there are two or three spoonfuls, so that there is good eating for one who is fond of picking heads. It seems that this fish makes them lascivious, for it is often observed that those who have caught any when they have gone fishing, have given them, on their return, to the women, who look for them anxiously....

As an employment in winter they make *sewan*, which is an oblong bead that they make from cockle-shells, which they find on the sea-shore, and they consider it as valuable as we do money here, since one can buy with it everything they have; they string it, and wear it around the neck and hands; they also make bands of it, which the women wear on the forehead under the hair, and the men around the body; and they are as particular about the stringing and sorting as we can be here about pearls. They are very fond of a game they call *Senneca*, played with some round rushes, similar to the Spanish feather-grass, which they understand how to shuffle and deal as though they were playing with cards; and they win from each other all that they possess, even to the lappet with which they cover their private parts, and so they separate from each other quite naked. They are very much addicted to promiscuous intercourse. Their clothing is [so simple as to leave the body] almost naked. In the winter time they usually wear a dressed deer skin; some have a bear's skin about the body; some a coat of scales; some a covering made of turkey feathers which they understand how to knit together very oddly, with small strings. They also use a good deal of duffel cloth, which they buy from us, and which serves for their blanket by night, and their dress by day.

The women are fine looking, of middle stature, well proportioned, and with finely cut features; with long and black hair, and black eyes set off with fine eyebrows; they are of the same color as the men. They smear their bodies and hair with grease, which makes them smell very rankly; they are very much given to promiscuous intercourse.

They have a marriage custom amongst them, namely: when there is one who resolves to take a particular person for his wife, he collects a fathom or two of sewan, and comes to the nearest friends of the person whom he desires, to whom he declares his object in her presence, and if they are satisfied with him, he agrees with them how much sewan he shall give her for a bridal present; that being done, he then gives her all the Dutch beads he has, which they call *Machampe*, and also all sorts of trinkets. If she be a young virgin, he must wait six weeks more before he can sleep with her, during which time she bewails or laments over her virginity, which they call *Coldatismarrenitten*; all this time she sits with a blanket over her head, without wishing to look at any one, or any one being permitted to look at her. This period being elapsed, her bridegroom comes to her; he in the mean time has been supporting himself by hunting, and what he has taken he brings there with him; they then eat together with the friends, and sing and dance together, which they call *Kintikaen*. That being done, the wife must provide the food for herself and her husband, as far as breadstuffs are concerned, and [should they fall short] she must buy what is wanting with her sewan.

For this reason they are obliged to watch the season for sowing. At the end of March they begin to break up the earth with mattocks, which they buy from us for the skins of beavers or otters, or for sewan. They make heaps like molehills, each about two and a half feet from the others, which they sow or plant in April with maize, in each heap five or six grains; in the middle of May, when the maize is the height of a finger or more, they plant in each heap three or four Turkish beans, which then grow up with and against the maize, which serves for props, for the maize grows on stalks similar to the sugarcane. It is a grain to which much labor must be given, with weeding and earthing up, or it does not thrive; and to this the women must attend very closely. The men would not once look to it, for it would compromise their dignity too much, unless they are very old and cannot follow the chase. Those stalks which are low and bear no ears, they pluck up in August, and suck out the sap, which is as sweet as if it were sugar-cane.

Source: J. Franklin Jameson, *Narratives of New Netherlands, 1609–1664* (New York: Charles Scribner's Sons, 1909), pp. 105–7. The original letter is in the National Archives at the Hague, and was translated by William I. Hull.

Study: Donna Merwick, *The Shame and the Sorrow: Dutch–Amerindian Encounters in New Netherlands* (Philadelphia: University of Pennsylvania Press, 2006).

3. A French Jesuit Missionary Reports on Life Among the Illinois, 1675

Jacques Marquette (1637–75) was a French Jesuit missionary who accompanied Louis Jolliet on the first French expedition down the Mississippi River in 1673. Born in France, where he joined the Jesuit order, he was sent in 1666 to Quebec, and served in several posts from Three Rivers (on the St. Lawrence) to the southwestern shore of Lake Superior. The 1673 expedition took Marquette down the Fox and Wisconsin Rivers to the Mississippi, which they then followed as far south as the mouth of the Arkansas River. Marquette took detailed notes in his journal (published in volume LIX of the Jesuit Relations*) of the topography of the region and the Indian peoples he encountered, as well as the commercial possibilities the Mississippi offered the French. The excerpt below describes the Algonquian peoples of the Illinois confederacy.*

WHEN one speaks the word "Ilinois," it is as if one said in their language, "the men," – As if the other Savages were looked upon by them merely as animals. It must also be admitted that they have an air of humanity which we have not observed in the other nations that we have seen upon our route. The shortness Of my stay among Them did not allow me to secure all the Information that I would have desired; among all Their customs, the following is what I have observed.

They are divided into many villages, some of which are quite distant from that of which we speak, which is called peouarea. This causes some difference in their language, which, on the whole, resembles allegonquin, so that we easily understood each other. They are of a gentle and tractable disposition; we Experienced this in the reception which they gave us. They have several wives, of whom they are Extremely jealous; they watch them very closely, and Cut off Their noses or ears when they misbehave. I saw several women who bore the marks of their misconduct. Their Bodies are shapely; they are active and very skillful with bows and arrows. They also use guns, which they buy from our savage allies who Trade with our french. They use them especially to inspire, through their noise and smoke, terror in their Enemies; the latter do not use guns, and have never seen any, since they live too Far toward the West. They are warlike, and make themselves dreaded by the Distant tribes to the south and west, whither they go to procure Slaves; these they barter, selling them at a high price to other Nations, in exchange for other Wares. . . .

I know not through what superstition some Ilinois, as well as some Nadouessi, while still young, assume the garb of women, and retain it throughout their lives. There is some mystery in this, For they never marry and glory in demeaning themselves to do everything that the women do. They go to war, however, but can use only clubs, and not bows and arrows, which are the weapons proper to men. They are present at all the juggleries, and at the solemn dances in honor of the Calumet; at these they sing, but must not dance. They are summoned to the Councils, and nothing can be decided without their advice. Finally, through their profession of leading an Extraordinary life, they pass for Manitous, – That is to say, for Spirits, – or persons of Consequence.

Source: Jacques Marquette, *Journal incomplet, adressé au R. P. Claude Dablon, supérieur des Missions* (1675), in Reuben Gold Thwaites, *The Jesuit Relations and Allied Documents* (Cleveland, Ohio: Burrows Bros. Co., 1896–1901), vol. LIX: *Lower Canada, Illinois, Ottawas, 1675–1677*, pp. 125–9.

Study: William C. Sturtevant, ed., *Handbook of North American Indians*, vol. 15: Bruce Trigger, ed., *Northeast* (Washington, DC: Smithsonian Institution, 1978).

4. Joseph Francis Lafitau, Portrait of Iroquois and Huron Culture, 1724

Joseph Francis Lafitau was a Jesuit priest, born in Bordeaux, who lived from 1712 to 1717 at Sault St. Louis, a village of Christianized Indians ("Praying Indians") across the St. Lawrence River from Montreal. Most of the villagers had roots in Mohawk and Oneida communities in New York, but during his tenure at Sault St. Louis, Lafitau also came in contact with Huron peoples, and he mastered Huron and Iroquoian dialects. After returning to France, Lafitau published in 1724 what might be called one of the first ethnographic studies about Native American peoples, Moeurs des sauvages amériquains comparées aux moeurs des premiers temps. Lafitau's purpose was to establish parallels between Native Americans and early Europeans, and he drew on classical literature, the writings of French Jesuit missionaries in Canada, and his own observations. The creation story, for example, recounted below and known by scholars as "The World on the Turtle's Back," had been recorded in different forms at least a century before Lafitau wrote, and he had access to these earlier accounts.

[Indian Women]

... [I]t is said that only the men among the Indians are really free and that the women are only their slaves. Nothing is more real, however, than the women's superiority. It is they who really maintain the tribe, the nobility of blood, the genealogical tree, the order of generations and conservation of the [72] families. In them resides all the real authority; the lands, fields and all their harvest belong to them; they are the soul of the councils, the arbiters of peace and war; they hold the taxes and the public treasure; it is to them that the slaves are entrusted; they arrange the marriages; the children are under their authority; and the order of succession is founded on their blood. The men, on the contrary, are entirely isolated and limited to themselves. Their children are strangers to them. Everything perishes with them. A woman alone gives continuity to the household, but, if there are only men in the lodge, however many they may be, whatever number of children they may have, their family dies out with them. And, although the chiefs are chosen among them, they are purely honorary. The Council of Elders which transacts all the business does not work for itself. It seems that they serve only to represent and aid the women in the matters in which decorum does not permit the latter to appear or act.

[Indian Men]

The men, who are so idle in their villages, make their indolence a mark of honour, giving it to be understood that they are properly born only for great things, especially for warfare. This exercise, which exposes their courage to the rudest tests, furnishes them frequent occasions to put in its brightest light all the nobility of their sentiments and the unshakeable firmness of a truly heroic greatness of mind. They like hunting and fishing which, after warfare, take their attention, only because they are the image of warfare. Perhaps they would leave these occupations as well as that of [getting] subsistence and all others to women if they did not consider hunting and fishing exercises which get them into shape to be a terror to enemies even more formidable than wild beasts.

[Iroquois Origins]

Here is the story that the Iroquois tell of their origin and that of the earth. In the beginning, there were, they say, six men. ... Whence had these men come? That is what they do not know. There was as yet no land. They wandered at the will of the wind. They had no women and they thought that their race was going to perish with them. Finally they learned, I do not know where, that there was a woman in the Heavens. They held a common council and decided that one of them named Hoguaho or the Wolf would go there. The enterprise appeared impossible but the birds of the sky in concert together, lifted him up there, making a seat for him of their bodies and sustaining each other. When he had reached there, he waited at the foot of a tree until this woman came out as she was accustomed to do, to draw water from a spring near the place where he had stopped. The man, who was waiting for her, entered into conversation with her and made her a present of bear fat which he gave her to eat. A curious woman who likes to talk and receives presents does not long delay in yielding. This one was weak even in heaven itself. She let herself be seduced. The master of the heavens perceived it and, in his wrath, drove her away and hurled her out. When she fell, the turtle received her on his back, on which the otter and the fishes, digging up clay from the bottom of the water, formed a little island which increased little by little and extended into the form in which we see the earth today. This woman had two children who fought one another. They had unequal arms whose force they did not know. Those of the one were dangerous and the other's could harm no one so that the former [latter] was killed without difficulty. All other men have their descent from this woman through a long succession of generations, and it is such a singular event as this which has served, they say, as a basis for the division of the three families of the Iroquois and Huron, into those of the Wolf, the Bear and the Turtle which, by their very names, are a living tradition bringing before their eyes the history of the first times. This tale's absurdity arouses pity although it is no more ridiculous than some of those invented by the Greeks who were such ingenious people.

Source: Father Joseph François Lafitau, *Customs of the American Indians Compared with the Customs of Primitive Times*, 2 vols., ed. and trans. William N. Fenton and Elizabeth Moore (Toronto: The Champlain Society, 1977), II, 69, 81–2, 98.

Study: Gordon M. Sayre, *Les Sauvages Américains: Representations of Native Americans in French and English Colonial Literature* (Chapel Hill: University of North Carolina Press, 1997).

Discussion Questions

1   Each of these depictions of Native American lives, as with three of the images in Chapter 2, was produced by a Euro-American, even when the account is presented as an unedited transcription (or image) of what a Native American said (or looked like). What does this do to the value of the document as a depiction of Native American life? In what sense do historians ever deal with "authentic" voices of peoples in different times, places, and cultures? What type of questions

is it appropriate to ask about such sources in evaluating what they can tell us about Native American life?

2   Are the values of the ethnographer who recorded the Costanoan story any less relevant (more "neutral") to evaluating that source than the values of the French Jesuits in evaluating their reports of Native American culture? In considering the Costanoan story, ask yourself not only why it was relevant to their world in the colonial past but why it was still relevant to the storyteller in the early twentieth century.

3   What do each of these sources tell us about gender relations and the roles of women and men in Native American societies?

4   In what ways do these sources depict quite different Native American peoples (as culturally distinct, for example, as the French and the English)? In what ways do they suggest certain commonalities among Native Americans? Are the two creation stories more similar or different?

5   In general, as you read these accounts, was the author looking for what made Native Americans different, unique, or "exotic," or looking for commonalities with Europeans and Euro-Americans?

Chapter 4   Borderlands

1. Dutch–Native American Relations Deteriorate: Kieft's War, 1640–1645

Kieft's War, 1640–5, like the Pequot War in New England and the assault on Native Americans during Bacon's Rebellion in Virginia, saw Europeans virtually exterminate hostile Native American populations. William Kieft was one in a series of directors of the Dutch West India Company's operations in New Netherlands. This war between Europeans and Native Americans was unusual in producing a number of accounts that were highly critical of the policies that led to the fighting. Such accounts were partisan (Kieft's supporters had their own story to tell), and, of course, "one-sided," as they did not include a Native American perspective, but they do provide some sense of the ways that even modest European settlement intruded on Native American life. The extract below comes from a 1644 account, drawn up by company officials in New Netherlands, of the situation in the colony.

But said population did not experience any special impulse until the year 1639, when the Fur trade with the Indians, which had been previously reserved to the Company, was thrown free and open to every body; at which time not only the inhabitants there residing spread themselves far and wide, but even new Colonists came thither from Fatherland; and the neighboring English, both from Virginia and New England repaired to us. . . . Although the hope was now entertained that the country would by such means arrive at a nourishing pass, yet it afterwards appeared that the abuses attendant on the free trade was the cause of its ruin.

First: because the Colonists, each with a view to advance his own interest, separated themselves from one another, and settled far in the interior of the Country, the better to trade with the Indians, whom they then sought to allure to their houses by excessive familiarity and treating. By this course they brought themselves into disrepute with the Indians, who, not having been always treated alike, made this, the cause of enmity.

Secondly: in consequence of the proximity to the Indians, whose lands lay unfenced, the cattle belonging to our people, straying without herdsmen; seriously damaged their corn or maize. This occasioned much complaint, and no redress following, they revenged themselves, killing both the cattle and horses.

Thirdly: not only the Colonists, but also the free traders proceeding from this country, sold for furs in consequence of the great profit, fire-arms to the Mohawks for full 400 men, with powder and lead; which, being refused to the other tribes when demanded, increased the hatred and enmity of the latter.

Fourthly: It happened, in addition to this, that the Director had, a few years after, imposed a contribution of maize on the Indians, whereby they were totally estranged from our people.

Hence arose divers threats and injurious occurrences, which finally broke out into acts of hostility; so that, first: the Raritan Indians attempted to make away with one of our sloops, and afterwards killed some hogs on Staten Island. Whereupon the Director dispatched eighty soldiers thither to avenge the act, who burnt their corn and killed three or four of their people. Both sides then desisted from further proceedings.

Next it happened that a Wechquaeakeck Indian murdered, about the year 1640, an old man in his own house with an axe; for which no satisfaction having been afforded by the tribe, 12 men, chosen from the Commonalty, afterwards resolved, in the year 1642, to revenge the murder by open war; but nothing was done at that time in consequence, of missing the enemy; who, observing what was designed against them, sued for peace.

Some time afterwards the Hackingsack Indians designedly shot, with an arrow, a Dutchman, who sat thatching a house. The Commonalty was very much troubled at this, dreading the recurrence of other such acts. And while the Director was seeking in vain for satisfaction, God seemed to have taken vengeance on those of Witqueschack, through the Mahikan Indians, who surprising, slew full 70 of them and led many women and children away into captivity. This obliged the remainder to fly to our people at the Manhattans, where they were received into the houses, and fed by the Director during fourteen days. Shortly after this, seized with another panic, they fled with the Hackingsacx, fully a thousand strong, to the vicinity of the fort, and over the river of Povonia. Some of the 12 men perceiving this, the Director... authorized an attack on the abovementioned

Indians, in the course of the night between the 27th and 28th of February, 1643, by a party of soldiers and burghers, who, with cruel tyranny, slew 80 of them, and took 30 prisoners. And although the Commonalty protested... on account of these hasty and severe proceedings; as having taken place without their knowledge or consent, they were obliged, notwithstanding, to declare open war against full eleven tribes of Indians, who rose in arms on that account. The consequence was that about one thousand of these, and many soldiers and colonists belonging to us, were killed.

Source: E. B. O'Callaghan, ed., *Documents Relative to the Colonial History of the State of New-York*, 15 vols. (Albany: Weed, Parsons & Company, 1853–87), XIII, 151–2. Translated from a document in the Royal Archives at the Hague.

Study: Evan Haefeli, "Kieft's War and the Cultures of Violence in Colonial America," in Michael A. Bellesiles, ed., *Lethal Imagination: Violence and Brutality in American History* (New York: New York University Press, 1999), pp. 17–40.

2. The Natural Wonders of California: Jose de Gálvez's Expedition, 1769–1770, as Recorded by Father (Franciscan) Juan Crespí

In 1769 Spain sent a military and religious mission from Lower (Baja) California to explore and secure the area between San Diego Bay and Monterey Bay. Jose de Gálvez headed the mission politically and militarily, but among those traveling in the various land and sea parties dispatched from Mexico were Franciscan friars. Juan Crespí (1721–82) had arrived in New Spain (Mexico) almost two decades earlier with other Franciscan missionaries. On the trip to California he kept a daily log of his observations, and from that log wrote a detailed account of the arduous journey of exploration. In preparing the published edition from which the extracts below are drawn, Alan K. Brown worked with fragments of Crespí trail notes, a draft made from the notes, and a revised "journal" based on the earlier draft.

(July 20th)... Having reached here today, Saint Margaret's day, we are christening it by the name of this holy virgin and martyr. On our reaching here, the whole village's worth of men, women, and boy and girl children soon came over, who must all have amounted to over sixty souls, all of them, young and old, having their whole bodies very much painted in all colors. The men have better features than the women. We have seen beads, Castilian ones, being worn around their necks; whether they will may have been preserved by them since General Vizcaino's time,[1] or whether there may be some nation further up that has given them to them, we cannot tell. Many of the heathens wear around their necks very thick claws which, so we have come to realize, must be bear claws, as they say these claws are from animals big as the mules, and there are some of these animals very close by now. Some beads were distributed to them. They all seem very tractable, with the men going naked and the women dressed like those I have mentioned on the past days' marches.

(September 2nd) . . . We were visited this morning by six very fine heathens, saying that there are two villages in this neighborhood. There are good-sized sand dunes upon one side of this lake here, and the other lake lies among dunes, so they say, with the whole edge of the sea (which since it can be heard very clearly is not very far from here) still being full of very tall dunes as far as the point of a high mountain range that we have in view from here, apparently making a kind of an embayment. Through these dunes here, there are a great many tracks of large bears. The soldiers shot and slew one yesterday afternoon, a very monstrously big, fearful creature. The hind feet are not under a third yard long, and are over a sixth yard in breadth; the forepaws are a good quarter-yard in length and over a sixth in breadth; with the toes, soles, and palms of the forepaws like a human's but with monstrously large digits, the nails being about a finger thick and three fingers in length. The head, and all of this creature, are a fearful thing to see, with two fangs a finger thick on both sides of its mouth. God deliver us from its clutches.

(October 8th) . . . The scouts came back from exploring what had been seeming to be pines, which they were not, but instead very straight very thick trees, quite tall, with a very short slight leaf. Some said they were savins; however, they are not so to my understanding, since the wood is red; but they are not junipers either. Whether or not they may be savins, who can tell. If so, they are not like any other that we have seen elsewhere.

Source: Juan Crespí, *A Description of Distant Roads: Original Journals of the First Expedition into California, 1769–1770*, ed. and trans. Alan K. Brown (San Diego, CA: San Diego University Press, 2001), pp. 284–7, 468–9, 554–7.

Study: Ramón A. Gutiérrez and Richard J. Orsi, eds., *Contested Eden: California before the Gold Rush* (Berkeley, CA: University of California Press, 1998).

---

[1] Sebastián Vizcaíno had traveled through the same region in 1602–3.

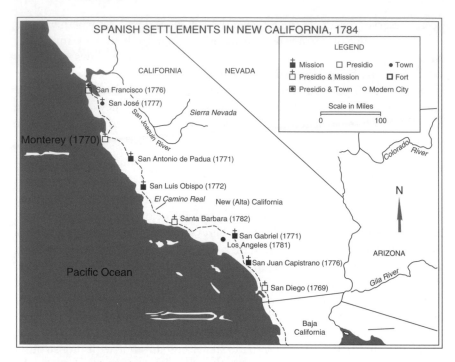

Map 3   Spanish settlements in New California, 1784
From David J. Weber, *The Spanish Frontier in North America* (New Haven: Yale University Press, 1992), p. 262. © 1992 by Yale University.

3. Pedro Fages Describes California Native Americans, 1775

Pedro Fages was among the Spanish officers who accompanied José de Gálvez's expedition into Upper California in 1769–70. He subsequently was appointed military commander of the region, and undertook at least two more exploratory trips of the San Francisco Bay area before writing his description of the region and its peoples. Fages wrote the document in Mexico, after being recalled from service in California in 1774. He would eventually return to California, and serve as governor from 1782 to 1791. His description would not be published until almost a century after his death around 1796.

The mission of San Carlos was, as originally established in June, 1770, founded near the Presidio de San Carlos de Monterey, [and] ... now stands, on the banks of the Carmel River. The new church, the dwelling, and the offices within the stockade, were built of good cedar and cypress, with earthen roofs.... The reverend fathers had already baptized, counting great and small, one hundred and sixty-two natives; of these, eleven had died, and there had been twenty-six marriages. These twenty-six families, with the single persons and children, made a total of one hundred and fifty-one persons, who formed the camp contiguous to the stockade, where they had their small houses built after the manner of the country. Three volunteer soldiers of my company had married recently baptized Indian women, and a servant had married another. The new Christians attend Mass and indoctrination regularly, and the natives of the neighboring villages are accustomed to frequent the mission in very orderly fashion. Only the residents of the village called *de los Zanjones*, six leagues distant toward San Diego, have been so bold as to attack postriders and travelers, but they have been punished, not without its having cost the lives of a few highway robbers, though they have not been able, thank God, to kill any of our men.

As to the temporal affairs of this mission, the reverend fathers have attempted to cultivate the soil in the best way possible, and the situation was improved when the mission was moved to where it now is, in the vicinity of the camp. The planting of corn turned out well, and the same is hoped of the wheat, although all that is sown will be exposed to the usual risks of excess or lack of rain, or of being sown out of season, since there is no means of taking irrigating water out of the river because the water flows deep in it and confined within a narrow bed. But God will be pleased to supply the needs of these unhappy people, for if they have to depend upon the mission for sustenance and the protection of a few clothes, their conversion will be an accomplished thing.

The Indians of this mission and its environs are well proportioned in body, but they do not have the best faculties of mind, and they are of feeble spirit. This apparently is attributable to their condition and the kind of life they lead, always fearful and unable to retire or make excursions of more than four or five leagues from the port of the Punta de Pinos, lest they come into conflict with their opponents who resist and persecute them on all sides. They love the Spaniards very much, and recognize in them a shelter and protection of which they were in absolute need. Nearly all of them go naked, except a few who cover themselves with a small cloak of rabbit or hare skin, which does not fall below the waist. The women wear a short apron of red and white cords twisted and worked as closely as possible, which extends to the knee. Others use the green and dry *tule* interwoven, and complete their outfit with a deerskin half tanned or entirely untanned, to make wretched underskirts which scarcely serve to indicate the distinction of sex, or to cover their nakedness with sufficient modesty.

They are governed by independent captains, both those near the mission and those who are more remote within the territory mentioned. They are warlike, as are the Indians everywhere else, and they inter their dead where they fall, having no chosen spot for burial. When they desire a truce in any battle, or to show themselves peaceful upon any other occasion, they loosen the cords of their bows in order that their intention may be understood. If two of the natives quarrel with each other, they stand body to body, giving each other blows as best they can, using what might be called spatulas of bone, which they always carry for the purpose of scraping off their perspiration while in the bath and during the fatigue of their marches. But as soon as blood is drawn from either of the combatants, however little he may shed, the quarrel is forthwith stopped, and they become reconciled as friends, even when redress of the greatest injury is sought.

They do not have fixed places for their villages, but wander here and there wherever they can find provisions at hand. Their houses are badly constructed, consisting solely of a few boughs placed in a circular arrangement. Their marriages, as in San Antonio, are celebrated with the barbarous practice of scratching each other when they cohabitate, a foolish practice committed even by the newly converted and baptized, though the reverend fathers labor much with them in order to dissuade them from it.... They have a game which is frivolous enough but which has interest supplied by wagers; it is like this: An Indian takes any little thing and hides it in one hand; closing both hands, he holds them out to the other player, who must guess in which hand the object is. All this is accompanied by various postures and gestures, the players and spectators singing while the guessing is in progress. The gain or loss amounts to a quiver, a skin, a handful of seeds, or some such thing.

These Indians have a kind of bath – although I do not know whether it deserves the name or not ... They erect a hut of branches, stakes, and fagots, after the fashion of an oven, without any air passage whatever. The Indian gets into it, and others make a fire for him with small pieces of wood near the door, and the one who is inside receives a good scorching for an hour, during which he perspires copiously, scraping himself with the poniard or spatula mentioned above. This done, he comes out quickly, and goes to wash himself all over in cold water wherever he may first find it. They have a custom of repeating this alternation, the first bath being in the morning, the others being at midday and at night. The women do not use these baths.

Source: Herbert Ingram Priestly, ed. and trans., *A Historical, Political, and Natural Description of California by Pedro Fages, Soldier of Spain* (Berkeley: University of California Press, 1937), pp. 63–8.

Study: David J. Weber, *The Spanish Frontier in North America* (New Haven: Yale University Press, 1992).

4. Natchez War in Louisiana, 1729–1730

In the 1720s, the Natchez were a Native American people who lived in scattered villages more than one hundred miles up the Mississippi River from the primary French settlements around New Orleans and on the Gulf Coast. A French outpost along the Mississippi near the Natchez villages included several "concessions," tobacco farms on lands nominally Native American, and now worked by enslaved Africans and Indians. Disease, disputes over trade relations, and a relentless demand by the Europeans for more of the rich farmland along the Mississippi fueled Natchez anger and exploded into a deadly assault on the French outposts in 1729. Escaped slaves fought alongside the Natchez, but the French also used black troops and Native American peoples against the Natchez. The document below, written by a Jesuit missionary in New Orleans, describes part of the French counteroffensive.

While our little army was repairing to the Tonikas [Tunicas], seven hundred Tchactas [Choctaws] mustered, and conducted by Monsieur le Sueur [Sieur Jean-Paul Le Seur], marched toward the Natches. We were informed by a party of these people that the Savages were not at all on their guard, but passed all their nights in dancing. The Tchactas took them therefore by surprise, and made a descent on them on the 17th of January, at the break of day. In less than three hours they had delivered 59 persons, both women and children, with the Tailor and Carpenter, and 106 Negroes or Negro women with their children; they made 18 of the Natches prisoners and took 60 scalps.…

Before the Tchactas had determined to fall upon the Natches, they had gone to them to carry the calumet, and were received in a very novel manner. They found them and their houses adorned with chasubles and drapery of the altars, many wore patens about their necks, and drank and gave to drink of brandy in the chalices and the ciboria. And the Tchactas themselves, when they had gained these articles by pillaging our enemies, renewed this profane sacrilege, by making the same use of our ornaments, and sacred vessels in their dances and sports. We were never able to recover more than a small portion of them. The greater part of their chiefs have come here to receive payment for the scalps they have taken, and for the French and Negroes whom they have freed. It is necessary for us to buy very dearly their smallest services, and we have scarcely any desire to employ them again, particularly as they have appeared much less brave than the small Tribes, who have not made themselves feared by their great number.

Every year disease diminishes this Nation, which is now reduced to three or four thousand warriors, Since these Savages have betrayed their disposition here, we have not been able to endure them longer. They are insolent, ferocious, disgusting, importunate, and insatiable. . . .

They have abandoned to the Tchactas three Negroes who had been most unruly, and who had taken the most active part in behalf of the Natches. They have been burned alive with a degree of cruelty which has inspired all the Negroes with a new horror of the Savages, but which will have a beneficial effect in securing the safety of the Colony. The Tonikas and other smaller Tribes have gained some new advantages over the Natches, and have taken many prisoners, of whom they have burned three women and four men, after having taken their scalps. Our own people, it is said, begin to be accustomed to this barbarous spectacle.

We could not forbear being affected, when we saw arrive in this City the French women whom the Natches had made slaves. The miseries which they had suffered were painted in their countenances. . . . The little girls, whom none of the inhabitants wish to adopt, have greatly enlarged the interesting company of orphans whom the Nuns are bringing up.

Source: "Letter from Father le Petit, Missionary, to Father d'Avaugour, Procurator of the Missions in North America," July 12, 1730, in Reuben Gold Thwaites, ed., *The Jesuit Relations and Allied Documents* (Cleveland, Ohio: Burrows Bros. Co., 1896–1901), vol. LXVII: *Travels and Explorations of the Jesuit Missionaries in New France*, pp. 120–223, at pp. 188–9, 194–9.

Study: Daniel H. Unser, *Indians, Settlers, & Slaves in a Frontier Exchange Economy: The Lower Mississippi Valley before 1783* (Chapel Hill: University of North Carolina Press for the Institute of Early American History and Culture, 1992).

Discussion Questions

1   What was a "borderland" in colonial America? What characteristics do the *places* discussed in these documents have in common?
2   Compare the accounts of Kieft's War and the French struggles with the Natchez. In what ways do both reflect the insecurities of settlers on the margins of empire?
3   Initial contact with a new frontier usually led to reports of the natural "wonders" of the area. What response does Juan Crespi record to the "wonders" of California? What parallels are there in the way these natural wonders were described and Pedro Fages' description of Native Americans in the same region?

Chapter 5   Founding Colonies

1. John Winthrop's *A Modell of Christian Charity*, 1630

John Winthrop (1588–1649) was elected the first governor of the Massachusetts Bay Colony in 1629 and led the Puritan migration to Massachusetts in 1630. Winthrop, a lawyer by education, and a substantial landowner, was also a devout Puritan lay preacher. His sermon, "A Modell of Christian Charity," may have been delivered in Southampton before he departed with other settlers on the Arbella; *rather than lay down his thoughts about the appropriate form of government for the New World colony that he was to lead, Winthrop used the occasion to remind his listeners that their success depended on remaining a community bound together by Christian love. Below are two extracts, in the first of which Winthrop explains the interdependence of poor and rich, and in the second of which he outlines the challenges facing the Puritan community.*

[Introduction]

God Almightie in his most holy and wise providence hath soe disposed of the Condition of mankinde, as in all times some must be rich some poore, some highe and eminent in power and dignities others meane and in subieccion.

THE REASON HEREOF.

1. REAS: First, to hold conformity with the rest of his workes, being delighted to shewe forthe the glory of his wisdome in the variety and differance of the Creatures and the glory of his power, in ordering all these differences for the preservation and good of the whole, and the glory of his greatnes that as it is the glory of princes to haue many officers, soe this great King will haue many

Stewards counting himselfe more honoured in dispenceing his guifts to, man by man, then if hee did it by his owne immediate hand.

2. REAS: *Secondly,* That he might haue the more occasion to manifest the worke of his Spirit: first, upon the wicked in moderateing and restraineing them: soe that the riche and mighty should not eate vpp the poore, nor the poore, and dispised rise vpp against theire superiours, and shake off theire yoake; 2ly in the regenerate in exerciseing his graces in them, as in the greate ones, theire loue mercy, gentlenes, temperance etc., in the poore and inferiour sorte, theire faithe patience, obedience etc:

3. REAS: Thirdly, That every man might haue need of other, and from hence they might be all knitt more nearly together in the Bond of brotherly affection: from hence it appeares plainely that noe man is made more honourable then another or more wealthy etc., out of any perticuler and singuler respect to himselfe but for the glory of his Creator and the Common good of the Creature, Man; Therefore God still reserues the propperty of these guifts to himselfe as Ezek: 16. 17. he there calls wealthe his gold and his silver etc. Prov: 3. 9. he claimes theire seruice as his due honour the Lord with thy riches etc. All men being thus (by divine providence) rancked into two sortes, riche and poore; under the first, are comprehended all such as are able to liue comfortably by theire owne meanes duely improued; and all others are poore according to the former distribution. There are two rules whereby wee are to walke one towards another: JUSTICE and MERCY. These are allwayes distinguished in theire Act and in theire obiect, yet may they both concurre in the same Subiect in eache respect; as sometimes there may be an occasion of shewing mercy to a rich man, in some sudden danger of distresse, and allsoe doeing of meere justice to a poor man in regard of some perticuler contract etc. There is likewise a double Lawe by which wee are regulated in our conversation one towardes another: in both the former respects, the lawe of nature and the lawe of grace, or the morrall lawe or the lawe of the gospell, to omitt the rule of justice as not propperly belonging to this purpose otherwise then it may fall into consideration in some perticuler Cases: By the first of these lawes man as he was enabled soe withall [is] commaunded to loue his neighbour as himselfe upon this ground stands all the precepts of the morrall lawe, which concernes our dealings with men. To apply this to the works of mercy this lawe requires two things first that every man afford his help to another in every want or distresse Secondly, That hee performe this out of the same affeccion, which makes him carefull of his owne good according to that of our Saviour Math: [7. 12] Whatsoever ye would that men should doe to you. This was practised by Abraham and Lott in entertaineing the Angells and the old man of Gibea....

[Conclusion]

Now the onely way to avoyde this shipwracke and to provide for our posterity is to followe the Counsell of Micah, to doe justly, to loue mercy, to walke humbly with our Gods for this end, wee must be knitt together in this worke as one man, wee must entertaine each other in brotherly Affeccion, wee must be willing to abridge our selues of our superfluities, for the supply of others necessities, wee must uphold a familiar Commerce together in all meekenes, gentlenes, patience and liberallity, wee must delight in eache other, make others Condicions our owne reioyce together, mourne together, labour, and suffer together, allwayes haueing before our eyes our Commission and Community in the worke, our Community as members of the same body, soe shall wee keepe the vnitie of the spirit in the bond of peace, the Lord will be our God and delight to dwell among vs, as his owne people and will commaund a blessing upon vs in all our wayes, soe that wee shall see much more of his wisdome power goodnes and truthe then formerly wee haue beene acquainted with, wee shall finde that the God of Israell is among vs, when term{?} of vs shall be able to resist a thousand of our enemies, when hee shall make vs a prayse and glory, that men shall say of succeeding plantatious: the lord make it like that of New England: for wee must Consider that wee shall be as a Citty upon a Hill, the eies of all people are vppon vs; soe that if wee shall deale falsely with our god in this worke wee haue undertaken and soe cause him to with-drawe his present help from vs, wee shall be made a story and a by-word through the world, wee shall open the mouthes of enemies to speake euill of the wayes of god and all professours for Gods sake; wee shall shame the faces of many of gods worthy seruants, and cause theire prayers to be turned into Cursses upon vs till wee be consumed out of the good land whether wee are goeing: And to shutt vpp this discourse with that exhort-ation of Moses that faithfull seruant of the Lord in his last farewell to Israell Deut. 30. Beloued there is now sett before vs life, and good, deathe and euill in that wee are Commaunded this day to loue the Lord our God, and to loue one another to walke in his wayes and to keepe his Commaundements and his Ordinance, and his lawes, and the Articles of our Covenant with him that wee may liue and be multiplyed, and that the Lord our God may blesse vs in the land whether wee goe to possesse it: But if our heartes shall turne away soe that wee will not obey, but shall be seduced and worshipp other Gods our pleasures, and proffitts, and serue them; it is propounded unto vs this day, wee shall surely perishe out of the good Land whether wee passe over this vast Sea to possesse it;

Therefore lett vs choose life,
that wee, and our Seede,
may liue; by obeyeing his
voyce, and cleaueing to him,
for hee is our life, and
our prosperity.

Source: *The Winthrop Papers*, 6 vols. (Boston: Massachusetts Historical Society, 1929–), II, 282–4, 294–5.

Study: Francis J. Bremer, *John Winthrop: America's Forgotten Founding Father* (New York: Oxford University Press, 2003).

2. Slave and Servant Codes in the Seventeenth-Century English West Indies: Barbados Laws for Servants (and Slaves), 1652

English settlers arrived in the West Indies in the 1620s, and they initially made a living planting tobacco with the labor of "indentured" English servants. By the 1650s, the planters on Barbados, the most populous and prosperous English outpost in the early Caribbean, had converted almost completely to sugar planting using enslaved Africans. In 1661 the Barbados Assembly passed a comprehensive slave code, which became a "model" for other English colonies, but well before that date numerous laws, some now lost, had been passed to regulate servants and slaves. The laws below come from a published 1654 edition of the colony's laws, and they reflect an earlier period when the primary worry of the planters was controlling their English servant population.

---

8. Item, that servant that shall lay violent hands on his, or her Master or Mistress or Overseer, and be convicted thereof before any Justice of the Peace of this Island, the said justice is hereby required and Authorized to order such servants to serve his Said Master or Mistress two years after his time by Indenture or Custom is expired.

10. Item, that on regard that the whole Wealth of the Inhabitants of the Island, consisteth chiefly in the labour of their servants, It is further established, that whosoever shall beget a woman servant with child, shall for such his offence personally serve the owner of such servant three years; or put one in his place for the said time, to recompence his loss and charge in bringing up the bastard Childe...And the said Woman servant

so offending, shall serve her said Master or Mistress, three years after her time of Indenture, or otherwise is expired...And the said man and woman, for their unlawfull copulation, are to suffer such further punishment, as by the Law of the Common-wealth of England is provided.

62. Whereas it hath been by dayly experience found, that many great mischiefs have risen in this Island, and to the particulars, Masters of Families, by the wandering of Servants and Slaves, on Sundayes, Saturdays in the afternoon, and other days wherein the said Servants, or Slaves do not work, and in such times as they can get out of their Masters Plantations, by stealing and filching their Masters goods and provisions, and bartering and selling the same, for remedy whereof: Be it enacted and ordained by the Government and Council, and with the consent of the Gentlemen of the Assembly, that every Servant that shall after Publication hereof absent himself out of his Masters Plantation, not having any License in writing under the hand of his said Master, or Overseer for the same, shall upon Conviction thereof, before any Justice of Peace within this Island, for every two hours absence be adjudged to serve his said Master one whole Month after his time by Indenture, or Custom, is expired...And be it further enacted...that it shall be lawfull for and all the Masters of Families and Overseers are hereby required to apprehend all Negro's whatsoever, so wandering, without the Masters or Mistress Ticket, or Overseers Licence, and they so apprehended moderately to whip and correct, which being done, they are to return them with a guard to their Masters or Mistress Plantation...

Source: *Acts and Statutes of the Island of Barbados, Made and Enacted since the Reduction of the same...and set forth the seventeenth day of September 1652* (London, 1654).

3. A Jamaica Act "For the better Ordering of Slaves," 1684

Jamaica was the largest, initially the most "disorderly" (as a haven for buccaneers who raided Spanish possessions and vessels), and eventually the most prosperous of the English sugar plantation colonies in the West Indies. The Jamaican planters adopted their slave code of 1664 from the Barbados code of 1661. The white Barbadians had declared their African slaves to be "an heathenish, brutish and an uncertaine, dangerous kinde of people." The laws below come from a 1684 published rendition of the code.

If any Negroe slave shall offer any violence by striking or the like, to any Person, shall for the first offence be severely whipt by the Constable, by Order of the Justice of the Peace; and for the second offence by like order shall be severely whipt, his or her Nose slit, and Face burnt in some place; and for the third offence, be left to two Justices and three Free-holders, to inflict Death or any other punishment according to their Discretion; *Provided*, such striking or conflict be not by Command of, or in Lawful defence of their owners Persons or Goods.

And it is further Enacted by the Authority aforesaid, That every Master or Mistress or Overseer of a Family in this Island, shall cause all their Slaves Houses to be diligently and effectually searched once every fourteen days, for Clubs, wooden Swords, and mischievous Weapons, and finding any, shall take them away and cause them to be burnt, and also upon any request made, to search the same for stolen Cloaths, Goods, or any other things or Commodities, particularly suspected Flesh, that is not given them by their Owners or Overseers , and honestly come by...

It is further Enacted by the Authority aforesaid, That if any Slave or Slaves shall commit any Murther, or make any Insurrection, or rise in Rebellion against his Majesties Authority, or make any preparation of Arms, as Powder, Bullets, or offensive Weapons, or hold any Conspiracies for raising Mutinies or Rebellion, the Offenders shall be tried by two Justices of the Peace, and three Free-holders... who are hereby impowered and required, to try the said Slaves so Offending, and inflict Death, or any other Punishment...

And it is further Enacted by the Authority aforesaid, That if any Slave, by punishment from the owner, for running away, or other Offence, shall suffer in Life and Limb, no person shall be liable to the Law for the same; but if any one out of wilfulness, wantonness, or bloudy mindedness, shall kill a Slave, he or she, upon due conviction thereof, shall suffer three Months Imprisonment, without Bail or Mainprize, and also pay the sum of Fifty Pounds to the owner of such Slave, but if the person so Offending be a Servant, he or she shall receive on his or her bare Back, nine and thirty Lashes, by order of any two Justices of the Peace... [and] be further liable to serve the owner or owners of such Slave the full term of Four Years.

Source: *The Laws of Jamaica Passed by the Assembly and confirmed by His Majesty in Council, April 17, 1684* (London, 1684).

Study: Jennifer Morgan, *Laboring Women: Reproduction and Gender in New World Slavery* (Philadelphia: University of Pennsylvania Press, 2004).

4. The Concessions and Agreements of the Proprietors, Freeholders, and Inhabitants of the Province of West New Jersey, 1676/1677

In 1676 the proprietors of New Jersey divided the colony into two provinces, East and West New Jersey, and West New Jersey passed into the hands of a group of Quaker trustees who sought to "lay the foundation for after ages to understand their liberty as men and christians, that they may not be brought in bondage, but by their own consent . . ." The Concessions committed the proprietors to a form of government based on the consent and participation of the governed and to protection, that Quakers had been denied in England, of religious belief and personal property. Some of the provisions of the Concessions would be reaffirmed in 1681, debated for the remainder of the decade as West New Jersey established its proprietary government, and then finally diluted in 1702 when the Jerseys were reunited as a royal colony.

Chapter XVI

That no men, nor number of men upon earth, hath power or authority to rule over men's consciences in religious matters, therefore it is consented, agreed and ordained, that no person or persons whatsoever within the said Province, at any time or times hereafter, shall be any ways upon any presence whatsoever, called in question, or in the least punished or hurt, either in person, estate, or priviledge, for the sake of his opinion, judgment, faith or worship towards God in matters of religion. But that all and every such person, and persons may from time to time, and at all times, freely and fully have, and enjoy his and their judgments, and the exercises of their consciences in matters of religious worship throughout all the said Province.

Chapter XVII

That no Proprietor, freeholder or inhabitant of the said Province of West New Jersey, shall be deprived or condemned of life, limb, liberty, estate, property or any ways hurt in his or their privileges, freedoms or franchises, upon any account whatsoever, without a due tryal, and Judgment passed by twelve good and lawful men of his neighborhood first had: And that in all causes to be tryed, and in all tryals, the person or persons, arraigned may except against any of the said neighborhood, without any reason rendered, (not exceeding thirty five) and in case of any valid reason alleged, against every person nominated for that service.

Chapter XXV

That there may be a good understanding and friendly correspondence between the proprietors freeholders and inhabitants of the Said province and the Indian Natives thereof

It is concluded and agreed that if any of the Indian natives within the said province shall or may doe any wrong or injury to any of the Proprietors Freeholders or inhabitants in person or estate or otherwayes howsoever upon notice thereof or Complaint made to the comissioners of any two of them they are to give notice to the Sachim or other chiefe person or persons that hath authority over the said Indian native or natives that Justice may be done and satisfaction made to the Person or persons offended according to Law.

And also in case any of the Proprietors or Inhabitants shall any wise wrong or injure any of the Indian natives there in person estate or otherwise the Comissioners are to take care upon complaint to them made or any one of them either by the indian natives or others that Justice be done to the Indian Natives and plenary satisfaction made them according to the nature and qualitie of the offence and Injury. And that in all tryalls wherein any of the said Indian Natives are concerned the tryall to be by six of the neighbour-hood and six of the said Indian Natives to be indifferently and impartially Chosen by order of the Comissioners and that the Comissioners use their endeavour to persuade the Natives to the like way of tryall when any of the Natives doe any waies wrong or injure the said proprietors Freeholders or inhabitants that they choose six of the Natives and six of the Freeholders or Inhabitants to Judge of the wrong and injury done and to proportion satisfaction accordingly.

Source: Aaron Leaming and Jacob Spicer, *The Grants, Concessions, and Original Constitutions of the Province of New-Jersey* (Philadelphia, 1756).

Study: Julian Boyd, ed., *Fundamental Laws and Constitutions of New Jersey, 1664–1964* (Princeton, NJ: Van Nostrand, 1964).

5. William Penn Purchases Land from the Lenape (Delaware) Indians, 1682

William Penn (1644–1718) was a son of a noted British admiral, but in 1667 he had joined the Quakers, a Christian, pacifist sect, which held some of the most radical religious and social ideas in England. Penn spent the 1670s as perhaps the most prominent religious dissenter in England, then in 1680

*petitioned the monarch, Charles II, for the right to establish a colony in the
New World. Penn hoped to profit from the enterprise, but also to establish
a uniquely tolerant society. That tolerance, at least as Penn envisioned his
"holy experiment," extended to the native inhabitants of the region, the
Lenape peoples. Penn hoped to trade profitably with the Lenape, and obtain
the land he needed for his colony as well (but insisted it be purchased, not
simply taken). In the first document extracted below, a promotional tract,
Penn describes Native American customs; the second extract comes from
the deed Penn negotiated with the Lenape for some of their land.*

[Of the Natives' Customs and Manners]

... in liberality they excel; nothing is too good for their friend. Give them
a fine gun, coat, or other thing, it may pass twenty hands before it sticks;
light of heart, strong affections, but soon spent, the most merry creatures
that live, feast and dance perpetually; they never have much, nor want
much. Wealth circulates like the blood, all parts partake; and though none
shall want what another has, yet [they are] exact observers of property.
Some kings have sold, others presented me with several parcels of land; the
pay or presents I made them were not hoarded by the particular owners; but
the neighboring kings and their clans being present when the goods were
brought out, the parties chiefly concerned consulted, what and to whom
they should give them? To every king then, by the hands of a person for that
work appointed, is a proportion sent, so sorted and folded, and with that
gravity that is admirable. Then that king subdivides it in like manner among
his dependents, they hardly leaving themselves an equal share with one of
their subjects; and be it on such occasions, at festivals or at their common
meals, the kings distribute, and to themselves last. They care for little
because they want but little; and the reason is, a little contents them.
In this they are sufficiently revenged on us; if they are ignorant of our
pleasures, they are also free from our pains. They are not disquieted with
bills of lading and exchange, nor perplexed with chancery suits and
exchequer reckonings. We sweat and toil to live; their pleasure feeds them,
I mean, their hunting, fishing, and fowling, and this table is spread everywhere. They eat twice a day, morning and evening; their seats and table are
the ground. Since the Europeans came into these parts, they are grown great
lovers of strong liquors, rum especially, and for it exchange the richest
of their skins and furs. If they are heated with liquors, they are restless
till they have enough to sleep. That is their cry, "Some more, and I will
go to sleep." But when drunk, one of the most wretchedest spectacles in
the world.

[Deed with the Delaware Indians]

15 July 1682. This indenture made the fifteenth day of July in the year of our Lord according to English account, one thousand six hundred eighty and two, between Idquahon, Janottowe, Idquoqueywon, Sahoppe for himself and Okanickon, Merkekowen, Oreckton for Nanacussey, Shaurwawghon, Swanpisse, Nahoosey, Tomackhickon, Westkekitt, and Towhawsis, Indian sachemakers of the one part, and William Penn, Esq., chief proprietor of the province of Pennsylvania of the other part. Witnesses that for and in consideration of the sums and particulars of goods, merchandise, and utensils hereinafter mentioned and expressed, that is to say: three hundred and fifty fathoms of wampum, twenty white blankets, twenty fathoms of stroudwaters, sixty fathoms of duffels, twenty kettles (four whereof large), twenty guns, twenty coats, forty shirts, forty pair of stockings, forty hoes, forty axes, two barrels of powder, two hundred bars of lead, two hundred knives, two hundred small glasses, twelve pair of shoes, forty copper boxes, forty tobacco tongs, two small barrels of pipes, forty pair of scissors, forty combs, twenty-four pounds of red lead, one hundred awls, two handfuls of fishhooks, two handfuls of needles, forty pounds of shot, ten bundles of beads, ten small saws, twelve drawing knives, four ankers of tobacco, two ankers of rum, two ankers of cider, two ankers of beer, and three hundred guilders, by the said William Penn, his agents or assigns, to the said Indian sachemakers for the use of them and their people, at and before sealing and delivery hereof in hand paid and delivered whereof and wherewith they, the said sachemakers, do hereby acknowledge themselves fully satisfied, contented, and paid.

The said Indian sachemakers (parties to these presents), as well for and on the behalf of themselves as for and on the behalf of their respective Indians or people for whom they are concerned, have granted, bargained, sold, and delivered, and by these presents do fully, clearly, and absolutely grant, bargain, sell, and deliver unto the said William Penn, his heirs and assigns, forever, all that or those tract or tracts of land lying and being in the province of Pennsylvania aforesaid, beginning at a certain white oak in the land now in the tenure of John Wood's and by him called the "Graystones" over against the Falls of Delaware River, and so from thence up by the riverside . . . together also with all and singular isles, islands, rivers, rivulets, creeks, waters, ponds, lakes, plains, hills, mountains, meadows, marshes, swamps, trees, woods, mines, minerals, and appurtenances whatsoever to the said tract or tracts of land belonging or in anywise appertaining. And the reversion and reversions, remainder and remainders thereof and all the estate, right, title, interest, use, property, claim, and demand whatsoever, as well of them the said Indian sachemakers (parties to these presents) as of all and every other the Indians concerned therein or in any part or parcel thereof. To have and to hold the said tract and tracts of land, islands, and all and every other the said granted premises, with their and every of their appurtenances unto the said William Penn, his heirs and assigns, forever, to the only proper use and behoof of the said William Penn, his heirs and assigns, forevermore. And the said Indian sachemakers and their heirs and successors and every of them, the said tract or tracts of land, islands, and all and every other the said granted premises with their and every of their appurtenances, unto the said William Penn, his heirs and assigns, forever, against them the said Indian sachemakers, their heirs and successors, and against all and every Indian and Indians and their heirs and successors claiming or to claim any right, title, or estate into or out of the said granted premises or any part or parcel thereof, shall and will warrant and forever defend by these presents. In witness whereof the said parties to these present indentures interchangeably have set their hands and seals the day and year first above written, 1682.

The mark of Idquahon, The mark of Janottowe, The mark of Idquoqueywon, The mark of Sahoppe, The mark of Merkekowen, The mark of Oreckton for himself and Nanacussey, The mark of Shaurwawghon, The mark of Swanpisse, The mark of Nahoosey, The mark of Tomackhickon, The mark of Westkekitt, The mark of Towhawsis.

Source: The description of the Lenape Indians is from "A Letter from William Penn ... to the Committee of the Free Society of Traders" (London, 1683). The treaty is from Jean R. Soderlund, *William Penn and the Founding of Pennsylvania, 1680–1684: A Documentary History* (Philadelphia: University of Pennsylvania Press, 1983), pp. 156–8, from the original in the Historical Society of Pennsylvania, Philadelphia.

Study: Paul A. W. Wallace, *Indians in Pennsylvania* (Harrisburg: Pennsylvania Historical and Museum Commission, 1968).

Discussion Questions

1   Each of these documents suggest different motives, intentions, and concerns that went into the founding of New World societies. Which are proscriptive – designs for the ideal way people ought to live? Which seem more a response to specific problems that settlers encountered in the New World?

2   What can we learn from colonial law codes? In what ways do the codes reflect the way people actually behave? Or do they tell us mostly about the hopes and fears of those who wrote the codes? In this context, can you reach any

conclusions about the relations between free and enslaved in the English West Indies? Or about relations between Euro-Americans and Native Americans in Pennsylvania?

3   What are the implications of John Winthrop's sermon for the way he hoped people would actually live in Massachusetts Bay Colony? If you were a settler, and took his strictures to heart, how would you fashion a system of government for the new colony?

4   Is the religious sentiment in Winthrop's sermon compatible with the governance of slaves that other English people initiated in the West Indies? Are the ideals of the West Jersey proprietors compatible with the slave codes of the West Indies? If so, why? If not, how would you explain these differences in the way English people thought about founding New World societies?

Chapter 6   Northern Colonies

1. Articles of Agreement Among the First Settlers of Springfield, Massachusetts, 1636

Most of the Puritans who came during the "Great Migration" of the 1630s to Massachusetts settled not in Boston but in small, corporate and pious towns radiating out geographically from Massachusetts Bay. When it was established in the Connecticut River Valley, Springfield was the furthest outpost of the Bay Colony, and the primary organizer of the undertaking, William Pynchon, expected to use the new town as a trading center with the Native American population. The agreement entered into by the founders is typical of the way Puritan towns were initially organized. Pynchon remained in Springfield until the 1650s and grew rich from the fur trade, but eventually left Massachusetts after being disciplined for publishing his unorthodox religious views.

May the 14th, 1636

We whose names are underwritten, being by God's Providence engaged together to make a Plantation at and over against Agaam [Agawam, renamed Springfield] upon Connecticut, do mutually agree to certain articles and orders to be observed and kept by us and by our successors, except we and every of us for ourselves and in our own persons shall think meet upon better reasons alter our present resolutions.

1^{ly}. We intend by God's grace, as soon as we can, with all convenient speed, to procure some Godly and faithful minister with whom we purpose join in church covenant to walk in all the ways of Christ [George Moxon arrived as minister in 1637].

2^{ly}. We intend that our town shall be composed of forty families, or, if we think meet after to alter our purpose, yet not to exceed the number of fifty families, rich and poor.

3^{ly}. That every inhabitant shall have a convenient proportion for a house lot, as we shall see meet for everyone's quality and estate.

4^{ly}. That everyone that hath a house lot shall have a proportion of the cow pasture to the north of End Brook tying northward from the town; and also that everyone shall have a share of the hassokey marsh over against his lot, if it be to be had, and everyone to have his proportionable share of all the woodland.

5^{ly}. That everyone shall have a share of the meadow or planting ground over against them, as nigh as may be on Agawam side.

6^{ly}. That the long meadow called Masacksick, lying in the way to Dorchester, shall be distributed to every man as we shall think meet, except we shall find other conveniency for some for their milch cattle and other cattle also.

7^{ly}. That the meadow and pasture called Nayas, toward Patuckett on the side of Agawam lying about four miles above in the river, shall be distributed [erasure] as above said in the former order – and this was altered with consent before the hands were set to it.

8^{ly}. That all rates that shall arise upon the town shall be laid upon lands according to everyone's proportion, acre for acre of house lots and acre for acre of meadow, both alike on this side and both alike on the other side, and for farms that shall lie further off a less proportion as we shall after agree; except we shall see meet to remit one half of the rate from land to other estate.

9^{ly}. That whereas Mr. William Pynchon, Jeheu Burr, and Henry Smith [Pynchon's brother-in-law] have constantly continued to prosecute this plantation when others fell off for fear of the difficulties, and continued to prosecute the same at great charges and at great personal adventure: therefore it is, mutually agreed that forty acres of meadow lying on the south of End Brook under a hillside shall belong to the said parties free from all charges forever – that is to say, twenty acres to Mr. William Pynchon and his heirs and assigns for ever, and ten acres to Jeheu Burr, and ten acres to Henry Smith, and to their heirs and assigns for ever – which said 40 acres is not disposed to them as any allotments of town lands, but they are to have their accommodations in all other places notwithstanding.

10^{ly}. That whereas a house was built at a common charge which cost 6£, and also the Indians demand a great sum to buy their right in the said lands, and also two great shallops [sail boats] which was requisite for the first planting: the value of these engagements is to be borne by inhabitants at their first entrance, as they shall be rated by us, till the said disbursements shall be satisfied. Or else in case the said house and boats be not so satisfied for, then so much meadow to be set out about the said house as may countervail the said extraordinary charge.

11^{ly}. It is agreed that no man except Mr. William Pynchon shall have above ten acres for his house lot.

12^{ly}. [Cancelled] It is also agreed that if any man sell any timber out of his lot in any common ground [and] if he let it lie above three months before he work it out, it shall be lawful for any other man to take it that hath present use of it.

13^{ly}. Whereas there are two cow pastures, the one lying toward Dorchester and the other northward from End Brook, it is agreed that both these pastures shall not be fed at once, but that the town shall be ordered by us in the disposing of [them] for times and seasons, till it be lotted out and fenced in severally.

May 16th, 1636

14. It is agreed that after this day we shall observe this rule about [the] dividing of planting ground and meadow: in all planting ground to regard chiefly persons who are most apt to use such ground; and in all meadow and pasture to regard chiefly cattle and estate, because estate is like to be improved in cattle, and such ground is aptest for their use. And yet we agree that no person that is master of a lot, though he have no cattle, shall have less than three acres of mowing ground; and none that have cows, steers, or year-olds shall have under two acres apiece; and [for] all horses not less than four acres. And this order in dividing meadow by cattle to take place the last of March next; so that all cattle that then appear, and all estate that shall then truly appear at 20£ a cow, shall have this proportion in the meadows on Agawam side, and in the long meadow [called] Masacksick, and in the other long meadow called Nayas, and in the pasture at the north end of the town called End Brook. . . . [Description of specific lot assignments excluded.]

It is ordered that for all highways that shall be thought necessary by the five men above named, they shall have liberty and power to lay them out where they shall see meet, though it be at the ends of men's lots, giving them allowance for so much ground.

Settlement

We testify to the order abovesaid, being all of us first adventurers and undertakers for the said plantation.

William Pynchon	Edmond Wood
Matthew Mitchell	the mark T
Henry Smith	of Thomas Ufford
the mark L	John Cable
of Jehu Burr	
William Blake	

Source: *New England Historical and Genealogical Register*, XIII (October 1859), 295–7.

Study: Stephen Innes, *Labor in a New Land: Economy and Society in Seventeenth-Century Springfield* (Princeton, NJ: Princeton University Press, 1983).

2. John Winthrop Describes Congregational Minister John Eliot's Work as a Missionary to the Native Americans in Massachusetts Bay Colony, 1647

John Eliot (1604–90) came from a similar background as John Winthrop; both were born into comfortable families and well educated. Eliot, however, became a minister and teacher, while Winthrop remained a lay preacher and became the first governor of Massachusetts Bay Colony. Eliot traveled to Massachusetts in 1631, a year after Winthrop, found a position in Roxbury as a teacher, and then became the town's minister in 1641, a position he held for the rest of his life. Eliot learned the Algonquian language of the neighboring Massachuset Indian peoples, preached to them in their own language, and helped establish several towns for "praying Indians." Many of Eliot's converts would die during King Philip's War (1675–6), after they had been removed to an island in Boston harbor, and deadly diseases swept through the refugee encampments.

Mention was made before of some beginning to instruct the Indians, etc, Mr. John Eliot, teacher of the church of Roxbury, found such encouragement, as he took great pains to get their language, and in a few months could speak of the things of God to their understanding; and God prospered his endeavors, so as he kept a constant lecture to them in two places, one week at the wigwam of one Wabon, a new sachem near Watertown mill, and the other the next week in the wigwam of Cutshamekin near Dorchester mill. And for the furtherance of the work of God, divers of the English resorted to his lecture, and the governor and other of the magistrates and elders sometimes; and the Indians began to repair thither from other parts. His manner of proceeding was thus; he would persuade one of the other elders or some magistrate to begin the exercise with prayer in English; then he took a text, and read it first in the Indian language, and after in English; then he preached to them in Indian about an hour; (but first I should have spoke of the catechising their children, who were soon brought to answer him some short questions, whereupon he gave each of them an apple or a cake) then he demanded of some of the chiefs, if they understood him; if they answered, yea, then he asked of them if they had any questions to propound. And they had usually two or three or more questions, which he did resolve. At one time (when the governor was there and about two hundred people, Indian and English, in one wigwam of Cutshamekin's) an old man asked him, if God would receive such an old man as he was; to whom he answered by opening the parable of the workmen that were hired into the vineyard; and when he had opened it, he asked the old man, if he did believe it, who answered he did, and was ready to weep. A second question was, what was the reason, that when all Englishmen did know God, yet some of them were poor. His answer was, 1. that God knows it is better for his children to be good than to be rich; he knows withal, that if some of them had riches, they would abuse them, and wax proud and wanton, etc., therefore he gives them no more riches than may be needful for them, that they may be kept from pride, etc., to depend upon him, 2. he would hereby have men know, that he hath better blessings to bestow upon good men than riches, etc., and that their best portion is in heaven, etc. A third question was, if a man had two wives, (which was ordinary with them,) seeing he must put away one, which he should put away. To this it was answered, that by the law of God the first is the true wife, and the other is no wife; but if such a case fell out, they should then repair to the magistrates, and they would direct them what to do, for it might be, that the first wife might be an adulteress, etc., and then she was to be put away. When all their questions were resolved, he concluded with prayer in the Indian language.

The Indians were usually very attentive, and kept their children so quiet, as caused no disturbance. Some of them began to be seriously affected, and to understand the things of God, and they were generally ready to reform whatsoever they were told to be against the word of God, as their sorcery, (Which they call powwowing,) their whoredoms, etc., idleness, etc. The Indians grew very inquisitive after knowledge both in things divine and also human, so as one of them, meeting with an honest plain Englishman, would needs know of him, what were the first beginnings (which we call principles) of a commonwealth. The Englishman, being far short in the knowledge of such matters, yet ashamed that an Indian should find an Englishman ignorant of any thing, bethought himself what answer to give him, at last resolved upon this, viz. that the first principle of a commonwealth was salt, for (saith he) by means of salt we can keep our flesh and fish, to have it ready when we need it, whereas you lose much for want of it, and are sometimes ready to starve. A second principle is iron, for thereby we fell trees, build houses, till our land, etc. A third is ships, by which we carry forth such commodities as we have to spare, and fetch in such as we need, as cloth, wine, etc. Alas! (saith the Indian) then I fear, we shall never be a commonwealth, for we can neither make salt, nor iron, nor ships.

Source: James K. Hosmer, ed., *Winthrop's Journal* (New York: Charles Scribner's Sons, 1908), pp. 318–21. See also the newer edition, Richard S. Dunn, James Savage, and Laetitia Yeandle, eds., *The Journal of John Winthrop* (Cambridge, MA: Harvard University Press, 1996), pp. 682–4.

Study: David Silverman, *Faith and Boundaries: Colonists, Christianity, and Community among the Wampanoag Indians of Martha's Vineyard, 1600–1871* (New York: Cambridge University Press, 2005).

3. The Raid on Deerfield, 1704

Located on the Connecticut River (approximately as far north as Albany, New York, was on the Hudson River), Deerfield, Massachusetts was situated on the colonial frontier of European settlement between English New England and French Canada. It was at the beginning of the eighteenth century a village of some 300 people, led by its Congregationalist minister, John Williams. During peacetime, Native Americans might stop to barter at Deerfield as they moved back and forth from New England to Canada, participating in a trade that both English and French officially tried to suppress but which nonetheless was conducted openly and participated in by French and English alike. During wartime, however, Deerfield became especially vulnerable to attack by the French and their Native American allies. On February 29, 1704, after war had broken out once again between England and France, a small contingent of French troops and 200 Abenakis, Hurons, and Mohawk Iroquois struck at Deerfield. Of the 300 or so people in the village, the raiders killed 48 and carried off another 140 to Canada.

Colonel Samuel Partridge, who had military responsibility for the Connecticut River Valley region, had warned Deerfield of its vulnerability before the attack, and arrived shortly after the raid. His "Account of Ye Destruction at Deerfld Febr 29, 1703–4" is the first document below. The raiders killed two of John Willliams' youngest children and also a family slave, but they carried off Williams, his wife, and four other children. The account of his son, then 9, written years later, and after he had been "redeemed" and returned to New England, is the second document. The third document is an account that is presumed to have been written by Joseph Kellogg, also a child at the time of his capture, dealing with his relations in Canada with Catholic Jesuit missionaries.

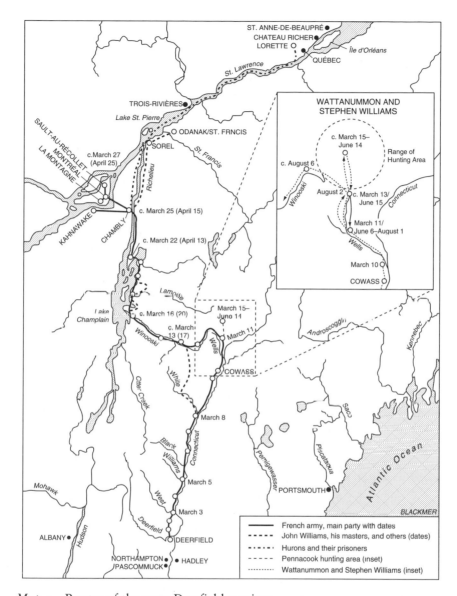

Map 4 Routes of the 1704 Deerfield captives
From Evan Haefeli and Kevin Sweeney, eds., *Captive Histories: English, French, and Native Narratives of the 1704 Deerfield Raid* (Amherst and Boston: University of Massachusetts Press, 2006), p. 98. © 2006 by University of Massachusetts Press.

1. *"An account of yᵉ destruction at Deerfd febr 29, 1703/4," by Samuel Partridge*

Upon the day of the date above about two hours before day, the French & Indian Enemy made an attack upon Deerfield, entered the Fort with Little discovery (though it is said the watch shot of a gun & cried Alarm, which very few heard) immediately set upon breaking open doors & windows took the the Watch &. others Captive, & had the men appointed to Lead them away, others improved in Rifling houses of provisions, money, clothing, drink, & packing up & sending away; the greatest part standing to their Arms, firing houses, & killing all they could that made any resistance; also killing Cattle, hogs, sheep, & sakeing & wasting all that came before them, Except some persons that Escaped in the Crowds, some by Leaping out at Windows & over the fortification.

Some ran to Capt Well his Garrison, & some to Hatfield with little or no clothing on, & barefooted, which with the bitterness of the season caused them to come of with frozen feet, & Lie Lame of them. One house, viz. Benoni Stebbins, they attacked Later than some others, yet those in it were well awakened, being seven men, besides Women & children, who stood stoutly to their Arms, fired upon the Enemy, & the Enemy upon them, caused several of the Enemy to fall, of which was one Frenchman, a Gentile man to appearance. The Enemy gave back, they strove to fire the house, our men killed three or four Indians in their attempt, the Enemy being numerous about the house, powered in much shot upon the house, the walls being filled up with brick, the force of the shot was repelled, yet they killed said Stebbins, and wounded one man & one woman, of which the survivors made no discovery to the Assailants, but with more then ordinary Courage kept firing, having powder & Ball sufficient in said house. The Enemy betook themselves to the next house & the Meeting house, both which [were] but about eight rod distant, other men yet plied their business & accepted of no quarter though offered by the Enemy, nor Capitulate, but by their Guns giving little or no Respite from the time they began (say some of the men in the house shot forty times, & had fair shots at the Enemy all the while) about one hour before day till the Sun about one hour & half high, at which time they were almost spent; yet at the very pintch, ready to yield, other men from Hadly & Hatfield, about thirty men, rushed in upon the Enemy & made a shot upon them, at which they quitted their Assailing the house & the fort also; the house at Liberty, women & children ran to Captain Wells his fort, the men with ours still pursued the Enemy, all of them vigorously, caused many of the Enemy to fall, yet being but about forty men pursued to far, imprudently, not altogether for want of conduct, for Captain Wells who led them called for a retreat, which they Little minded, the Enemy discovering their numbers having ambushments of men, caused other men to give back though to Late, being a Mile from the Fort; in the drawing of & at the Fort Lost eleven of our men . . .

[A]bout midnight the same night were gathered of our upper & Lower Towns near about eighty men which had thoughts with that number to have Assaulted the Enemy that Night, but the snow being at Least three foot deep & impassable without snow shoes (which we had not a supply of) & doubtful whether we could attack them before day, being in no Capacity to follow them but in their path, they in a Capacity to flank us on both sides, being fitted with snow shoes, & with treble our Number, if not more, & some were much concerned for the Captives, Mr. Williams family, Especially, whom the Enemy would kill if we come on, & it was concluded we should too much Expose or men . . .

Source: From the *Proceedings of the Massachusetts Historical Society*, IX (1866–7), 478–81.

2. *"Account of the Captivity of the Rev. Doctor Stephen Williams, Written by Himself"*

What befell Stephen Williams in his Captivity. On the last of February 1703–4, the French and Indians came and surprised our fort and took it, and they had broken into our house and took us prisoners, they barbarously murdered a brother and sister of mine, as they did several of our neighbours. They rifled our house and then marched away, with us that were captives, and set our house and barn on fire, as they did the greatest part of the town. When the greatest part of the enemy were gone out of the town, there came some English from the next town that drove those Indians that remained in the town away; but they were quickly driven back again by the rest of the army. Nine of them were slain as they retreated. Then they marched a little further and stopped, for they had several wounded men that hindered them. There they told us that if the English pursued they would kill us, otherwise they would not, but they quickly proved themselves liars, for before they departed from the place they barbarously murdered a child of about two years old. There master took away my English shoes, and gave me Indian ones in the room of them, which I think were better to travel in. Then we marched five or six miles further where took up our lodgings. Then one Englishman ran back to Deerfield, which provoked them much. They told us that if any more ran away they would burn the rest. There they slew our negro man. The next morning we travelled about two or three miles, when they murdered my ever honored mother, who having gone over a small river, which water running very swift flung her down, she being wet, was not able to travel any farther. We travelled eight or nine miles further and lodged that night ...

We rested on the Sabbath day; they gave my father liberty to preach. Here we sang a psalm, for they requested of us a song. The next day we travelled a great way farther than we had at any time before. About the middle of the day, some that were in the rear fired at some geese that flew over, which put them into considerable fright, for they thought that the English were come up with them. Then they began to bind the prisoners, and to prepare themselves for battle, but when they understood what was the matter, they shot a volley for joy, boasting that the English could not overtake them ...

The next day was a tempestuous day, and I froze my great toe of my left foot; the day after, which was Wednesday, my master bid me go down to the river with him very early in the morning, which startled me, for he did not use to be so early. There that river parted, and I went up one branch and my father with my brother and sisters another. I never saw my father for fourteen months. I did not eat any thing in the morning, yet must travel all day, yea I travelled till about nine o'clock at night without one morsel of victuals. I travelled about fifty miles that day and night. For my supper I had one spoonful of Indian corn, in the morning five or six kernels, but must travel. Then we left the river and travelled about noon on the west side of that river. We came to two wigwams, where we found the signs of Indians but no Indians, (in those wigwams they left their sacks and went a hunting, if perhaps they might find some moose buried in the snow by the hunting Indians but could not find any.)

I, wandered about and lost myself and hollowed. My master came to me, and was very angry with me. He lifted up the breach of his gun in order to kill me, but God kept back his hand, for which I desire his name might be praised. The Indians will never allow any body to hollow in the woods. Their manner is to make a noise like wolves or other wild creatures, when they would call to one another. My master sent the Indian lad and I to those wigwams, but he himself took his gun and went a hunting (now there were only we three in company, we had left all that army.) We made a fire but had no victuals to dress, only a moose's paunch and bones, which the Indians had left. We took the paunch and boiled it without cleansing of it, for what was on it served for thickening the broth. There we tarried that night, and the next day till about noon, then there came an Indian girl and brought us some moose's meat dried, which I thought was the best victuals ever I eat. We travelled with the Indian girl about ten miles where was two wigwams. My master that left us the day before was got there. While we tarried here, the French that were in the army passed by. Within a day or two we travelled seven or eight miles northward to a place where they had killed some moose, where they made wigwams (for their manner was when they killed any moose to move to them and lie by them till they had eaten them up.) ...

I went with the messenger, and after a tedious day's travel came to my master's family. He gave me to his brother with whom I continued two or three months thereabouts hunting moose, bears, and beavers. But when I first arrived here they were extraordinary kind, took care of my toe which was frozen, would not suffer me to do any work, gave me deer skin to lie on, and a bear skin to cover me withal, but this did not last long, for I was forced to carry such a pack when I travelled that I could not rise up without some help, was forced to cut wood, and carry it sometimes a considerable way on my back. After that manner I lived till their hunting time was over, without any society but the inhuman pagans....

[In French Canada, Williams lived with his Indian captors, among other captives, and became a "slave" – he might be bought by the French or redeemed for a price by the English.] I lived here, I observed that some English children would scoff at me (when before the Indians, worse than the Indian children) but when alone they would talk familiarly with me in English, about their own country, &c. whereas when before the Indians they would pretend that they could not speak English. Here the Indians did say something to me about religion, but not much, being eastern Indians were not zealous as the Macquas are.

The French Governor after he heard I was in the country, because of my father's intreaties, was often sending to the Indians to buy me, who were quite wearied out because of the many messages he sent. The Governor was not willing to give above thirty crowns, whereas they stood for forty. At length being wearied out, my master went to the Jesuit, and got pen, ink, and paper, would have me write to my father (for we had heard he was learned, and had two hundred pounds a year allowed him, which I believe some of them believed.) After he had got paper he takes another Indian with him that could speak good English who were to indite for me. The substance of the letter was this, that if they did not buy me before spring, they would not sell me afterwards, and that he must give forty crowns for me. They carried it to the Jesuit, who could speak English, to read, to see whether I had written as they ordered me, and when they found I had they were well pleased.

My master had a mind to go hunting, and would have taken me with him, but because he sent such word, that they must buy by such a time, he left me at home, that I might be ready if they should send to buy me, and when Capt. Livingston and Mr. Sheldon were come to Canada, my mistress thought there would be an exchange of prisoners, and lest the French should then take me away for nothing, she removed up in the woods, about half a mile from the river, that if they came they might not find me; while on a certain day my mistress went to a French house to get victuals, and ordered me to spend my day in getting wood, but it proved a tempestuous day, and we had half a cart load at the door, which is a great deal for Indians to have, so that I did not get any. When she came home, being disturbed by the French, asked what I had been doing, they replied nothing, at which she was very angry. I will not beat you myself; says she, for my husband ordered me to the contrary, but will tell the Jesuit, the next time he comes. Now they were not gone so far but that the Jesuit knew where they were, who often visited them. Within a day or two the Jesuit comes. She was as good as her word, did complain. He takes me out and whipt me with a whip with six cords, several knots in each cord.

After a few days, he comes again, and brings me a letter from my father, by which I understood he was a prisoner as well as I, which I told the Indians, who said they believed it. He likewise said in his letter that the Governor of New-England would take care we should be redeemed.... [which he eventually was, and returned to New England in 1705].

Source: Stephen W. Williams, *A Biographical Memoir of the Rev. John Williams, First Minister of Deerfield, Massachusetts* (Greenfield, MA: C. J. J. Ingersell, 1837), pp. 102–10.

3. "When I Was Carryed to Canada," attributed to Joseph Kellogg of Deerfield

When I was Carryed to Canada, I was forced by my Master to go to Church. he forced me to cross my self when I was unwilling he threatened to beat me, & would by force take my hand, & make it for me, would deny me Victuals unless I would conform to them. by the Priests means all the grown persons were put away. then they used all their arts to make us in love with their religion, were often crying against our Religion. told us our bibles were defective and did not contain all. showed us so many leaves as contained the Apocrypha books and said the English had taken all that out of their bibles, told us the Rise of our religion was King Henries the eight Wickedness, that he killed two Wives, & marryed his own Daughter, that he had Six wives one after another for which wickedness he was Excommunicated by the Pope; and that then by means of Luther's and Calvin's apostasie he made himself Lord & master of Religion, they said Calvin and Luther were very wicked, that Luther himself said he had eaten a bushel of Salt with the [Devil] that Calvin was enraged because when a Canon expecting a Bishoprick he failed in it, and in discontent he ran away, and took a nun with him with whom he lived in whoredom, and that for these wickednesses he was whiped and branded. [They] often told us their Religion was confirmed by miracles. . . . One Priest Monsieur Rena told me he had heard of great miracles wrought by Saint Katherine. Here note that this Saint Katherine was a Macqua Squaw that was dead & Sainted, but he did not believe them and was now Strook deaf, and after some time he thought how he had Reproached her and went to her tomb, & confessed his sin and asked her pardon, and prayed that he might be restored, & was immediately cured . . .

Source: Simon Gratz Collection, Case 8, Box 28 (The Rev. John Williams and Family Papers), unnumbered folder, "Papers Relating to the Attack on Deerfield," Historical Society of Pennsylvania, Philadelphia.

Study: John Demos, *The Unredeemed Captive: A Family Story from Early America* (New York: Alfred Knopf, 1994).

Discussion Questions

1   While all of the northern colonies were not Puritan and not all communities supported a Congregationalist church, these three sets of documents do come from Puritan settlements. Is there a religious theme in each document? How do the themes in the documents relate to the notions in Winthrop's *Modell of Christian Charity* in the last chapter?

2   Documents such as Winthrop's description of John Eliot's work as a missionary tell us something about how Europeans understood themselves and their relationship to Native Americans as well as about the way they went about trying to transform Native American cultures. Do they provide any hint about the way Native Americans accepted, adapted to, and resisted such efforts?

3   Captivity was one of the experiences that brought different cultures into immediate contact and forged some type of mutual understanding. Reading the story of the Deerfield raid from three different perspectives (and different points in time), how did the different narrators explain the motives for the raids and the captivity that followed? How do you think captivity changed the captives themselves?

4   What differences do you see between the Deerfield raid and the violent conflict between Native Americans and the Dutch and French described in earlier documents?

5   Traditional histories of New England were written from documents such as Winthrop's *Modell of Christian Charity* and the agreement of the first settlers of Springfield as well as the sermons of Puritan ministers. Relations with Native Americans seldom figured in these accounts. What hints do these documents provide about the way in which intercultural contact affected the lives of ordinary European settlers in New England?

Chapter 7   Southern Colonies

1. Richard Frethorne's Letter from Jamestown to his Parents in England, 1623

In 1623, when Richard Frethorne wrote this letter, the Virginia Company's colony along the James River had just withstood a devastating attack by the Powhatan Indians (1622). For those who survived, life was laborious, brutal, and usually short, to paraphrase Thomas Hobbes. Despite the introduction earlier of tobacco as a cash crop, within a year, the Virginia Company would be dissolved and its effort to turn a profit in its colony abandoned. Virginia became a royal colony. Frethorne was a young indentured servant (committed by "indenture," or contract, to labor for his owner for at least seven years), unusual in that he was literate, and he lived on one of the private "plantations" in Virginia, Martin's Hundred. His letter, one of the classics of colonial American literature, may have been occasioned and undoubtedly survived, as Emily Rose has shown, because it was a useful propaganda piece in the battle over the Virginia Company's fate.

LOVING AND KIND FATHER AND MOTHER:
My most humble duty remembered to you, hoping in god of your good health, as I myself am at the making hereof. This is to let you understand that I your child am in a most heavy case by reason of the country, [which] is such that it causeth much sickness, [such] as the scurvy and the bloody flux and diverse other diseases, which maketh the body very poor and weak. And when we are sick there is nothing to comfort us; for since I came out of the ship I never ate anything but peas, and loblollie (that is, water gruel).

As for deer or venison I never saw any since I came into this land. There is indeed some fowl, but we are not allowed to go and get it, but must work hard both early and late for a mess of water gruel and a mouthful of bread and beef. A mouthful of bread for a penny loaf must serve for four men which is most pitiful. [You would be grieved] if you did know as much as I [do], when people cry out day and night – Oh! That they were in England without their limbs – and would not care to lose any limb to be in England again, yea, though they beg from door to door. For we live in fear of the enemy every hour, yet we have had a combat with them . . . and we took two alive and made slaves of them. But it was by policy, for we are in great danger; for our plantation is very weak by reason of the death and sickness of our company. For we came but twenty for the merchants, and they are half dead just; and we look every hour when two more should go. Yet there came some four other men yet to live with us, of which there is but one alive; and our Lieutenant is dead, and [also] his father and his brother. And there was some five or six of the last year's twenty, of which there is but three left, so that we are fain to get other men to plant with us; and yet we are but 32 to fight against 3000 if they should come. And the nighest help that we have is ten mile of us, and when the rogues overcame this place [the] last [time] they slew 80 persons. How then shall we do, for we lie even in their teeth? They may easily take us, but [for the fact] that God is merciful and can save with few as well as with many, as he showed to Gilead. And like Gilead's soldiers, if they lapped water, we drink water which is but weak.

And I have nothing to comfort me, nor is there nothing to be gotten here but sickness and death, except [in the event] that one had money to lay out in some things for profit. But I have nothing at all – no, not a shirt to my back but two rags, nor clothes but one poor suit, nor but one pair of shoes, but one pair of stockings, but one cap, [and] but two bands [collars]. My cloak is stolen by one of my fellows, and to his dying hour [he] would not tell me what he did with it; but some of my fellows saw him have butter and beef out of a ship, which my cloak, I doubt [not], paid for. So that I have not a penny, nor a penny worth, to help me too either spice or sugar or strong waters, without the which one cannot live here. For as strong beer in England doth fatten and strengthen them, so water here doth wash and weaken these here [and] only keeps [their] life and soul together. But I am not half [of] a quarter so strong as I was in England, and all is for want of victuals; for I do protest unto you that I have eaten more in [one] day at home than I have allowed me here for a week. You have given more than my day's allowance to a beggar at the door; and if Mr. Jackson had not relieved me, I should be in a poor case. But he like a father and she like a loving mother doth still help me.

For when we go to Jamestown (that is 10 miles of us) there lie all the ships that come to land, and there they must deliver their goods. And when we went up to town [we would go], as it may be, on Monday at noon, and come there by night, [and] then load the next day by noon, and go home in the afternoon, and unload, and then away again in the night, and [we would] be up about midnight. Then if it rained or blowed never so hard, we must lie in the boat on the water and have nothing but a little bread. For when we go into the boat we [would] have a loaf allowed to two men, and it is all [we would get] if we stayed there two days, which is hard; and [we] must lie all that while in the boat. But that Goodman Jackson pitied me and made me a cabin to lie in always when I [would] come up, and he would give me some poor jacks [fish] [to take] home with me, which comforted me more than peas or water gruel. Oh, they be very godly folks, and love me very well, and will do anything for me. And he much marvelled that you would send me a servant to the Company; he saith I had been better knocked on the head. And indeed so I find it now, to my great grief and misery; and [I] saith that if you love me you will redeem me suddenly, for which I do entreat and beg. And if you cannot get the merchants to redeem me for some little money, then for God's sake get a gathering or entreat some good folks to lay out some little sum of money in meal and cheese and butter and beef. Any eating meat will yield great profit. Oil and vinegar is very good; but, father, there is great loss in leaking. But for God's sake send beef and cheese and butter, or the more of one sort and none of another. But if you send cheese, it must be very old cheese; and at the cheesemonger's you may buy very good cheese for twopence farthing or halfpenny, that will be liked very well. But if you send cheese, you must have a care how you pack it in barrels; and you must put cooper's chips between every cheese, or else the heat of the hold will rot them. And look whatsoever you send me – be in never so much – look, what[ever] I make of it, I will deal truly with you. I will send it over and beg the profit to redeem me; and if I die before it come, I have entreated Goodman Jackson to send you the worth of it, who hath promised he will. If you send, you must direct your letters to Goodman Jackson, at Jamestown, a gunsmith. (You must set down his freight, because there be more of his name there.) Good father, do not forget me, but have mercy and pity my miserable case. I know if you did but see me, you would weep to see me; for I have but one suit. (But [though] it is a strange one, it is very well guarded.) Wherefore, for God's sake, pity me. I pray you to remember my love to all my friends and kindred. I hope all my brothers and sisters are in good health, and as for my part I have set down my resolution that certainly will be; that is, that the answer of this letter will be life or death to me. Therefore, good father, send as soon as you can; and if you send me any thing let this be the mark.

Richard Frethorne, Martin's Hundred

Source: Richard Frethorne, letter to his father and mother, March 20, April 2 and 3, 1623, in Susan Kingsbury, ed., *The Records of the Virginia Company of London* (Washington, DC: Government Printing Office, 1935), 4: 58–62. The original of the letter was in the Public Record Office, London, but sold in 1970, according to Emily Rose, and its current whereabouts are unknown.

Study: Emily Rose, "The Politics of Pathos: Richard Frethorne's Letter Home," in Robert Appelbaum and John Wood Sweet, eds., *Envisioning an English Empire: Jamestown and the Making of the North Atlantic World* (Philadelphia: University of Pennsylvania Press, 2005), pp. 92–108.

2. Witchcraft Trial of Jeane Gardiner, Bermuda, 1651

Bermuda was founded, in the words of historian Richard Dunn, when "Sir George Somers, admiral of the Virginia Company, ran his ship on to Bermuda's coral reef in 1609; he liked the beautiful islands so much that he came back to hunt and fish, ate too many wild hogs, and died of acute indigestion." The bountiful island filled up quickly with English colonists. As in Virginia, the settlers eventually made a living as tobacco planters; as in New England, most of the settlers were Puritans; and as in New England, the colony officials prosecuted numerous witchcraft cases – nearly two dozen during the second half of the seventeenth century.

An assize and generall Goale deliverie held at St Georges from the nineteenth daye of Maye to the 22nd daye of the same month, 1651. Captain Josias fforster Governor &c.

(1) The Jury for our Soveraigne Lord the kinge Doe present Jaene Gardiner the wife of Ralph (Gardiner) of Hambleton tribe for that the said Jeane on or about the Eleaventh day of Aprill 1651 feloneously deliberately and mallitiously did saye that she would Crampe Tomasin a mullatto woeman in the same tribe, and used many other threatenninge words tending to the hurt and injurie of the said mullatto woeman, and within a while after by practice and combonason with the Devill felloneously did practice on the said Mullatto the diabollicall craft of witchcraft, insoemuch that the said Mullatto was very much tormented, and struck blind and dumbe for the

shape of twoe houres or thereabouts, and at divers tymes in other places did practice the said devilish craft of witchcraft on severall persons to the hurt and Damage of their bodyes and goods Contrary to the peace of our Souveraigne lord the Kinge his crowne and dignitie.

To which indictment she pleaded not guilty but beinge the grand inquest found a trewe bill and for her forther triall did put herself uppon God and the Countrey, which beinge a Jury of 12 sworne men, did find her guilty, whereuppon the sentence of death was pronounced upon her, and accordingly shee was executed on Munday the 26th day of this Instant May at Saint Georges before many Spectators.

(2) The proceedinge against this woman was longe and teadious, by reason of many accusacons. The Govr. and counsell was very carefull in findinge out the trewth. The[y] caused a jury of woemen to search her and one Goody Bowen wch was suspected; they returned as followeth. Havinge made diligent searche accordinge to our oathes we cannot find any outward or inward mark soe far as wee can p.ceave whereby wee can in conscience find them or either of them guilty of witchcraft, onely in the mouth of goody Gardiner there is a blewe spott which being prickt did not bleed and y^t. place was incencible but being prickt close by it, it bled the which wee leave to the judgment of Phisitians. Mc Hooper and the chirurgions being appointed to viewe that spott the day that she was to com to her triall and it was fallen away and flatt, and being prickt it bled acid it was knowne to be there 18 yeares, and for farther triall she was tried and throwne twice in the Sea. She did swyme like a Corke and could not sinke. These signes and other stronge evidences in Court condemme her, yet neverthelesse shee would confesse noethinge att her death. Shee was demanded in court if she could give a reason why shee did not sinke. She Answered that she did open her mouth and [bubles?] but could not sinke.

(3) The names of the Jury of woemen appointed to search the bodies of Anne Bowen and Goody Gardiner: –

Mrs. Ellen Burrowes	Allice Sparkes
Mrs ffiora Wood	Eliz. Brangman.
Mrs. Eliz. Stowe	

And seven others whose Christian names only can now be read.

Source: J. H. Lefroy, *Memorials of the Discovery and Early Settlement of the Bermudas or Somers Islands, 1511–1687*, 2 vols. (London, 1879, 1932), II, 602–3, corrected from the original by Michael Jarvis. The quote is from Richard S. Dunn, "The Downfall of the Bermuda Company: A Restoration Farce," *William and Mary Quarterly*, 3rd ser., XX (October 1963), 488.

Study: Michael Jarvis, "'In the Eye of All Trade': Maritime Revolution and the Transformation of Bermudan Society, 1612–1800" (Ph.D. diss., College of William and Mary, 1998).

3. Cases Before the Maryland Provincial Court in the 1650s

Although Maryland had been established as a proprietary colony almost two decades before, in 1652 it was still a sparsely settled and oftentimes a politically volatile place. The court system had the primary responsibility for maintaining an ordered society, and the most important court was the Provincial Court, which had sole jurisdiction over serious criminal matters, and heard appeals in civil cases. Court cases, such as the three that follow, record unique and somewhat unusual events, and must be used cautiously when drawing conclusions, but they also provide invaluable detail, available from no other type of records, about daily life in the early colonies.

A Case of Adultery/Fornication, 1652

Susan Warren and Captain William Mitchell came to the Chesapeake on the same ship about 1650. Warren was a free woman; Mitchell was appointed to the Governor's Council, making him one of the most important men in the province, and owned at least 2,000 acres of land. Warren apparently had been married and widowed twice. Mitchell lived with a woman he considered his wife but was not legally married to her. Mitchell had allegedly subjected Warren to physical and verbal abuse while on board the ship bringing them to the Chesapeake, mostly over the ownership of goods that Warren claimed belonged to her father. Once in Maryland, they were both brought to trial for their "scandalous course of life," which in Mitchell's case included adultery, blasphemy, and an effort to get Warren to induce a miscarriage. The Provincial Court recorded almost two dozen depositions from people who knew them in England as well as the Chesapeake. The two excerpted below concern the charge of adultery/fornication.

The Deposition of Susan Warren widdow aged 21 Sworn & examined 24th Aprill Saith
That when Cap' Mitchell he perceived She bred Child by him he prepared a potion of Phisick over night unknown that it was for herself in the Morning

calls Martha Webb & bids her poach an Egg and bring it to him presently which She did Soe, he put this Phisick into that Egg and come to her as She was in bed. and bid her take this, and She requesting to know for what, he: Said if She would not take it he would thrust it down her throat, Soe She being in bed could not withstand it, Soe Shutting all out of the room but himself for all that day but only Martha Webb knew and none of the house else, but they all told her afterwards, that they knew it was her that tooke the Phisick, for all Capt Mitchell Soe dissembled th[at] when any body came to knock, he would take a towell and put it about his neck and Soe lie down as if it had been himself that had taken Phisick, Soe Some two or three days after he told her that if She was with Child, he would warrant that he had frighted it away, Soe when She heard him Say Soe She answered him again if She had thought that She would not have took it for a world, for it was a great Sin to get it, but a greater to make it away and further Saith not at present.

The Deposition of Susan Warren Wid[ow] aged 21 Sworn and exam^d 24th Aprill Saith
That when Cap' Mitchell came to the Crosse Since his last arrival Said to the Said Susan Warren that he heard She had had a Child. I She Said Soe She had and that it was by him and She Said by none else, and he further Said that he heard She had Suffered much disgrace for his Sake, I now if She pleased he would make her amends if Marriage of her would whereto She made Answer She would for She was fittest for him, for being it was through him that her great Misfortune and disgrace was occasioned; She hearing that his wife was dead, and he being a Single man, She did think that he would not twitt her with what She had done as another Might because he did it, and further this Deponent Saith not at present.

Mary the wife of Daniel Clocker being exam^d & Sworn by vertue of her former Oath taken in open Court testifieth as followeth. That She was the Midwife to Susan Warren and in the time of her delivery charged the Said Susan Warren to Speak the truth and to give Such an Answer as She would give an accompt of to God and man, and whether those things that She had Spoken of Concerning Capt Mitchell that he was ffather of the Child, and had given her Phisick to destroy it were true or noe, and She answered that they were all true. . . .

And the said Susan Warren being called to her Answer and the Said Charge [adultery, fornication, and "blasphemous expressions" that "much dishonoured God and given great Offence and Scandal to the Government"] read unto her could not deny the Offence of ffornication the same appearing by her own Confession upon Record . . . and she acknowledging her Offence humbly desired the Court would be favourable unto her But in regard of the Great Scandal to the Government by her lewd Course of life Soe publick and notorious It is thought fit and Soe Ordered, that She be forthwith whipped with thirty nine lashes upon her bare back, and Soe to be discharged of her Imprisonment in that particular which punishment She received accordingly with Some Mittigation upon the Intercession of Some of the Counsell and Others to the Govr on her behalf.

Capt William Mitchell this day referred himself wholly to the derminacon and Judgment of the Court... This Court therefore takeing the matter into Serious Consideracon upon the perusal of the proofs and in pursuance of the verdict of the Grand Jury for the Several Offenses of Adultery ffornication and Murtherous intention, and in respect of his lewd and Scandalous Course of life... doth Order that the Said Capt Mitchell Shall forthwith pay ffive thousand pounds of Tobacco and Cask... And to enter into bond for his good behaviour, And that hc and his now pretended wife Joan be Separated till they by Joyned together in Matrimony in the usual Manner...

A Case of Murder, 1653

The Examination of Mary Warrow widdow taken this day [September 26, 1653] Upon Oath in open Court.
That upon Thursday in the last week of July last about Noon the Same day four Indians, whom this deponent then knew not, came after a bould Manner into the house of Cap' Daniell Gookins upon the South River in Annarundell County this Deponents then husband Jacob Warrow, this Deponent and Jacob their Son a child of about Seven years of age being then in the Said house where they dwelt being Servants to the Said Cap, Gookine, And after the Said Indians had Stay'd in the Same house about an hour her Said husband Stooping down upon Some Occasion, Upon a watch word or Notice from one of the Said Indians: three of them whereof one is now here prisoner, in a Violent Sudden Manner fell upon her Said Husband and with their weapons or Tomohawks wounded him Soe that he died, And further this Deponent upon her Oath Sayeth that as Soon as She perceived that the Said three Indians were resolved to Murther her Said Husband She not being able as She conceived any wayes to help him & desireing if it might please God to Save her Self and her Said Child from Slaughter tooke up the Child thinking to fly away with him but as She was goeing out of the door, the fourth of the Said Indians who is now here prisoner felled this Deponent to the Ground with his weapon or Tomohawke wounding her in Such a Manner as that She fell down Senceless for Some time before the door, And

that upon her Comeing to her Self againe She Saw her Said Child to be Dead being wounded in the head, And perceiving the Said Indians or Some of them busie as She conceived in pillaging or robbing the Said house She by Gods assistance used meanes to Creep into the weeds by the Said house and Soe by Gods providence escaped with Life, And further this Deponent Sayeth that at the time when the Said Murther was Committed as aforesaid there were in the Said house three Gunns Some Good quantity of powder and Shott and divers wearing Clothes and bed Clothes Some pewter and three hatts to a good Value, All which the Said Indians as She Verily believeth and for ought She could Ever understand to the Contrary Stole out of the Said house and Carryed away with them and further Sayth not. Sworne in open Court.

[The same day the Attorney General to the Lord Proprietor brought in an indictment:] I doe hereby by way of Indictm[ent] declare against Skightam-Mongh and Couna-weza the two piscatoway Indian prison[ers] here present, Shewing that they upon Thursday in the last week of July last or Some other time this last Sumer with the Assistance of or as Assistant or consort with two other Indians in a felonious Manner entred into the house of Capt Danicll Gookin in the County of Annarundell w[ith]in this Province of Maryland, and then and there in a Most barbarous inhumane Cruell felonious Manner Murthered one Jacob Warrowe a Negro Servant of the Said Capt Gookins and a Child of the Said Negroes about Seven Yeares of age, and alsoe then and there in like Manner Grieviously wounded the Said Negroes wife Leaving her for Dead ...

Whereupon the prisoners were Arraigned and brought to their Answers by Interpreters being confronted by Mary Warrow the Negro woman that escaped, and with a Gun and Severall parcells of Clothes which had been taken out of the house, where the Murther was Committed and found in their Custody, and Sent down by Warcosse the Emperor as though taken from the Murtherers, and the prisoners as appeared by their Interpreters, acknowledged they knew the Negro woman, and that they were both present when the Negro man and child were killed, Sometimes confessing and Sometimes denying as fearfull & desireing to conceale their Guiltness.

And thereupon out of divers freemen of the County of S' Maries Summoned for that purpose a Jury of 24 able persons was impannelled for the Tryall ... They returned their joint Verdict to the Court in these words following vizt If one or both of these Indian prisoners had not consented to the Murther of Capt Daniell. Gookins Negroes, they ought to have withstood the other Indins in their intended Murther or revealed it by Some means, But doing neither and receiving Stoln Goods (as they confess) as hired to conceal it. We find them Guilty of the foresaid Murther.

Upon the bringing of which Verdict and Serious consideration thereupon had, by the Court. Judgm^t or Sentence passed upon the prisoners, That they Should be returned to close prison as formerly, and from thence to be conveyed to the place of Execution, there to be hanged by the Neck till they were Dead, which the Sheriffe was to See pformed and Soe God have Mercy upon their Souls, which Execucon was performed the Same Evening accordingly.

An Agreement about Marriage, 1657

Articles of Agreement...made the 24th of September 1657 Between Peter Sharpe of Putuxent Country in the Province of Maryland...of the one parte and Robert Harwood of the Same country planter of the other parte.

Whereas there has been a Suit Commenced by the said Peter Sharpe before the Governour and Councell of this province against the above-named Robert Harwood on the behalf of Elizabeth Gary Daughter of Iudith now wife of the Said Peter Sharpe, for reparation for Slaunders, and unhandsome attempts Charged to be acted and reported by the Said Robert Harwood to the great Detriment of the Said Elizabeth, and of the Said Peter Sharpe his wife and family.

And Whereas the Said Robert Harwood for his own Vindication, Both much insist upon a former promise of Marriage Grounded upon a Mutuall declared affection between him the Said Robert Harwood and the Said Elizabeth Gary, obtained after a long familiaritie and Sollicitation, which the Said Peter Sharpe and Iudith his wife are much dissatisfied in, yet are willing in Case the Said Elizabeth Gary have Such an affection and resolution of Marriage to and with the Said Robert Harwood to Consent thereunto upon Consideration whereof It is Agreed in Manner following viz.

1. Imprimis the Said Peter Sharpe doth...agree to and with the Said Robert Harwood, that the Said Elizabeth Gary Shall within fifteen dayes after the date hereof, be Conveyed to the house of m^r Thomas Davis at the Cliftes and there She is to remaine for the Space of Six weekes, after fifteen days be Expired, And the Said Robert Harwood is to have during all the Said Time, full free and perfect Liberty (bringing one or more of the Neighbours with him) to have all freedom of discourse with the Said Elizabeth Gary and to use all faire and Lawfull Endeavours with her to Marry or Contract Marriage to and with the S[aid] Robert Harwood, one or more of the Neighbours being alwayes present with the Said Robert Harwood & Elizabeth Gary when they are in Company together, The Said Robt Harwood paying for the Said Elizabeth Gary her Entertainment during her Stay at the Said Thomas Davis his house.

2. Item the Said Peter Sharp doth farther...agree to and with the Said Robert Harwood that he the Said Peter Sharpe Shall not nor will not directly or indirectly...Endeavour to obstruct the Said Robert Harwood, and Elizabeth Gary from Contracting or Marrying each to other within the time mentioned in the precedent Article, nor from Marriage after the Said time be Expired, if the Said Elizabeth Gary Shall within the Said time fully Consent thereunto, But if it Shall by Gods permission, So happen that the S[aid] Elizabeth Gary Shall within the Said perfixed time give her Consent, then the Said Marriage Shall be permitted to take Effect without obstruction, And the Said Elizabeth Gary be fully and freely left to her own will and pleasure to dispose of her Self in Marriage accordingly at her own discretion.

3. Item the Said Robert Harwood doth...agree to and with the Said Peter Sharpe and Iudith his wife, That in Case he Shall not within the time perfixed, procure the Said Elizabeth Gary to give her Consent to intermarry with him the Said Robert Harwood, That then he the Said Robert Harwood Shall and will from thence forth, totally and absolutely discharge the Said Elizabeth Gary from all former promise and Contracts in relation to Marriage and Shall never after by himself, or any other person or persons, either by words Letters or any other way directly or indirectly Endeavour to gaine the affection of the Said Elizabeth Gary, or to procure any familiaritie or discourse with her or willingly to Come into her Company ...

Source: William Hand Browne, ed., *Judicial and Testamentary Business of the Provincial Court*, vol. 2: *1649/50–1657* (Baltimore: Maryland Historical Society, 1891), pp. 173–85, 293–6, 531–3 (vol. X of the *Archives of Maryland*), from original records in the Maryland State Archives, Annapolis.

Study: Lois Green Carr and David William Jordan, *Maryland's Revolution in Government, 1689–1692* (Ithaca, NY: Cornell University Press, 1974).

4. Hans Sloane, Observations on Living in Jamaica, 1707

Hans Sloane (1660–1753) was a prominent English doctor and botanist who in 1687 traveled to the West Indies as the personal physician to Christopher Monck, second duke of Albemarle, the newly appointed royal governor of the English colony of Jamaica. After the death of the duke, Sloane returned to England, and over the next decades published his observations on the West Indies. His best-known work, Voyages to the islands ... , *appeared in two volumes, the first published in 1707, and the second in 1725.*

The Meat of the Inhabitants of Jamaica, is generally such as in England, as Beef, Pork, and Fish, salted and preserved, and sent from hence and Ireland, Flour, Pease, salted Mackrels etc. from these Places, and New-England, or New York; on which not only Masters feed, but also they are oblig'd to furnish their Servants both Whites and Blacks with three Pounds of Salt Beef, Pork, or Fish, every week, besides Cassada Bread, Yams, and Patatas, which they eat as Bread, and is the natural Product of the Country.

Although there is here in the Savannas great plenty of Cattle, yet they cannot keep Beef past some few days, and that salted, otherwise in three or four hours 'tis ready to corrupt. Butchers always kill in the morning just before day, and by seven a Clock the Markets for Flesh-Meat are over ...

Plantains are the next [...] most general support of Life in the island. They are brought in from the Plantain-Walk, or place where these Trees are planted, a little green; they ripen and turn yellow in the House, when, or before they are eaten. They are usually roasted, after being first clear'd of their outward Skins, under the Coals ...

The common suddling Liquor of the more ordinary sort is Rum-Punch, to the composition of which goes Rum, Water, Lime-juice, Sugar, and a little Nutmeg scrap'd on the top of it. This as 'tis very strong, so 'tis sower, and being made usually of the Sugar-Pot-bottoms, is very unhealthy, and because 'tis cheap, Servants and other of the poorer sort are very easily suddled with it, when they come from their Masters Plantations ...

The better sort of People lie as in England, though more on Quilts, and with few, is any Coverings; they hold here that lying expos'd to the Land Breezes, is very unhealthy, which I do not believe to come so much from the qualities of the Air... as from this, that the Air is, when one goes to sleep here, very hot, the Sun beams having heated it so long, it retains this heat from some considerable time in the night, which afterwards wearing away, it grows towards morning very cold, and affects one so much as by the coldness sometimes to awake one of sleeping. This must of necessity check insensible transpiration, and so may be the cause of many Diseases. To avoid this, Negros and Indians sleep not without a Fire near them.

Hamacas are the common Beds of ordinary white People, they were in use amongst the Indians, and are much cooler than Beds, so cool as not to be lain in without Clothes... Indians and Negros lie on the Floors, most generally on Mats made of Bull-Rushes, ordinary Rushes, Ribs of Plantain Leaves, or the Spathe, or Vagine of Cabbage-tree-Flowers, with very little or no coverings, and a small Fire near them in their Cottages. Hence they and ordinary white Servants, who lie not in Beds, are not said to go to Bed, but to go and Sleep; and this Phrase has generally obtain'd all over the Plantations ...

The Inhabitants of Jamaica are for the most part Europeans, some Creolians, born and bred in the island Barbados, the Windward Islands, or Surinam, who are the Masters, and Indians, Negros, Mulatos, Alcatrazes, Mestises, Quaterons, &c. who are the Slaves. The Indians are not Natives of the Island, they being all destroy'd by the Spaniards, ... but are usually brought by surprize from the Musquitos or Florida, or such as were Slaves to the Spaniards, and taken from them by the English ...

Clothing on the island is much as in England, especially of the better sort, that of the Indians and Negros is a little Canvass Jacket and Breeches, given them at Christmas. It seems to me the Europeans do not well, who coming from a cold Country, continue here to Cloth themselves after the same manner as in England, whereas all Inhabitants between the Tropics go even almost naked, and Negros and Indians live almost so here, their Clothes serving them but a very small part of the year ...

The Buildings of the Spaniards on this island were usually one Story high, having a Porch, Parlour, and at each end a Room, with small ones behind for Closets, &c. The built with Posts put deep in the ground, on the sides their Houses were plaistered up with Clay on Reeds, or made of the split Truncs of Cabbage-Trees ... The Lowness, as well as fixing the Posts deep in the Earth, was for fear their Houses should be ruin'd by Earthquakes, as well as for Coolness.

The Houses built by the English, are for the most part Brick, and after the English manner, which are neither cool, nor able to endure the shocks of Earthquakes ...

The Negros Houses are likewise at a distance from their Masters, and are small, oblong, thatch'd Huts, in which they have all their Moveables or Goods, which are generally a Mat to lie on, a Pot of Earth to boil their Victuals in, either Yams, Plantains, or Potatoes, with a little salt Mackarel, and a Calabash or two for Cups and Spoons.

Source: Hans Sloane, *A Voyage to the Islands. Madera, Barbados, Nieves, S. Christophers, and Jamaica, with the Natural History of the Herbs and Trees, Four-Footed Beasts, Fishes, Birds, Insects, Reptiles, &c. Of the last of those Islands; to which is prefix'd An Introduction, Wherein is an Account of the Inhabitants, Air, Waters, Diseases, Trade, &c., of that Place* ..., 2 vols. (London, 1707, 1725), I, xv–xlviii.

Study: Richard S. Dunn, *Sugar and Slaves: The Rise of the Planter Class in the English West Indies, 1624–1713* (Chapel Hill: University of North Carolina Press for the Institute of Early American History and Culture, 1972).

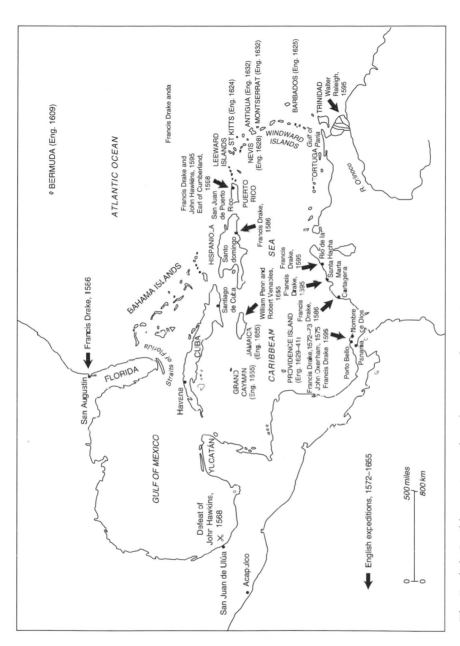

Map 5 The English Caribbean, sixteenth and seventeenth centuries
From James Walvin, *Atlas of Slavery* (New York: Pearson Education Ltd, 2006), p. 44; after A. Porter, ed., *Atlas of British Overseas Expansion* (London: Routledge, 1991), p. 25.

Discussion Questions

1   Each of these documents provides some sense of everyday life in the seventeenth-century southern colonies. Places like Bermuda, Virginia, and Jamaica were established primarily for the financial gain of those who backed or participated in the settlement process. As you read the documents, consider what they tell us about daily life. In what ways was life affected by the scramble for personal betterment?

2   Do the documents suggest that life was relatively secure and ordered? More or less so than in New England?

3   In what ways do the documents indicate that colonists lived or tried to live as they had in England? In what ways do they suggest that traditional ways of living had broken down?

4   What do the documents tell us about class and gender relations in the southern colonies? Is this what you would expect from the documents you read in chapter 1?

Part II　The Eighteenth Century

Chapter 8   Politics

1. Address of the House of Representatives of the Massachusetts Bay to the King. November 22, 1728

Puritan Massachusetts had originally had considerable autonomy in ordering its political affairs, but even after its original charter was revoked in 1684 by the English Crown, and it was made a royal colony in 1691, the popularly elected assembly (General Court) continued to battle any intrusion of British authority into local affairs. Most of these contests occurred with the Crown-appointed royal governors. In the address below, the assembly protested a plan to remove its authority to fix the salary of the new governor, William Burnet. As the governor had the explicit responsibility of enforcing English political orders and trade regulations in the colony, control of the governor's salary gave the assembly crucial leverage in countering intrusive, distant, and "tyrannical" power.

We your Majesty's loyal and dutifull subjects, the Representatives of yor. Province of the Massachusetts Bay in the General Court assembled humbly beg leave to approach yor. Royal Presence and offer the reasons and grounds of our proceedings and conclusions concerning a fixed salary on the Governor of this province, which is directed to, by your Majesty's twenty third Instruction to your present Governor here. Nothing less than the prosperity or welfare of this yor. Most dutifull Province could have prevailed with us to have done anything disagreeable to Yor. Majesty's Instruction; This Province is under that natural disadvantage, by reason of its distant situation, that it cannot be under yor. Majesty's immediate inspection and care, as Great Britain our happy Mother is; it is and has been very well known, in this as well as other nations and ages, that Government have great opportunities and sometimes too prevailing inclinations, to oppress the people. And it is almost impossible for the Prince, who is the most carefull Father of his subjects, to have such matters set in a true light. We humbly crave leave therefore to suggest that it is very much for yor. Majesty's interest and very necessary to the tranquility and flourishing of this your Province that the Governor should be induced by his own interest, as well as duty to yor. Majesty, to consult the interest and welfare of the people, but should we fix a sallary; the Governor's particular interest would be very little affected (while thus settled) by serving or disserving the peoples interest, and we should do more than has ever been done by the wisdom of Great Britain, notwithstanding the Nation, and your subjects in the most distant parts of yor. Dominions, have so intire a confidence in your Majesty and yor. interest and glory, and that of your Royal Posterity, are inseparable from the prosperity and welfare of your people, for we are all yor. inheritance; Yet the Civil List is settled for yor. Majesty's life only, whereas neither the happiness nor adversity of this Province; affect a Governor's interest, when he has once left us, and the raising and disposing of money from time to time, of our free will and assent, for the defence and support of the Government and protection and preservation of the inhabitants; is the great priviledge, which as Englishmen by Magna Charta and by the Charter granted by King William and Queen Mary of glorious Memory, the General Assembly, (as wee humbly conceive) have a right unto. For these reasons the house of Representatives were perswaded they could not in duty to your Majesty, and truthfullness to the people of this Province; settle or fix a sallary, when your Majty.'s Instruction for that end was first laid before them, and in this conclusion the House had the concurrence of yor. Majesty's Council here: and since that, in the course of the Governor's administration, we have had no encouragemt. to do it from any grounds or reasons for such special confidence in him, but the treatment we have met with, in the methods that have been used to bring us into a stated sallary, hath tended to confirm and abundantly strengthen us in our first determination; for instead of the Governor's laying our conclusion on that affair before yor. Majesty, and waiting your direction to him, and consulting in the mean time the benefitt and welfare of the people, we were told by him that we were met for that end, and so should continue, till we had finisht it; and when we were desirous to rise that we might consult our constituents; it was denied us, and we have been compelled, to sitt for some months, when the affairs of the Province have not required it, for no other end but to bring us into the settlement of a sallary, which we have often declared we could not do; and when this method did not prevail, we were removed from the house and Records belonging to the Generall Assembly in Boston, to Salem, a town about twenty miles from Boston, upon a pretence that the people in Boston influenced the representatives against settling a sallary; and altho' since our being at Salem, we have assured him that we acted freely therein, and that the same reasons that prevailed with us at Boston, would go with, and influence us everywhere, yet we are still kept sitting there, to the great disservice of yor. Majesty's interest, and previous hurt and damage of the Province. And all this has been (as we humbly conceive) without any provocation from the Assembly or people here. Your Majesty's Governor at his first arrival was received with the highest respect and greatest expence by much that ever was on such an occasion, the Assembly took care for his entertainment in a very honourable manner, according to the dignity of his station at a private gentleman's house, till the Province house was prepared for him, and altho' the Province is under great difficulties, by being a barrier to your Majesty's other plantations against the Indian savages, which in a warr brings an excessive charge sometimes of about fifty thousand pounds p. anm., and has left a load of debt on the Province of about two hundred thousand pounds, and how soon a warr may break out again with them, we cannot tell, and now in peace with them, the Province is at the annual charge of many thousands of pounds to preserve it; yet soon after the Governor's arrival the Assembly granted seventeen hundred pounds to him; fourteen hundred pounds to enable him to manage the publick affairs, and three hundred pounds to defray the charges of transporting his goods and servants here, and informed him that at the usual times, this and succeeding Assemblies, would undoubtedly afford a support suitable to the dignity of his person and station; and since that, upon the first opportunitys in the usual time of the year for the second grant, as soon as the fall of the year was arrived, notwithstanding then had been kept sitting all the while; to the great damage of the Province, they granted sixteen hundred pounds more, and since those grants were passed, we have once and again earnestly desired him to take both the one and the other; these sums are far beyond what has ever been granted to any Governor heretofore, and we doubt not but succeeding Assemblies, according to the ability of the Province, will come into as ample and honourable support from time to time, and should they not, we acknowledge your Majesty will have just reason to spew yor. displeasure with them; but while we continue to grant a support so honourable, (as we humbly conceive) we have since the present Governor's arrival, beyond other Plantations, considering the charge we are otherwise exposed to, and load of debt lying upon us; we hope we shall always enjoy your Majesty's Royal Grace and Favour which this universally loyall people, above all things desire; that the Crown may long flourish on your Royal Head, and continue so in your most illustrious family to the latest posterity is the sincere and hearty prayer of etc. *Signed* by the Order of the House of Representatives, William Dudley, Speaker. Copy.

Source: *Calendar of State Papers, Colonial Series, America, and West Indies, 1728–1729* (London, 1937), pp. 311–14; from C.O. 5, 870. fos. 154, 155–157^v, 159^v, British Public Record Office, London.

Study: Richard Beeman, *The Varieties of Political Experience in Eighteenth-Century America* (Philadelphia: University of Pennsylvania Press, 2004).

2. A Virginia Election Dispute, 1740

In Virginia, most adult free white males could vote for their county's delegates to the House of Burgesses, the colonial assembly. The delegates themselves were generally members of the "gentry" (large landholders), but as one member of the gentry usually ran against another for office, they each had to win the approval of their "lesser" constituents. No one campaigned openly or on the issues as in a modern election; rather, voters were expected to assess a candidate's virtues or status in the community. The report of an election dispute suggests other ways that candidates attracted support.

Mr. Conway reported, That the Committee of Privileges and Elections had had under their Consideration the Petition of Mr. Samuel Buckner, to them referred, complaining of an undue Election and Return of Mr. *Beverley Whiting*, to serve as a Burgess in this present General Assembly, for the County of Gloucester; and had heard as well the Petitioner, as the sitting Member, by their Council, and examined divers Witnesses on both Sides, upon the Matter of Complaint: Whereupon it appear'd to the Committee, That a greater Number of Freeholders did vote at the Election for Mr. *Whiting*, the sitting Member, than for Mr. *Buckner*. . . . [T]he Day of issuing the Writ of Election, one *John Ellis* did sollicit one *William Keys* to vote for Mr. *Whiting*, the sitting Member, and *Keys* promised to vote for him And thereupon Ellis carried the said *Keys* to the said *Beverley Whiting*, and told him there was a Man would vote for him, which the said *Keys* then promised Mr. *Whiting* to do: And upon that, Mr. *Whiting* gave *Ellis* an *English* Shilling; and bid him go and buy a Bowl of Punch, and drink his Health. That the same Day *at Night*, one of the Servants belonging to the Ordinary-keeper at the Court House brought his Master a Guinea, and said he had it of

Mr. Whiting for Liquor; but it did not appear to the Committee to what Use the Liquor had been applied. That the same Night, Mr. *Whiting,* the sitting Member, was in Company with Six or Seven persons *more,* at the said Ordinary, and Wagers being offer'd on the Election, Mr. *Whiting* said, that several of Mr. *Buckner's* Friends, who had promised him their Votes, would not come to the Election; and if their Fines were under One Hundred Pounds, he would pay them: And that Mr. *Whiting* then also said, the Election would cost him Forty or Fifty Pounds. That the Day after the Teste of the Writ, at a Private Muster in that County, under Capt. *Thomas Hayes,* one Capt. *Robert Bernard* came into the Muster Field, and sollicited the Freeholders to vote for Mr. *Whiting:* And that the next Day, at a Muster of his own Company, the said Bernard brought 40 Gallons of Cyder, and 20 Gallons of Punch into the Field, and treated his Men, solliciting them to vote for Mr. *Whiting,* as they came into the Field; and promised one *James Conquest,* to give him Liquor, if he would vote for Mr. *Whiting,* which *Conquest* refused; and then *Bernard* said he should be welcome to drink, tho' he would not vote for him: That the said *Bernard* promised one *Gale,* a Freeholder, to pay his Fine, if he would stay from the Election; which *Gale* accordingly did: That the Day of Election, the said *Bernard* treated several Freeholders, who said they would vote for Mr. *Whiting,* at one *Sewell's* Ordinary: And that, at the Election, one of the Freeholders said, he was going to vote for Mr. *Whiting,* because he had promised Capt. *Bernard* so to do; but that he had rather give Half a Pistole [coin] than to do it: And other Freeholders, who were indebted to Col. *Whiting,* said, that Capt. *Bernard* told them, that Col. *Whiting* would be angry with them, if they voted against Mr. *Whiting:* which the said *Bernard* denied, upon his Oath, before the Committee: But that it did not appear to the Committee, That any of *Bernard's* Transactions were done at the Instigation, or with the Privity of Mr. *Whiting.* And that upon the whole Matter, the Committee had come to several Resolutions; which he read in his Place, and afterwards delivered in at the Table: Where the same being twice read, and Mr. *Whiting* ordered to withdraw, Part thereof was agreed to, by the House.

Resolved, That that Freedom which ought to be maintained in all Elections, hath been greatly invaded by *Robert Bernard* ...

Ordered, That *Robert Bernard:* be taken into the Custody *of the* Serjeant at Arms, and brought immediately to the Bar of the House, to answer for his Misdemeanor and Breach of Privileges: And being brought to the Bar, Mr. *Speaker* informed him of the Resolution of the House; and that the House expected he would make an Acknowledgement of his Offence, and Breach of Privilege, and ask the Pardon of this House for the same: which he accordingly did, and then withdrew.

Ordered, That an Address be made to the Governor, to order a new Writ to issue for Electing a new Burgess to serve in this present General Assembly, for the County of *Gloucester,* in the Room of Mr. *Beverley Whiting,* who is not duly qualified to serve for the said County.

Source: Proceedings of June 11, 1740, as reported in *The Journal of the House of Burgesses: At a General Assembly...in the Thirteenth Year of His Said Majesty's Reign, and in the Year of our Lord, M,DCC,XL...* (Williamsburg, Virginia, 1740), pp. 41–2.

Study: Charles S. Sydnor, *American Revolutionaries in the Making: Political Practices in Washington's Virginia* (New York: The Free Press, 1965). Originally published as *Gentlemen Freeholders* in 1952.

3. A Contested Election in Pennsylvania, 1742

In most colonies, white, male landowners voted for their representatives in the lower house or assembly of the colonial government. Many elections were uncontested. When there were contests for a seat in the assembly, they usually turned on the prominence and reputation of the candidates, not on organized political support for a party or position. Mid-eighteenth-century Pennsylvania was an exception. There two factions, or political "parties," squared off in most colony-wide elections. One represented the interests of the proprietary family (the Penns); the other was associated with leading Quaker families. Both had to build coalitions to win elections.

Richard Peters was a British-born clergyman who, when he arrived in Philadelphia in the mid-1730s, found employment with the Penn family and provided vigorous support for their political interests. In this letter to the proprietors, he describes some of the tactics used in the 1742 election campaign for seats in the Pennsylvania colonial Assembly.

Honour'd Prop[rietors]

Having put all Business into a distinct by it selfe I shall in this take the freedom to give you a History of the late Eleccon.

The Governor's friends came early to Resolution of endeavouring a Change of Representatives & began to make Interest as soon as the Assembly had finish'd the Business of the year & were separated. Robert Buchanan and Samuel Smith the Justice happening to be in Town & declaring their Sentements that the old members might easily be thrown out in their County. Mr. Allen & Mr. James Hamilton prevailed with them to use their Endeavours to do it & I believe were instructed by the Governor to give Robert Buchanan assurances that in case of success he woud name him as Trustee for Lane & Co. This had its effect & they promised to do all in their power...

Mr. Allen had a Conference with the Heads of the Dutch at Germantown & had brought them to this Resolution that they would vote for 4 new Members, if the [Governor] would give them assurances provided there was no French War there should be no Militia, or if it should be necessary either by reason of War or of the Kings Orders that a Militia should be established, that such Foreiners as were religiously & conscientiously persuaded ag[ainst] bearing arms should have the same exemption as Quakers, and they were to appoint some of their Body to wait on the Go[vernor] & receive his answer...

There is a L[etter] in the book [?] of Susan Wrights own hand writing & of her & Sam's [Samuel Blunston] composing w[hich] was sent to every Presbyterian Congregation in the County & read at all publick Meetings of the Party. You'l see by it to what Lengths a vindictive Spirit will carry people without the restraints of Honor & Conscience: could any one believe that Susy could act so unbecoming & unfemale a part as to be employ'd in copying such infamous stuff & to take her stand as she did at Lancaster in an upper Room in a publick House and to have a ladder erected to the Window & there distribute Lies & Tickets all the day of the Eleccon?

Source: Richard Peters Letterbook, Richard Peters Papers, The Historical Society of Pennsylvania, Philadelphia. Peters' letterbooks for 1739–41 and 1741–3 have been combined in a volume of photocopies, and the above letter is to be found on pages 131–40.

Study: Craig Horle et al., *Lawmaking and Legislators in Pennsylvania: A Biographical Dictionary*, vol. 2: *1710–1756* (Philadelphia: University of Pennsylvania Press, 1997).

Discussion Questions

1 Read through the documents and list all those political practices you consider to be similar to modern political practices. Then list those practices you think are distinctive to the eighteenth century.
2 How did the members of the Massachusetts House explain their relationship to the British Crown and British empire? Were they asserting their independence? If not, what did they believe their rights to be?

3 What do you think was at issue in the Virginia and Pennsylvania elections
   described in the documents? In what way did politics differ in the two colonies?
   In which colony was politics more egalitarian (or less based on class standing)?
4 In one of the documents there is a mention of a woman's involvement in
   politics. Does the document suggest that this was unusual? Accepted? Thought
   scandalous?

Chapter 9   Economy

1. Commerce at the Port of Bristol, Great Britain, July 2, 1731

London was by far and away the most important port in Great Britain, but much of the trade with the colonies was conducted through other ports (known as the "outports") in England and Scotland. The record below lists the ships entering the second most important English port in the Atlantic colonial trades on one day during the summer of 1731. The name of each ship is followed by the name of its master and the origin of its cargo. Below the ship name are the names of merchants entering specific cargoes and the primary duty in pounds, shillings and pence paid for the cargo. "Cwt" was the abbreviation for "hundredweight," or 112 pounds; while a quarter was 28 pounds. Goods listed without a duty were those that the English government was trying to encourage the colonists to produce.

Table 9.1 Commerce at the Port of Bristol, Great Britain, July 2, 1731

Vessels and Merchandise Entering from Overseas:

In the Stockwell William Cowherd from Virginia

James Laroche for Charles Bewser	4 cwt sassafras wood	0	4	0
Thomas Chamberlayne per ships company	20,000 lbs tobacco	62	10	0

In the John & Ann Thomas Morse from Virginia

John King	9,000 lbs tobacco	28	2	6

In the Jenny Edward Bryan from Philadelphia

Joseph Bradley & company	488 lbs tobacco	1	10	6

In the Arent Samuel Bourdell from New York

L. Casamajor	18 lbs half drest deer skins	0	1	1

In the Jenny Edward Bryan from Philadelphia

William Jenkins	11 cwt 22 lbs common turpentine	0	5	1
Joseph Bradley	2 cwt 14 lbs muscovado sugar	0	3	2

In the Katherine Roger Wigmore from Jamaica

George Packer for Edward Freeman	65 gallons rum	0	5	5
Thomas Watts	168 gallons rum	0	14	0
John Gwatkin	7 cwt 3 quarters 15 lbs muscovado sugar	0	11	10
Joseph Bradley & Cp	3 cwt 2 quarters 11 lbs muscovado sugar	0	5	4
Richard Farr	7 cwt 25 lbs muscovado sugar	0	10	10
John Elbridge	6 cwt 3 quarters 17 lb muscovado sugar	0	10	4
Executor of Cicelia Morgan	1 cwt 1 quarter 21 lbs muscovado sugar	0	2	2
Isaac Hobhouse	6 cwt 4 lbs muscovado sugar	0	9	1
James Ward	2 cwt 2 quarters muscovado sugar	0	3	9

		£	s	d
In the Content William Bragginton from Jamaica				
William Bragginton	110 cwt muscovado sugar	8	5	o
	300 gallons rum	1	5	o
	200 lbs pimento	o	5	c
	70 lbs ginger	3	10	c
	300 lbs cotton wool			
	16 cwt mahogany			
Richard Farr	50 cwt muscovado sugar	3	15	o
	150 gallons rum	o	2	6
Humphrey Smith	18 cwt muscovado sugar	1	7	o
	115 lbs indigo			
John Worsley	7 cwt cotton wool			
In the Ann and Mary Joseph Langdon from Jamaica				
William Turton	70 cwt muscovado sugar	5	5	o
William Turton	22 cwt 2 quarters muscovado sugar	1	13	9
Thomas Dolman & Cp	180 cwt muscovado sugar	13	10	o
Michael Atkins	29 cwt 1 quarter 15 lbs muscovado sugar	2	4	1
Michael Atkins	6 cwt 3 quarters 7 lbs muscovado sugar	o	10	3
In the Scrope Mathew Cooper from Jamaica				
Michael Atkins	18 cwt 3 quarters 21 lbs muscovado sugar	1	8	5
James Hilhouse	10 cwt 2 quarters 26 pounds muscovado sugar	o	16	1
In the Union Thomas Dolman from Jamaica				
Thomas Willing	23 cwt muscovado sugar	1	14	6
Isaac Hobhouse & Cp	32 cwt 3 quarters 21 lbs muscovado sugar	2	9	5

(Continued)

Table 9.1 (Continued)

In the Freke John Bartlett from Barbados				
John Bartlett	222 gallons rum	0	18	6
Isaac Hobhouse & cp	25 cwt 1 quarter 20 lbs muscovado sugar	1	18	2
Thomas Chambury as executor	13 lbs elephant teeth	0	0	5
In the Aurora Thomas Davis from Barbados				
Richard Champion & Cp	4 cwt 3 quarters 9 lbs muscovado sugar	0	7	3
In the Blanford William Skutt from Mountserett				
Richard Hawksworth for Richard Kenvill	393 gallons rum	1	12	9
Richard Hawksworth for Richard Kenvill	6 cwt 23 lbs muscovado sugar	0	9	4
William Turton & Cp	80 cwt muscovado sugar	6	0	0
In the Marlborough Robert Freels from Rotterdam				
Barnes Hunt Smith & Cp	60 reams blew paper for sugar bakers	1	10	0
Cors. & Fra^s Rogers	1625 old sheets	6	1	11
	25 cwt crop madder for dyers use			
Paul Fisher	2 basketts quantity 300 flasks Spanish water	0	8	0
Joseph Franter for Francis Humphry	745 ells holland linen under 1 ell	9	6	3
	35 cwt long steel	2	12	6
In the Combe Robert Denton from Riga				
William Donne	20 tons 5 cwt Russia Iron (duty not clear)			
Henry Combe & Cp	235 cwt rough hemp	7	16	8
Robert Denton	1 quarter 6 lbs Russia Deals above 20 ft long	0	4	6
	1 cwt handspikes	0	1	0
	3 cwt hogshead staves	0	1	0

	£	s	d
In the Kyrle George Wadmore from Bremen			
Richard Bayly			
8 cwt 3 quarters 3 ells hessens canvas	1	10	9
John Wraxall			
64 cwt 2 quarters 22 ells narrow Germany linen	12	18	9
30 cwt 3 quarters 3 ells narrow Germany linen	6	3	1
Robert Smith & Son			
378 cwt 3 quarters 2 ells narrow Germany linen	75	15	1
46 cwt 8 ells hessens canvas	8	1	3
In the Prince William Elias Perryman from Dunkirk			
William Lane			
318 gallons Flemish Brandy	1	5	3
Francis Williams			
2 ton & 44 gallons Flemish Brandy	0	13	6
Jonathan King			
15 yards Diaper Tabling of Holland 2 ells under 8 ells in breath	0	6	9
In the Harry John Woollen from Malaga			
Robert Deverett			
10 cwt raisins solis	1	0	0
400 canes or reeds	0	1	0
William Hart			
11 tons Spanish wine unfitted for sale	28	18	2
Thomas Bruton			
1 ton Spanish wine unfitted for sale	2	6	10
In the Thornbury Thomas Littlewood from Malaga			
David Barry			
120 gallons Spanish wine unfitted for sale	1	2	4
In the Farmer James Barrell from Malaga			
Ann Wraxall			
90 cwt raisins solis	9	0	0
50 tons Spanish wines unfitted for sale	117	0	0

Source: Bristol Port Books, E 190/1206/3 and 1207/1, British Public Records Office, from microfilm records in the Virginia Colonial Records Project, Micfilm 7477, Reel 744, Alderman Library, University of Virginia.

Study: Kenneth Morgan, *Bristol and the Atlantic Trade in the Eighteenth Century* (Cambridge: Cambridge University Press, 1993).

2. A New England Farmer's Expectations of Profit, 1742

Francis Brinley was a third-generation New Englander, born around 1690. His grandfather (also Francis) had come to Rhode Island from Barbados, amassed a considerable estate, and served as a judge in the Rhode Island court system. The grandson inherited the family property, and then moved to Roxbury, Massachusetts, where he lived until his death in 1765. He held appointed office in the Massachusetts colonial government, was a prosperous farmer, and with his wife, Deborah Lynde Brinley, raised more than half a dozen children. The document below, then, does not represent the calculation of a typical New Englander householder, but rather the self-appraisal of a comfortably situated large landowner. All values are in pounds, shillings, and pence.

Table 9.2   A New England Farmer's Expectations of Profit, 1742

Francis Brinley, A Ruff Computation of the Charges of My Farme att Framingham and what it may Produce if rightly Conducted	
D[ebit], March 1742	
Men and Boys now on it this year	
Ebenezer Hager overseer (one man more) & 2 boys, one 16 yr other 12 years old wages	105-0-0
Conrad Hotsens & 2 boys one 15 y, other 10 years old	30-0-0
James Berry on hyre & Priviledge	30-0-0
Women Maids and Girls	
Mrs Hager her daughter & maid wch are all women grown	60-0-0
[Total]	225-0-0
Provisions to Support Them	
50 Score of Pork at 18	75-0-0
1 ox wt 30 Score at 8	20-0-0
10 Sheep & Lambs for fresh meat	10-0-0
4 calves for ditto	12-0-0
Pottery now and then	3-0-0
Spice, Sugar, Plumb, Molosses & Rum	40-0-0
The mill will supply meal for the House	35-0-0
yet we allow a bush a week at 14/ extra wooll, cotton, flaxs &c for clothing	

(Continued)

Table 9.2   (*Continued*)

The spinning & weaveing all at home		30-0-0
[Total, all above]		450-0-0
To buy 3 negroes and their clothing		
with Interest profit & loss on them		50-0-0
for which the discharge two men next		500-0-0 [Total]
year whose wages is 90-0-0		
C[redits]		
By 800 Bush. of Indian Corn at 10/		400-0-0
By 1 Tunn & 1/2 of Hemp at 10 p LL		150-0-0
By 400 wt of Flaxs at 3/		48-0-0
By 150 Bush of oats at 7/		52-0-0
By 60 ditto of wheat at 15/		45-0-0
By 80 Bush of Rye at 12/		48-0-0
By 100 Bush of Barley at 10/		50-0-0
By 150 Score of Pork at 18		225-0-0
By Syder 2 hundred Barrells at 20/		200-0-0
By 100 Bush of apples at 6/		30-0-0
By Proffat on Fatt Cattle		100-0-0
By what sheep & Lambs I shall raise		
and dispose of	60-0-0	
By wooll 250 wt of wooll at 4/	50-0-0	110-0-0
By 20 calves to raise	60-0-0	
By 1000 wt of Butter to Sell at 2/6	125-0-0	
By 5000 wt of cheese at 18	375-0-0	560-0-0
By Patatoes 50 Bush Turnips 50 Bush,		
and Garden Stuff		50-0-0
[Total]		2068-0-0
By the mills a 100 Bush of meal		50-0-0
By the Tanyards		100-0-0
[Total]		2218-0-0
My Expenses Backwards & Forwards &		
Friends abt 50-0-0		500-0-0
[Balance]		1718-0-0

Source: Brinley Family Papers, 1742, Archives, University of Massachusetts, Amherst.

Study: Stephen Innes, *Creating the Commonwealth: The Economic Culture of Puritan New England* (New York: W. W. Norton, 1995).

3. The Business of a South Carolina Commission Merchant, 1738 and 1740

Robert Pringle was a Scottish-born merchant who arrived in Charleston, South Carolina in the 1720s, to work as a factor (agent) and commission merchant for traders in other ports. A fortuitous marriage in 1734 into a resident merchant family helped his career, as did his second marriage in 1751 to a wealthy and prominent widow. In the first of the two letters below, Pringle explains to a merchant from Hull (England) how the commission business operates. In the second letter, Pringle writes to a correspondent in Portugal (where much of Carolina's rice was being shipped in the middle of the eighteenth century) to request a favor.

Robert Pringle, Charles Town, to Richard Thompson, Hull, 2 September 1738

SIR:

A few days agoe came to hand your very agreeable favours of the 27th May, through the Recommendations of my good Friend Mr. Robert Scotts of Madeira, & Duly Observe the Contents. Agreeable to your Request this is to advise you that Mr. Scott ought Certainly to know better than to Inform you that a Vessell to come here with a Cargoe of Wines may be Loaded Directly with Rice as soon as She has Deliver'd said Cargoe for doe assure you a Cargoe of Wines cannot be Dispos'd of here & turn'd into Cash in less than Six Months at least, & you may be Sencible that the Commission of 5 per cent is not worth while to be in advance when the Interest of money is at 10 per cent as Rice is always bought of the Planters with present money. And as for Madeira Wine I cannot much Encourage your sending any Quantity here there being a pretty Deal at present on hand unsold, & more expected next Vintage, as also from the Canarys, & this is a place of not great consumption for Wines & the Market very Precarious.

Our Rice is now beginning to be Cutt Down & will Continue to Cutt it in all this Month of September. Of which we have the greatest Crop has yet been in the Province & will be double the Quantity of what we had last year. We generally begin to ship about the first of November & so continue Shipping off Briskly via the month of May & in that time we expect to Load above One hundred sail of Ships for Europe with Rice only. The most proper time for a Ship to Load Rice here I take to be in the Months of December, January, February, & March. As we have a very good Crop, it is expected that Rice will be much lower in price than it has been for some years past, but that Cheifly depends upon the number of Shipping that come here to Load therewith.

This province takes off yearly a very great Quantity of all manner of dry goods from Europe & Ports in England that are Cheifly supply'd from are London, Bristol, Topsham, & Liverpool & our manner of Trade in Dry goods is by giving the Planters Credit from Crop to Crop, so that a ship to come here with a Cargoe could not be Immediately Loaded with Dispatch with the proceeds of what she brings. However doubt not but a Trade May be carried on here from your Port & to as good Account as from any where Else, there being a great many Articles from your ports that are very Suitable for this Province. & on the other side we have a List of what goods are generally Imported. We Likewise export besides Rice a great Quantity of Pitch, Tar, Turpentine, Rosin, & Deer Skins, a great Quantity as also Logwood & Brazilleto Wood [Jamaican wood used for dyes] of which you have Inclosed of the Current prices. There are between Two and Three hundred sail of shipping yearly Loaded from this port & the Chief part are Large ships for London & to London especially.

The proper Season for Importing Woolen Goods is to have them arrive here in the Month of August or September & for Summer Goods to be here in the Months of February & March. I am of opinion that for your Vessell to sell her Cargoe of Madeira Wine in Barbadoes or Antigua & invest same in Rum, Sugar, & Molassis for this Place would answer much better there than Madeira Wine, having a great Consumption for same here & is of a Quick & Ready Sale. If you are Inclinable to make a Tryal of this Trade either by sending Goods in a Vessell here directly or by shipping goods by way of London, shall be very glad to Receive your Commands. I shall always endeavour my utmost to perform them to your best advantage & very readily Contribute all in my power to Cultivate & Improve a Lasting & agreeable Correspondance with you, mean time heartily Salute you & am most Respectfully &c.

Goods proper for So Carolina Vizt. Course Cloths & Heavies, Camblets of all sorts & Colours & Silk Camblets, Linnen & Cotton Checks. Huckaback for Tables & Napkins, Diapers & Damask for ditto. Sheeting Linnen. Bagg & Gulix & Holland Cambricks. Gun Powder. A Large Quantity 3/4 & 7/8 Garlix low pric'd. Brown Osnaburggs, Dowlas & Russia Linnen. Indian Trading Guns with two Sights & Gun Flints, Non so pretties. Small Shott put up in Small Keggs, Bullets in small Keggs & Swan Shott. White, Bleue, & Green plains for Negro Cloathing. Sagathys & Duroyss & worsted Damask, Ship & Duffill Blanketting. Ruggs for Negroes Beds. Bed Blanketts fine. Strouds blue & Red. Felt hatts mens & Boys. Course Worsted stockings

For Negroes. Course Leather Shoes. Womens Course ditto. Nails, vizt. 20d, 10d, 8d, 6d, 4d, Clasp in small Casks. Single reffin'd Loaf Sugar a Large Quantity, Bohea Tea in Cannisters. Black pepper & Spices of all Sorts. China Ware & Punch Bowls. Earthen ware in Crates. Florence & Linseed Oyl, mens & womens Lamb Gloves. Painted Callicoes, Shirts & Handkes. Indian Goods of all sorts. Scarlett, blue, & Superfine Broad Cloth. Mens thread Hose of all sorts. Cordage vizt. Cables, Hawsers & Running Rigging. Pewter plates, Dishes, & Spoons, sorted hand mixte, & 1/3 Common mixte Tobacco, Shortt Pypes called Hunting in Boxes or Barrels. Writting paper, & Brown ditto, bottle Casks, Osnaburggs, Thread, Cheshire Cheese a small Quantity. Canvas or Sail Cloth. Hamburg Lines English Salt. English Bricks & New Castle Coals for Ballast.

Prices of Goods in Charlestown So Carolina vizt. Rice, at present none, but supposed next Crop to be sold at 40/ to 45/per Ct. Currency & the barrels of about 500 lb. each at 10/per piece. The last Crop Rice was sold from £3 to £4 per Ct., but expect it wont be more than the above price this Crop. Pitch 40/per Barell, Tarr 32/per ditto, Turpentine 10/per Ct., Deer Skin 17/6 per lb., Logwood £56 per ton, Brazilletto wood £35 per ditto. Commission on buying 5 per cent & all of the Shipping Charges on board may be Reckoned at 2½ per cent more. Commission on selling 5 per cent & Storeage a 2½ per cent more. Dry Goods sold at 900 per cent advance on the Invoice of Sterling Money. Exchange to London £800 Currency per £100 Sterling or 8 per 1.

Robert Pringle to Edward and John Mayne, Lisbon, Portugal,
19 September 1740

... This will be delivered you by Capt. Robert Thompson, Commander of the Snow *Dorsett*, & please receive Inclosed Bill of Loading for a Negro Girl nam'd Esther, which I take the Liberty to Consign to your address by said Capt. Thompson for Sale & Desire you'll please receive her & dispose of her to my best advantage in Case you have not Occassion for her your Self at your House. She is a Very Likely Young Wench & can doe any House Work, such as makeing Beds, Cleaning Rooms, Washing, attending at Table, &c. & talks good English being this Province Born, & is not given to any Vice, & have always found her honest. The only Reason of my sending her off the Province is that she had a practice of goeing frequently to her Father and Mother, who Live at a Plantation I am Concern'd in about Twenty Miles from Town from whence there was no Restraining her from Running away there, & Staying every now & then, which determin'd me to send her off & hope may sell her to good Advantage. She is valued at Twenty pounds

Sterling here & hope may be worth as many Moydores' with you. However desire you may Sell her Off for the Most you Can. Capt. Thompson has been so Good as to give me Her passage free. He tells me that she is Lyable to a Duty at Lisbon, which he will Likewise Endeavour to Save me and the Neat proceeds of whatever She Sells for, you'll please to Remitt on my Account to my Brother in London. . . .

Source: Walter B. Edgar, ed., *The Letterbook of Robert Pringle*, 2 vols. (Columbia: University of South Carolina Press, 1972), I, 29–32, 247, from originals in the South Carolina Historical Society.

Study: Cathy D. Matson, *Merchants & Empire: Trading in Colonial New York* (Baltimore: Johns Hopkins University Press, 1998).

Discussion Questions

1   If we assume that the trade depicted in the Bristol document above was typical, which areas of the New World were the most valuable to Great Britain commercially?
2   The New England farmer in the second document clearly thought what he was producing was commercially valuable. How did his production plans differ from the goods sent to Bristol? For whom was he producing these products?
3   What can you determine about the business practices of colonial merchants from the South Carolina documents? What factors, which might not be of concern to a modern business person, were critical to the success of this merchant?
4   The sale of colonial produce through ports like Bristol paid for the goods shipped to the colonies. What type of goods did American consumers purchase? The documents in chapter 12, on "Everyday Life," may help you expand on your answer.

Chapter 10   Empire

1. A Memorial Concerning the Fur Trade of the Province of New York: Cadwallader Colden to William Barnet, Governor of New York, November 10, 1724

Cadwallader Colden, New York's surveyor general, wrote a long letter of advice to the colony's royal governor, William Burnet, on how to win the fur trade with Native Americans away from the French in Canada. The letter is instructive for the way it lays out the geographic (colonial and international) and political dimensions of the fur trade.

It has of late been generally believed that the Inhabitants of the Province of New York are so advantageously situated with respect to the Indian Trade and enjoy so many advantages as to Trade in General, that it is in their Power not only to rival the French of Canada who have almost entirely engrossed the Fur Trade of America, but that it is impossible for the French to carry on that Trade in competition with the People of this Province. The enquiring into the Truth of this Proposition may not only be of some consequence as to the riches and honor of the British Nation for it is well known how valuable the Fur Trade of America is, but likewise as to the safety of all the British Colonies in North America.

New France (as, the French now claim) extends from the mouth of the River Mississippi to the Mouth of the River St Lawrence by which the French plainly shew their intention of enclosing the British Settlements and cutting us off from all Commerce with the numerous Nations of India that are every where settled over the vast continent of North America. The English in

America have too good reason to apprehend such a design, when they see the French Kings Geographer publish a Map by which he has set bounds to the British Empire in America and has taken in many of the English Settlements, both in South Carolina and New York within these Boundaries of New France – And the good Services they intend us with the Indians but too plainly appear at this day by the Indian War now carried on against new England.

I have therefor for some time past endeavoured to inform myself from the writings of the French and from others who have travel'd in Canada or among the Indians how far the People of this Province may carry on the Indian Trade with more advantage than the French can, or what disadvantage they labour under more than the French do . . .

[The Advantages of the French]
. . . the French have an Easy communication with all the Countrys bordering upon the River of St Lawrence and its Branches with all the countrys bordering upon these inland Seas [the Great Lakes] and the Rivers which empty themselves into these Seas and can thereby carry their Burden of Merchandize through all these countrys which could not by any other means than Water carriage be carried through a vast Tract of Land. This however but half furnishes the view the French have as to their commerce in North America many of the Branches of the River Misissipi come [so] near to the Branches of several of the Rivers which empty themselves into the great Lakes that in several places there is but a short land carriage from the one to the other as soon as they have got into the River of Missisipi they open to themselves as large a feild for Traffic in the Southern Parts of North America as was before mentioned with respect to the Northern Parts. . . .

The French have with much industry settled small Colonys and built Stockada Forts at all the considerable Passes between the Lakes except between Cataracqui Lake (called by the French Ontario.) and Lake Erie, One of our five Nations of Indians, whom we call Sinnekes and the French Sonontouons having hitherto refused them leave to erect any buildings there. The French have been indefatigable in making discoveries and carrying on their Commerce with Nations whom the English know nothing but what they see in the French Maps and Books. The Barrenness of the Soil and the coldness of the Climate of Canada, obliges the greatest number of the Inhabitants to seek their living by travelling among the Indians or by trading with those that do travel. The Governour and other officers have but a scanty allowance from the King, & could not subsist were it not by the perquisites they have from this Trade Neither could their Priests find any means to satisfy their ambition and Luxury without it So that all heads & hands are employed to advance it, and the men of best parts think it the surest way to advance themselves by travelling among the Indians and learning the Languages even the Bigotry & Enthusiasm of some hot heads has not been a little useful in advancing this commerce. For that Government having prudently turned the Edge of the Zeal of such hot spirits, upon converting the Indians many of them have spent their lives under the greatest hardships, in endeavoring to gain the Indians to their religion, and to love the French Nation while at the same time they are no less industrious to represent the English as the ennemies of Mankind . . .

[The Disadvantage of the French Position]
But notwithstanding all these advantages the French labor under difficultys that no art or Industry can remove. The mouth of the river of St Lawrence and more especially the Bay of St Lawrence lyes so far North and is thereby so often subject to tempestuous weather and thick Fogs that the Navigation there is very dangerous and never attempted but during the summer months. . . .

Besides these difficultys in the Transportation the French labor under greater in the purchasing of the principal goods proper for the Indian Market for the most considerable & most valuable part of their Cargo, consists in Strowds, Duffils Blankets and other Woollens, which are bought at a much cheaper rate in England than in France – The Strowds which the Indians value more than any other Clothing, are only made in England, and must be transported into France before they can be carried to Canada, Rum is an other considerable Branch of the Indian Trade which the French want, by reason they have no commoditys in Canada fit for the West India Markets – This they supply with Brandy at a much dearer rate than Rum can be purchased at New York tho of no more value with the Indians, generally all the goods used in the Indian Trade except Gunpowder, and a few trinkets are sold at Monreal for twice their value at Albany. To this likewise must be added the necessity they are under of laying the whole charge of supporting their Government on the Indian Trade, I am not particularly informed of their duties or imposts, but I am well assured that they commonly give six or 700 Livres for a Licence for one canoe in proportion to her largeness to go with her loading into the Indian Country to trade . . .

[Dislodging the French]
King Williams Peace put an end to [war between the English, the French, and their Indian allies], but the Peace lasted so short a while that the people of this Province had hardly time to resettle their Farms on the Frontiers which they had deserted in the time of War, much less to adventure trading in the Indian Countrys so lately the Scene of so much Cruelty. But both Colonies having now an abhorrence of the crueltys of the last war, agreed

on a kind of Neutrality for the Indians during Queen Ann's War. Since which time we lost much ground with our own Indians. For the French having learned by dear Experience that it was not possible for them to conquer our five Indian Nations resolved to try all means to gain their affections, and in this art the French are always more successful; than in that of War; and the English failing in two ill concerted expeditions against Canada the Indians lost much of the opinion they had of the English Power and Valor.

In the time of this last war the clandestine trade to Monreal began to be carried on by Indians from Albany to Monreal. This gave rise to the Konuaga or praying Indians who are entirely made up of Deserters from the Mohawks and River Indians and were either enticed by the French Priests or by our Merchants in order to carry goods from Albany to Monreal or run away from some mischeif done here. These Indians now consist of about 80 fighting men and live about four leagues above Monreal: They neither plant nor hunt but depend cheifly upon this private Trade for their subsistence these Indians in Time of War gave the French intelligence of all designs here against them. By them likewise the French engaged our Five Nations in a War with the Indians Friends of Virginia; and from them we might expect the greatest mischeif in time of war seeing every part of the Province is as well known to them as to any of the inhabitants. But if this Trade were entirely at an end we have reason to beleive that these Indians would return to their own Tribes for they [then] could not long subsist where they now are . . .

Source: E. B. O'Callaghan and Berthold Fernow, eds., *Documents Relative to the Colonial History of New York*, 15 vols. (Albany, NY: Weed, Parsons, Printers, 1856–87), V, 726–32.

Study: Daniel K. Richter, *The Ordeal of the Longhouse: The Peoples of the Iroquois League in the Era of European Colonization* (Chapel Hill: University of North Carolina Press for the Institute of Early American History and Culture, 1992).

2. Lieutenant Governor William Gooch of Virginia to the Board of Trade, on the Need for a Tobacco Inspection Act, June 29, 1729 and February 27, 1731

William Gooch (1681–1751) served as Virginia's royal [lieutenant] governor from 1727 to 1749, among the longest tenures for a governor during the colonial period. He formed an effective alliance with the colony's ruling gentry, whose interests as tobacco planters, he supported assiduously. In the late 1720s and early 1730s, Gooch tried to protect Virginia planters from

*legislation British merchants wanted to make debt collection in Virginia easier,
and from legislation that West Indian sugar planters sought to prohibit trade
between the mainland colonies and the French Caribbean islands. At the same
time, he worked to convince the Virginia gentry and British officials of the
need to enact legislation to improve the quality of tobacco shipped to Great
Britain. Gooch's correspondence below with the Board of Trade (which
advised the British Parliament on colonial matters) illustrates his these efforts
in support of tobacco inspection.*

[June 29, 1729]
As the state of the tobacco trade calls for a speedy remedy, as well to prevent
an apparent loss to H.M. revenue, as a great blow to the manufactures of
Great Britain, if the planters discouraged from making tobacco by the
lowness of the price, should be driven to the necessity of laying that aside,
and should provide themselves with their own cloathing from the materials
this country affords. . . . It is evident that the duty have been and is a strong
temptation to many to contrive all possible ways of defrauding the Crown
by running the tobacco in Great Brittain: and the success they have had
therein, has likewise given occasion to the buying up all the mean and trash
tobacco, purchased here by agents and sailors who well know how to
dispose of it without paying any duty. And this sort of traffique has encouraged the planters to cure a great deal or all of their trash, which otherwise
must have been thrown away; Thus is the market for the good tobacco
damp'd by the fraudulent importation of the bad, and the fair trader and
honest and industrious planter greatly discouraged. I have taken some pains
to find out a remedy for this great evill, and to that purpose have consulted
divers of the principal inhabitants of this Province as well merchants as
others, and find it generally agreed that the only effectual means to prevent
the abuse which long since crept into this trade; will be to bring all the
tobacco under a strict examination by sworn Officers; before it be allow'd
to be ship'd of for Great Brittain; that all that is found bad be destroy'd, and
none exported but what is really good and merchantable, and that an
account of the true weight of every hogshead or cask shall be transmitted
to the Commissioners of H.M. Customs, by which the fraudulent practice of
breaking open of hogsheads and ruining of the tobacco may be more easily
detected and prevented. I now send to your Lordships also the heads of what
I propose for the improvement of the tobacco trade, hoping that when your
Lordships have consider'd them, they may be approved and immediately
put in practice, either by obtaining H.M. letters mandating to the Governors of Virginia and Maryland to pass them into laws, or, which would be

much more efficacious, an Act of Parliament to put all the tobacco made in the Plantations under the regulation therein proposed; for it must be confess'd that though the judicious and honest part of the people here are well inclined to these measures, there are too many of a different character, who are ready to oppose everything that is not suited to their narrow conceptions and private views. If these proposals are thought by your Lordships to deserve encouragement and to pass in the Parliament there is one thing not mentioned that must be provided for, and that is the nomination of the officers to inspect the tobacco, who must be men of character and understanding in that commodity which may be left, unless your Lordships shall order otherwise, to the appointment of the Governours, who must also ascertain their sallarys in proportion to their trouble; for some places where storehouses must be built, will have much more tobacco brought to them than others.

[February 27, 1731]
Almost all the tobacco made by the common people, (and they make the best), is sold to the merchants in this country and the factors from the out-ports, for cloathing and other necessaries which the planters want *etc.* Their manner of dealing hitherto hath been that if a planter wants but a pair of shoes at one of these stores, he must lay out a whole hogshead of tobacco, seeing the merchant will not receive a less quantity, neither will he deal at all, unless the tobacco lyes convenient to his Receiver; and by this means the poor planter is often obliged to take goods that are of little or no use to him, and at what price his neighbouring storekeeper pleases to impose, because he cannot otherwise have what he really hath occasion for; This has indeed proved a discouragement to many industrious people, and must in time obliged them to leave off planting, and apply their labour to better purpose. But by this act the greatest encouragement is given to the common people to make tobacco that could be then thought of: for after their tobacco hath passed an inspection, they may take as many notes for it as they please; i.e., notes for fiftys or hundred pounds, dividing their tobacco into what parcels they think proper; these notes, the same as money, will be accepted as payment at any store or shop, and as it is much easier for a planter to carry home his goods, than to remove his tobacco to the conveniency of the merchant, he will not henceforward be confined to one particular merchant, but will be at liberty to deal where he can meet with the best goods and the best purchase.

These advantages being what the common planters see their account in, they are, and will be, more particularly fond of the method proposed for payment in these transfer notes, and will thereby be incited to apply themselves to this manufacture with greater attention than they have hitherto done, under the disadvantage of being stinted in their plants, a low price and an useless return. As to lessening the consumption by advancing the price, I can see no ground to apprehend such a consequence: for since the rich and even people of middling fortunes will ever be fonder of smoking good than bad tobacco, be the price what it will; so custom having made smoaking as necessary as food to the labourer and mechanick, it will not be an half-penny, or penny pr. pound that will lessen the consumption of what they find necessary to the gratification of their desires : but 'tis rather to be expected that a more agreable tobacco will draw them into a greater inclination to use a much larger quantity.

Source: *Calendar of State Papers, Colonial Series, America and the West Indies, 1728–1729* (London, 1937), pp. 417–18; from C.O. 5, 1322, Public Record Office, London; *Calendar of State Papers, Colonial Series, America and the West Indies, 1731* (London, 1937), pp. 47–8; from C.O. 5, 1322.

Study: John M. Hemphill, *Virginia and the English Commercial System, 1689–1733: Studies in the Development and Fluctuations of a Colonial Economy under Imperial Control* (New York: Garland Publishing, 1985); an unrevised reprint of the author's 1964 Princeton University Ph.D. dissertation.

3. James Oglethorpe Promotes a New Colony in Georgia, 1732

James Oglethorpe (1696–1785) was a military officer and Member of Parliament. An early interest in prison reform blossomed into a utopian scheme to found a colony in America to give Britain's unemployed a chance at a better life. One of the pieces he published (anonymously) in the early 1730s, Select Tracts Relating to Colonies, *to promote the colonization plan reprinted several well-known and skillfully edited essays explaining the benefits, romance, and grandeur of colonization.*

Nothing so much improves the Mind, and directs the Judgment to right Determination as Experience and the Opinions of wise Men. As new Colonies are now so much talked of, it may be agreeable to the Public, to see what has been writ upon that Subject by Philosophers, Statesmen, and Merchants, Men of different Professions, living in different Ages and Countries, who could have no common View in deceiving. To save the Reader therefore the Trouble of hunting their Opinions out in many Books, the following Tracts are collected and published.

The first is by one whose Genius was not only an Ornament to the Nation and Age he lived in, but an Honor to Mankind. It is by Tradition deliver'd down, that he writ his Treatise on Plantations upon the following Occasion.

Sir Walter Raleigh the excellent Historian, Soldier, Statesman, and Philosopher, made Attempts to settle in America, went twice in person to Guiana and once to Virginia, the latter of these was granted to him by Queen Elizabeth, who loved great Designs, carried her Views far, and studied the Welfare of England in future Generations as well as in her own Age. Under her Countenance he settled the first Colony in Virginia, so named in Compliment to her Majesty. The Queen died, and with her expired all Encouragement to noble Undertakings. Raleigh not fit for a weal Mixture of timorous and arbitrary Measures was disgraced, condemned, imprisoned; the Plantation neglected, and all Thoughts of America given over by the Court.

But tho' Sir Walter was destroyed, his Spirit survived...The Earl of Southampton and Sir Edwin Sandys, among many other very considerate Men, were of that Council [the Virginia Company], and they being intimate Friends of Sir Francis Bacon, prevailed with him to write Instructions concerning the new Colony. This was afterwards printed amongst his Essays, and is here annexed.

The next consists of Passages taken out of different Parts of the Florentine Historian. He treats of Colonies as a Politician, and therefore mentions them as they may be useful or prejudicial towards the preserving or increasing the Power of the Prince or State. Being thoroughly conversant with the Ancients, he from the Roman Maxims chalks the Outlines of a Plan for peopling a whole Country in a regular Manner, and by that Means remedying the Inconveniences of Climate, Air, and Soil. He shows the Difference between supporting Conquests by garrisons of Colonies, and supporting them by mercenary Troops, and just sketches out the only Plan upon which he seems to think they can be successfully founded, viz. Religion, Liberty, good Laws, the Exercise of Arms, and Encouragement of Arts...

The third Tract was writ by John De Witt the famous Pensionary of Holland, who being both a Statesman and a Merchant mixes political with trading Considerations...

The fourth Tract is writ by William Penn Proprietary of Pennsylvania. It was printed in the Year 1680, about the Time that he began to settle that Colony, and given amongst his Friends...Foreseeing the Effects of Justice, Liberty, and wise Regulations he formed the Plan to admit of great Increase; he chose a Situation between two navigable Rivers, and designed a Town in Form of an oblong Square....He left proper Spaces for Markets, Parades, Keys, Wharfs, Meeting-houses, Schools, Hospitals, and other future publick Buildings. In the Province there is now eighty Thousand Inhabitants and in the Town of Philadelphia a great Number of Houses...

The fifth Tract is a Discourse by Sir Josiah Child. He writ with an excellent Intention, that of undeceiving the People, by exposing several vulgar Errors; the twelfth of which vulgar Errors, and which in this discourse he labors to confute is, "That our Plantations depopulate, and consequently impoverish England..." Men have since the publishing of his Book been undeceived, and the Plantations have been continually encouraged by Parliament, to the great Increase of the Wealth, Trade and people of the Kingdom.

Source: [James Oglethorpe], *Select Tracts Relating to Colonies* [London, 1732].

Study: David Armitage, *The Ideological Origins of the British Empire* (Cambridge: Cambridge University Press, 2000).

4. James Ramsay on the Abolition of the British Slave Trade, 1784

James Ramsay (1733–89), an Anglican minister, had lived in St. Kitts in the British West Indies, where he had experienced firsthand, as he tried to preach to slaves, the arrogance of the powerful sugar planters of the islands. He formulated a critique both of the conditions under which slaves labored and of the slave trade in the 1770s, but didn't publish his opinions until after the American Revolution. Ramsay was among a number of early critics of slavery in an era described by one historian as that of "antislavery without abolitionism," but the one who most clearly recognized that reform could only be carried out if the colonies had less, rather than more, autonomy within the British empire. Britain, of course, would eventually impose emancipation on its colonies, while the newly independent United States would need a civil war to resolve the issue. In the first extract below Ramsay argues for the extension of law (police) to master–slave relations as an aid to religious conversion of the slaves. In the second, he lists objections to the end of the slave trade, and answers each.

[From *Conversion of African Slaves*]

We have observed, that slaves are hardly in any instance considered as objects of police, being abandoned to the management, or rather caprice, of their several masters. Nor doth law take notice of them, but to enforce power, which, without further assistance, too frequently lays reason and humanity bleeding at its feet. Our laws, indeed, as far as they respect slaves, are only licensed modes of exercising tyranny on them; for they are not made parties to them, though their lives and feelings be concluded by them. As well may directions for angling be said to be laws made for dumb fish, as our colony regulations for whipping, hanging, crucifying, burning negroes, be called law made for slaves. To make them objects of civil government must therefore be an essential part of every plan of improvement that respects slaves; so that while obnoxious to the penalties of the law, they must be entitled to its security; and while law leaves them under management of the master, it must protect them from his barbarity.

[From *Objections*]
Object. 9. *Parliament has given its sanction to the trade by regulating it.*

Answ. 9. If the countenance given by parliament to this horrid trade, has constantly been procured by the representation of interested people, must government be charged with the consequences arising from the imposition? Because we had laws that once fixed a commutation for murder, were we thereby precluded from ever improving our police? But this shows how cautious we should be, by any regulation, to give sanction to oppression and murder.

Object. 11. *Dr. Burton, Secretary of this Society* [Society for the Propagation of the Gospel, which ran a slave plantation in Jamaica] *wrote a letter to Mr.* [*Anthony*] *Benezet* [English-born, Philadelphia Quaker and abolitionist], *under the direction of an eminent prelate, which acknowledged the lawfulness of slavery, as mentioned in the Bible.*

Answ. 11.... The abstract question, "is slavery lawful?" is not now agitated. We must allow its lawfulness in any case, where it can be proved, that injustice, murder, oppression, and avarice, has not been exercised. The present question is, "may Liverpool merchants fit their ships with arms, chains, baubles, and brandy, to bribe Africans to rise against their countrymen, to murder some, to enslave others; to be delivered up to them to be chained, suffocated, starved; to be transported to the sugar colonies to work for planters without food, rest, or raiment; to be ill treated without cessation, without remedy." The Doctor, writing on the first question, leaves it as he found the practice to be in the times of the apostles. The Liverpool slave trade was not before him; and even could the highest human sanction be produced in its favour, nature would revolt and refuse her assent to the decision....

Object. 13. *To imprison debtors, and impress men to serve in war, are violations of moral law, equally with domestic slavery....*

Answ. 13. He who runs in debt knows the consequences; but all is a force upon the poor negroe. Many men enter into the sea and land service willingly; and those who are impressed are treated as volunteers are. But we never heard of an African offering himself to be received on board, of having been put on a footing with the ship's crew. But the impressed sailor is among his countrymen, and serves his country. What common tie subsists between the African, living 1200 miles from the sea-coast, and a West-Indian planter, to induce him to submit to be tied neck and heel, to die a thousand suffocating deaths on ship board; to go and be beaten, half starved, and abused, in the cultivation of a plant, from which he reaps no profit?

Source: James Ramsay, *An Essay on the Treatment and Conversion of African Slaves in the British Sugar Colonies* (Dublin, 1784); and *Objections to the Abolition of the Slave Trade with Answers. To Which are Prefixed Strictures on a Late Publication, Intitled, "Considerations on the Emancipation of Negroes, and the Abolition of the Slave Trade, by a West India Planter"* (London, 1784, 1788).

Study: Christopher Leslie Brown, *Moral Capital: Foundations of British Abolitionism* (Chapel Hill: University of North Carolina Press for the Omohundro Institute of Early American History and Culture, 2006).

Discussion Questions

1   Each of these documents assumes a notion of empire in making an argument about a particular political goal of the author. What notion(s) of empire – commercial, geographic, cultural – does each author have?
2   Where in these letters and essays do you see tensions between different regions of the empire?
3   Where in these letters and essays are empire and imperial interests defined *against* some other empire?
4   What sense do the documents give of the place of Native Americans in the British notion of empire?
5   In what ways does Ramsay connect the British empire to the slave trade? Why does Oglethorpe, in promoting a colony that would become a slaveowning society, not mention slavery?

Chapter 11   Slavery

1. Lieutenant Governor William Gooch of Virginia to the Board of Trade, Comments about African American Slaves in Virginia. June 29, 1729

William Gooch's reports to the Board of Trade concerned more than commercial matters (see Gooch's comments on tobacco inspection in the chapter 10 on "Empire"). Here he comments on slavery in Virginia.

Some time after my last [letter] a number of negroes, about fifteen, belonging to a new plantation, on the head of James River formed a design to withdraw from their master and to fix themselves in the fastnesses of the neighbouring mountains : they had found means to get into their possession some arms and ammunition, and they took along with them some provisions, their cloaths, bedding and working tools; but the Gentleman to whom they belonged with a party of men made such diligent pursuit after them, that he soon found them out in their settlement, a very obscure place among the mountains, where they had already begun to clear the ground, and obliged them after exchanging a shot or two by which one of the slaves was wounded, to surrender and return back, and so prevented for this time a design which might have proved as dangerous to this country, as is that of the negroes in the mountains of Jamaica to the inhabitants of that island. Tho' this attempt has happily been defeated, it ought nevertheless to awaken us into some effectual measures for preventing the like hereafter, it being certain that a very small number of negroes once settled in those parts, would very soon be encreas'd by the accession of other runaways and prove dangerous neighbours to our frontier inhabitants....

[I hope further to] inform your Lordships that upon the bruit of many wonderful cures performed by a negro slave in the most inveterate venerial distempers, I thought it might be of use to mankind, if by any fair method I could prevail upon him to discover to me the means by which such cures were effected, which the negro had for many years practiced in this country, but kept as a most profound secrett; as the fellow is very old, my endeavours were quicken'd, lest the secrett should dye with him: therefore I immediately sent for him, and by good words and a promise of setting him free, he has made an ample discovery of the whole, which is no other than a decoction of the root and barks I have sent over to a phisitian, that the Colledge may have the oppertunity of making an experiment what effect it will have in England; and I flatter myself, by the ingenuity of the learned in that profession, it may be reduced into a better draught than he makes of it, which they tell me is nauseous enough.

Source: *Calendar of State Papers, Colonial Series, America and the West Indies, 1728–1729* (London, 1937), pp. 414–15, 419; from C.O. 5, 1322, Public Record Office, London.

Study: Gerald Mullin, *Flight and Rebellion: Slave Resistance in Eighteenth-Century Virginia* (New York: Oxford University Press, 1972).

2. New York Conspiracy Trials of 1741

In the mid-eighteenth century, many white New Yorkers owned slaves. These slaves had, relative to southern agriculture workers, a great deal of autonomy to move about the city to carry out tasks for their masters or hire themselves out (for the masters' and their own benefit). Others were seamen who resided temporarily in the city when a ship they were working on was in port. But if slavery gave slaves greater autonomy in New York City than it might elsewhere, it could be, and often was, equally brutal.

In the winter of 1741, several New York City slaves stole goods from a local shopkeeper and then "fenced" the goods through John and Sarah Hughson, husband and wife, and tavernkeepers. When the theft was followed by a series of mysterious fires, some whites concluded that there was a conspiracy afoot, also involving the Hughsons and various slaves and free blacks, to burn New York. An ongoing war between Spain and Great Britain, and fear of "papist plots" against Protestant New York, heightened anxieties. Witnesses, often facing death themselves if they didn't point the finger at others, would eventually bring a group of black sailors captured during the war, held in New York City, and known as the "Spanish prisoners," into the story of conspiracy, as well as incriminate a local dancing master (John Ury), who the court would determine was the Spanish Catholic mastermind of the conspiracy. The key witness in a spiraling set of accusations was the Hughsons' servant, Mary Burton.

The grand jury investigations and trials stretched over several months, amidst growing anxiety, and led to the execution of 30 slaves and four whites. The primary record of the proceedings came from Justice Daniel Horsmanden, who published an account to prove that there had in fact been a conspiracy, and that its brutal repression – some of those convicted were burned to death – was justified. What follows below are excerpts from his account about Mary Burton's testimony. Also included is Horsmanden's summary of the confession of an Indian slave, Wan.

WEDNESDAY, APRIL 22
Deposition, No. 1. -Mary Burton, being sworn, deposeth,

1. "That Prince and Caesar brought the things of which they had robbed Mr. Hogg, to her master, John Hughson's house, and that they were handed in through the window, Hughson, his wife, and Peggy receiving them, about two or three o'clock on a Sunday morning.
2. "That Caesar, Prince, and Mr. Philipse's negro man (Cuffee) used to meet frequently at her master's house, and that she had heard them (the negroes) talk frequently of burning the fort; and that they would go down to the fly and burn the whole town; and that her master and mistress said, they would aid and assist them as much as they could.
3. "That in their common conversation they used to say, that when all this was done, Caesar should be governor, and Hughson, her master, should be king.
4. "That Cuffee used to say, that a great many people had too much, and others too little; that his old master had a great deal of money, but that, in a short time, he should have less, and that he (Cuffee) should have more.
5. "That at the same time when the things of which Mr. Hogg was robbed, were brought to her master's house, they brought some indigo and bees wax, which was likewise received by her master and mistress.
6. "That at the meetings of the three aforesaid negroes, Caesar, Prince, and Cuffee, at her master's house, they used to say, in their conversations, that when they set fire to the town, they would do it in the night, and as the white people came to extinguish it, they would kill and destroy them.

7. "That she has known at times, seven or eight guns in her master's house, and some swords, and that she has seen twenty or thirty negroes at one time in her master's house; and that at such large meetings, the three aforesaid negroes, Cuffee, Prince, and Caesar, were generally present, and most active, and that they used to say, that the other negroes durst not refuse to do what they commanded them, and they were sure that they had a number sufficient to stand by them.

8. "That Hughson (her master) and her mistress used to threaten, that if she, the deponent, ever made mention of the goods stolen from Mr. Hogg, they would poison her; and the negroes swore, if ever she published, or discovered the design of burning the town, they would burn her whenever they met her.

9. "That she never saw an white person in company when they talked of burning the town, but her master, her mistress, and Peggy.

This evidence of a conspiracy, not only to burn the city, but also destroy and murder the people, was most astonishing to the grand jury, and that any white people should become so abandoned as to confederate with slaves in such an execrable and detestable purpose, could not but be very amazing to every one that heard it; what could scarce be credited; but that the several fires had been occasioned by some combination of villains, was, at the time of them, naturally to be collected from the manner and circumstances attending them.

FRIDAY, JUNE 19
Confession of Wan, Indian man of Mr. Lowe, before the grand jury.

1. He said that about twelve months ago he met at the water-side, John, a free Indian, late of Cornelius Cosine, who carried him to Hughson's, where they drank a mug of beer, and paid for it: when John went away, but Hughson stopped him (Wan) and told him a law was made to sell no liquor to slaves, bid him not tell: Wan said he would not; then Hughson bid him swear on a book he held to him, to do what he should tell him, and Wan said he would; and he put his hand on the book and swore after what Hughson said, to burn his master's house. and to kill his master and mistress, and to assist to take the town.

2. That Ticklepitcher and Bastian were there when he swore; and being asked if any one else? he said none.

3. That John, the Indian, met him afterwards, and seeing him melancholy, asked him what was the matter? He (Wan) told him what he had done, on which John said it was good for him.

4. That Cuffee (Gomez's) and Francis (Bosch's) told him, they were to set
   their master's house on fire, and one day asked him if he was ready, and
   he told them yes.
5. That being asked what they were to do when they took the town? he
   answered, they were to kill the white people, the men, and take their
   wives to themselves.

Source: Daniel Horsmanden, *A Journal of the Proceedings in the Detection of
the Conspiracy formed by Some White People, in Conjunction with Negro and
other Slaves, for Burning the City of New-York in America, and Murdering the
Inhabitants*... (1744).

Study: Serena R. Zabin, author and editor, *The New York Conspiracy Trials of 1741:
Daniel Horsmanden's* Journal of the Proceedings *with Related Documents* (Boston:
Bedford/St. Martin's, 2004).

3. A Virginia Planter Instructs his Plantation Manager about Enslaved Workers, 1743/4 and 1754

> *Joseph Ball owned Morattico, a plantation in Lancaster County, Virginia, but
> lived in Great Britain with his English-born wife, and there practiced law. He
> nonetheless returned frequently to Virginia, and had detailed knowledge of his
> large land holdings in the colony. In 1743 Ball employed his nephew Joseph
> Chinn to manage his plantation, and sent him detailed instructions about
> planting crops, the care of the livestock, the hiring of overseers, and the
> supervision of slaves. The extracts below come from Ball's initial instructions
> to Chinn in 1743, and from a letter in 1754 detailing his concerns about one
> of his slaves, Aron Jameson.*

Stratford 18 February 1743/4. Instructions for my nephew Joseph Chinn in
Virginia to observe about my affairs there.
Morattico. I will have what Goods I send to Virginia to the use of my
Plantation there, kept in my House at Morattico.
  If I Should not send Goods enough, you must Supply the rest out of the
stores there with my Tobacco.
  The Coarse Cotton, I sent by Bowman, was assign'd for blankets for my
Negroes: there must be four yards and a half to each Blanket. They that
have not two blankets already; that is one tolerable old one, and one pretty
good one, must have what is wanting to make it up, 4½ yards in a blanket.
And Every one of the workers must have a Good Suite of the Welsh Plain

made as it should be. Not to Scanty, nor bobtail'd. and Each must have Two shirts, or shifts, of the ozenbrigs. And Each of the Children must have a Coat of Worser Cotton, or Plaiory of Virginia Cloth, and two shirts or shifts of ozenbrig and the Workers must Each of them have Summer Shirts of the brown Rolls. And all the workers must have Good strong Shoes, & stockings: and they that go after the Creatures [livestock], or Much in the Wet, must have two pair of Shoes. Bess, Winny, Nan, Hannah, and frank must have their Shifts, and Linen Petticoats, and their Children, Linen, Cutout, and thread and needles given them, and they must make them themselves; and they must not be cut too Scanty, nor bobtail'd. The rest of the folks must have their Linen made by Some body that will make it as it should be. And you must get a Taylor to make their Woollen Cloths strong, & well and all must be done in Good time; and not for the Winter to be half over before they get their summer Cloths; as the Common Virginia fashion is.

If any of the Negroes should be sick, let them ly[e] by a Good fire; and have fresh Meat & broth; and blood, and vomit them, as you shall think proper; though I think both to be proper in most Cases. I would have no Doctor, unless in very violent Cases: they Generally do more harm than Good.

I would have you make the overseer take Care that they have Good wood enough always at ye Door, Especially in Cold weather, which may be readily done, if every one Carries a Stick home with them when they going and Cart some sometimes, as they will always have a Cart. A Good fire is the Life of a Negro.

When any of the Negroes take a vomit, I would always have it workt with Strong Cardury Tea: there is enough grows at Morattico: I us'd to pull it in Good time and hang it upon the Kitchen Loft; and keep it all the year. pray order it to be done. Polly knows how to do it.

Let not the overseers abuse my People. Nor let them abuse their overseer.

Let the Breeding Wenches have Baby Cloths, for wh[ic]h you may tear up old sheets, or any other old Linen, that you can find in my house. (I shall Send things proper hereafter) and let them have Good Midwives; and what is necessary. Register all the Negro Children that shall be born and after keep an account of their ages among my Papers.

I left an account of the ages of all my young Negroes in my Bureau: pray send me Aron's and Pat's ages from it.

Stratford 23^d of April 1754 [Ball to Chinn]
I have sent you by Capt Teage in the Lydia for York River my Man Aron, to whom I have given the Surname of Jameson, who & his Things w[hi]ch are pretty many, as much as fill a Large Harness Barrell as big as an Eighty

Gallon Cask, a small Chest & a box, Containing a Seabed, a large Mattress Stuffed well with flocks and Stitched with tufts, and a bolster filled with feathers, the Mattress & Bolster both besides their ticks having Ozenbrigs Cases; and two new coverlids, and other old Bed Cloths, and Three suits of wearing Cloths (one New) and Two pair of new shoes; and several pair of Stockings, a pair of boots, and Twelve shirts Eight of which are New, A small Iron pot & hooks and Rack to hang it on, an iron Skillet, a Copper Sauce pan, an old Bridle & Saddle a Cheese, a Narrow ax, a Tin pint pot, Three hats, Twelve Neckcoths, two Handkerchiefs, one Violin and some Spare strings, a small spit, an old pewter basin, Two pair of sheets, and several other things, which Aron very well knows of Cap. Teage has promised to deliver at my house at Morattico. I would have him used kindly Especially this year, and not put into the Crop for any part of a Share; but I would have him work at the plow [?] but not Constantly this year, for perhaps he may not be able to bear it, not having been used to hard Labor; but you may between whiles Imploy him about one odd Jobb or other; But the next year he must be put in for a full share....

His Bed[d]ing is Quite New & Clean and I would have it kept So; and to that End would have him to ly[e] in the Kitchen Loft when he is at Morattico; and in Some Clean Place when he is in the Forrest [quarter]. I would forth with after his arrival have one of the worst of my old Bedsteads Cut short to fit for his Mattress, and have a Cot and hide for it.

And as soon as Can be I would have a framed House Twelve foot Long, and ten foot wide built for him ...

He must have all his Household Goods and other things in his own Custody in his own Little House. The Narrow ax sent with him is for him to work with. He cann work a little with it, and will soon learn to do it very well. You must keep him to the hoe [?] ax & maul. I would have his House built at Morattico between the End of the Quarter and the pond. He must have his own Meat to himself in a Good Little powdering Tub to be made [made] on purpose; and he must have his own fat & milk to himself; and be allowed to Raise fowls. I would have him have the Liberty of a Horse to Ride to Church, or where else you shall think it to be Convenient, and not be too nice about it but he must have one of the worst; but I would not have him to have Liberty to Ride out Stroling on Nights; neither must he strole about much on nights Either on foot or horseback. With Prudent Management he will be a very good hand....

Source: Joseph Ball Letterbook (1743–59) in Correspondence of Joseph Ball, 1743–1780, Ac. No. 13,257 (microfilm copy), Library of Congress. I owe this source to Lorena Walsh.

Study: Lorena Walsh, *From Calabar to Carter's Grove: The History of a Virginia Slave Community* (Charlottesville, VA: University Press of Virginia, 1997).

4. Runaway Servant and Slave Advertisements, as Published in Colonial Newspapers

The first continuously issued colonial newspaper was the Boston News-Letter, which ran from 1704 to 1776; the Boston Gazette followed in 1719, and the Philadelphia American Mercury (at which a young Benjamin Franklin worked) in the same year. New York had a weekly by 1725, Maryland in 1727, and South Carolina and Rhode Island in 1732. By the time of the American Revolution there were more than three dozen newspapers being published in the thirteen colonies. Colonial newspapers seldom reported local news, instead including verbatim stories that had appeared in the British newspapers or papers from other colonies, but they regularly carried local advertising, from merchants, shopkeepers, artisans, landowners selling their properties, and even dancing and music instructors. Most of these advertisements offered rewards for the return of runaway laborers – white servants, African American slaves, or Native American slaves.

Pennsylvania Gazette

September 26, 1765 Kent County, Maryland, Sept. 14. FIVE POUNDS REWARD.

RUN away, the first Instant, from the Subscriber Boat, Thomas Dorney Skipper, between Hell Point and Grayfin Creek, Chester River, one John Taylor (the Son of Bray Taylor of Kent County, formerly of Baltimore County) a Taylor by Trade, but has lately used the Water; he is of a very low Stature, well set of a boyish Look has had one of his Legs broke, on which is a Scar, and his Hair has been lately cut off: Had on a light coloured Saggathy Coat, Nankeen Jacket, an old white Shirt, a half worn Philadelphia made hat, with Silver Loops, a Silver Lace round the Brown, with a large Stone Buckle, Check Trowsers, a ruffled Shirt, and a Pair of Cotton Stockings of Thomas Gresham. He likewise stole the Canoe from the Boat, which is almost new, made of Chesnut; he also stole out of the Boat between Eighteen and Nineteen Pounds, in Dollars. Whoever takes up the said Runaway, and secures him, so that he may be brought to Justice, shall receive the above Reward, paid by R. GRESHAM.

November 3, 1768. RUN away from the subscriber, living in Sadsbury township, Chester county, a servant girl, named CATHERINE JONES, born in

Ireland, of a very red complexion, long nose, and long black hair; had on, when she went away, a chip hat, with a red ribbon about the crown of it, a striped linen gown, red flannel petticoat, a striped linsey ditto, a black silk handkerchief, an old tow shift, with flaxen sleeves, a pair of worsted stockings, and neats leather shoes, and took with her a short cloth cloak, and white linen apron. Whoever takes up said Catherine Jones, and secures her, so that her master may have her again, shall have TWENTY SHILLINGS reward, and reasonable charges, paid by THOMAS DAVIS.

Virginia Gazette

January 30, 1752. STOLEN, or ran away, from the Subscriber's Plantation, in King and Queen County, on Sunday, the 17th of November last, a likely young Eboe Negroe Man Slave, who was imported last Summer in the Ship Williamsburg, Capt. Tate; he is a short well-set Fellow, with a small Scar on his right Cheek, and a Parcel of small Scars on his Forehead, which is suppos'd to be his Country Mark; he was well cloathed with Cotton and Canvis, and a Pair of Virginia Shoes; went by the name of Cuffee, and can speak but few words of English: If stolen, I do hereby offer a Reward of Ten Pistoles to any Person that will apprehend the Thief, so as he may be brought to Justice; and Two Pistoles, besides what the Law allows, if taken up as a Run-away. Benjamin Scott.

March 26, 1767. N.B. Run away, about the 15th of December last, a small yellow Negro wench named HANNAH about 35 years of age; had on when she went away a green plains petticoat, and sundry other clothes, but what sort I do not know, as she stole many from the other Negroes. She has remarkable long hair, or wool, is much scarified under the throat from one ear to the other, and has many scars on her back, occasioned by whipping. She pretends much to the religion the Negroes of late have practiced, and may probably endeavour to pass for a free woman, as I understand she intended when she went away, by the Negroes in the neighbourhood. She is supposed to have made for Carolina. Whoever takes up the said slave, and secures her so that I get her again, shall be rewarded according to their trouble, by STEPHEN DENCE.

South Carolina (paper as noted)

Run Away from Stephen Ford, of John's Island, an Indian Woman named Sarah, brought up to Household Work, about 23 Years of Age, and speaks good English, has no Marks on her Face. she had on when she went away a strip'd flannel Gown, and has been gone about 15 Days. Whoever takes up the said Wench, and delivers her to Stephen Ford or Thomas Fleming in Charlestown, shall have 50s Reward and reasonable Charges paid, by Stephen Ford or Thomas Fleming. (*South Carolina Gazette*, June 17 to June 24, 1732)

July 17, 1767: FIFTY POUNDS REWARD. Ran Away last week from my Cowpen, and took with him a Horse; a short well set fellow, named BEN, upon the yellowish or mustee cast, very hairy about the legs, and has a down look, is very sensible, and was once the property of Hugh Bryan. He is supposed to be enticed away to the Creek Nation by one Henry Snap, though it is not improbable but he may endeavour to go to North-Carolina, or East-Florida, being well acquainted with most parts of the back country, or he may attempt to pass for a free man. The horse he took away is branded x, or CE being the brand of Charles Elliott, Esq; who bred him.

Whoever... will apprehend and deliver the said... Jacob Kittles, or Hardy Daloatch... Savannah River, or to the warden of the work house shall receive a reward of FIFTY POUNDS currency from WILLIAM WILLIAMSON. (*The South Carolina & American General Gazette*)

Source: Newspapers as noted.

Study: Philip Morgan, *Slave Counterpoint: Black Culture in the Eighteenth-Century Chesapeake and Lowcountry* (Chapel Hill: University of North Carolina Press for the Omohundro Institute of Early American History and Culture, 1998); David Waldstreicher, *Runaway America: Benjamin Franklin, Slavery and the American Revolution* (New York: Hill & Wang, 2004).

Further exploration: The *Pennsylvania Gazette* is available online from 1728 to 1800 through a library subscription to Accessible Archives Inc., and can be searched by keywords for the entire text. Thus it is possible to enter terms such as "servant," "run away," or "slave" and pull from the newspaper as a whole many of the runaway advertisements.

Discussion Questions

1   Why did William Gooch include the discussion of slaves in his report to the Board of Trade? Can the report be read to reveal things about slavery in Virginia that Gooch did not realize or wish to convey?
2   What does Mary Burton's testimony in the New York conspiracy trials reveal about the relationship between whites and slaves in the city? Do we have to believe that her statements were true, or that there actually was a conspiracy, to use the testimony as a historical source?

3 How would you characterize Joseph Ball's approach to the management of his farm and his enslaved laborers in Virginia? What indications are there that he sought to make as much money as possible from his farm? What indications are there that he was concerned about the welfare of his workers? If the overseer carried out Ball's commands, would slaves have been left with much autonomy?

4 In reading the advertisements for runaways, keep in mind that owners had good reason to be as accurate and detailed as possible in describing their lost "property," but that their accounts were also extensions of the class, gender and racial assumptions of such property owners. What can you tell about the attitudes of white owners toward the runaways? What can you tell about life of coerced laborers from the way they are described in the advertisements? What do the advertisements suggest about why and how slaves and servants escaped coerced labor?

Chapter 12   Everyday Life

1. Examination of Daniel Tice, 1765

In colonial America, neighbors or local government were responsible for those too poor to provide for themselves. In Pennsylvania this responsibility fell to townships, the administrative units into which counties were divided. When a dispute arose about which township was responsible for the maintenance of an indigent residence, an examination like the one below was conducted to resolve the issue. Daniel, in testifying about Hannah Tice, provides a unusually detailed account of his life as an indentured servant and poor free person. Lancaster and Chester Counties lay west of Philadelphia, and both were home to numerous prosperous landowners and skilled artisans who bought servants, and occasionally slaves, and employed wage laborers.

This 28th Day of February in the Year of Our Lord 1765. Before me William Moore Esqr &c Came Daniel Tice who being Sworn on the Holy Evangelist did Depose and Say That in the Year of One thousand Seven Hundred and fifty Three he came from Germany into the City of Philadelphia and in order to pay his passage money which was Advanced by Nicholas Teetrick he agreed to Serve him five years and for that purpose Executed an Indenture [contract] of Servitude for that Term. That the said Nicholas immediately carried him Up Strasburg Township in Lancaster County Where he served with the Said Nicholas five weeks or thereabouts From wheance the Said Nicholas Removed to his Brother in Laws, Baltes Pesser where he thinks he Lived two months with Said Nicholas, and from thence was Removed by the Said Nicholas to a Plantation of the Said Nicholas where he Believes he compleated One Years Servitude with him, But Being Cross Examined Says he Believes he Lived with his Master After Removing from Baltes Pesser About five or Six Months But Does Not know in what Township his Masters Said Plantation is Situate. That thereupon he was Sold to Fredrick Peckle with whome he thinks he Lived One Year in the Same Township Where the Said Nicholas Resided when he lived with his Brother in Law Baltes Pesser which he thinks was in Earl Town Township Lancaster County. But Being Cross Examined Says he Cannot Remember in what Township he Lived with Frederick Peckle that Afterwards he was Sold to Fredrick Sagar with Whome he thinks he Lived about a Year and Two Months But does not Remember the name of the Township, After which he Enlisted in the Kings Service Under Col. Bouquette and Served three Years & Untill After the Term of his Indenture was Expired, And the Said Deponant further Saith that After his Return & Discharge from his Majesties Service he came to Haverford where he was Married to Hannah Huster, the woman Lately Sent as a Poore person to Newtown Township by whome he had three children Christopher & Catherine Now a Live and Mary Now Dead, And that he is Certain that the Two Children Aforesaid now Alive ware Both Born in Marple where he Lived with his wife About two Years and a half. That he was married By a Duch Luteran Minister in Haverford But has forgot his Name and further this Deponant Saith Not.

his

Daniel X Tice

mark

Source: Examination, Daniel Tice, February 28, 1765, Chester County Quarter Session Records, Chester County Archives and Records Service, West Chester, Pennsylvania. Laurie Rofini, the Chester County archivist, provided this document and headnote.

Study: Billy Smith, ed., *Down and Out in Early America* (University Park: Pennsylvania State University Press, 2004).

2. Brinton Farmhouse, Birmingham Township, Chester (Delaware) County, Pennsylvania, 1704

This substantial colonial farmhouse was built in 1704 by William Brinton, an early settler in Chester County; by the 1790s, the house was in the possession of George Brinton, one of the more prosperous farmers of what was now

Delaware County, in southeastern Pennsylvania. The photographs displayed here are part of the Historic American Buildings Survey of the Library of Congress. The HABS documentation for the house, dating from 1958, includes an inventory of goods in the house in 1777 and "wasted" by General William Howe's British troops at the time of the Battle of Brandywine. Brinton claimed to have lost, among other goods, 200 bushels of wheat, 4½ tons of hay, seven cows, and almost £100 in bedding – indications of the prosperity that went with a house such as the one pictured here.

Figure 12.1   Brinton farmhouse.

Figure 12.2   Brinton farmhouse kitchen.

Source: Brinton 1704 House, Oakland Road (Birmingham Township), Dilworthtown vicinity, Delaware County, PA, The Historic American Buildings Survey, Prints and Photographs Division, Library of Congress, Washington, DC.

Study: Paul G. E. Clemens and Lucy Simler, "Rural Labor and the Farm Household in Chester County, Pennsylvania, 1750–1820," in Stephen Innes, ed., *Work and Labor in Early America* (Chapel Hill: University of North Carolina Press for the Institute of Early American History and Culture, 1988), 106–43.

3. Everyday Life in the Colonies as Seen through Probate Inventories and Wills

When a free male adult or a widow died, their estate entered probate. A colonial court would order an inventory taken of the decedent's possessions and an account made of the debts owed by and to the decedent. Once this was done, the court could then order the estate distributed to heirs and creditors under the terms of a will (or the intestate laws of the colony if there was no will). Inventories did not record all the property of a decedent (except in the New England colonies, for example, land was not inventoried) and the estates of the poorer members of society often did not enter probate (while slaves and servants never had inventories taken). That said, inventories and wills provide a snapshot of the material culture of many ordinary colonists. All inventories in pounds, shillings and pence of local currency. The totals given for inventory values are in the original document and are not always the correct total of values.

Inventory of Archibald Curry, Laborer, Darby, Chester County, October 24, 1764

Table 12.1 Inventory of Archibald Curry, Laborer, Darby, Chester County, October 24, 1764

Horse	12	o	o
Sythe (?)	o	2	6
Grubbing hoe	o	5	o
Ax	o	3	o
Ditching shovels	o	3	o
Two pair of stockings	o	o	o
Wearing clothes	o	5	o
Five account balances	14	8	6
Total	26	17	o

Source: Chester County Probate Inventories, No. 2168.

Inventory and Will of Sarah McWilliams, East Nottingham, Chester County, March 15, 1765

9th March 1765

Being Sick and weak of body but of perfect mind and memory and Knowing that I must Die and having Some Estate which God hath been pleased to bless me with I do make this to be my last will and testament, Revoking all other wills heretofore by me made. First, my will is that my body be decently buried in my husband's grave next my will is that there be a head or tomb stone put to our grave also my funeral Expenses and just Debts to be paid. The Stone to be such as my Executors think best. Item give to my son William my silver buckles and chest. Item I give to my son John five shillings – and what remains to be divided in three Equal parts two parts of which I give to my Daughter Mary. And third part to my kinswoman Isabella Stockman. Lastly I ordain constitute and appoint John Hauthorn and Archibald Job to be my Executors to this my last will and testament.... Sarah McWilliam her mark.

Table 12.2 Inventory and Will of Sarah McWilliams, East Nottingham, Chester County, March 15, 1765

Cash	0	10	0
Account against James Johnson	6	1	6
Account against James Stockman	4	0	0
Same on John Huston	0	1	3
Same on Robert Harvey	0	10	0
One Calico Gown	0	15	0
Calico Gown and Coat	0	4	0
Great Coat	0	7	6
Two petticoats apron and gown	0	7	6
Two quilted coats	0	5	0
Clock and Riding Skirt	0	3	6
Petticoat Gown and apron	0	15	0
Two aprons	0	1	0
Three paid shoes	0	5	0
Two pairs stockins	0	1	0
Shift and two aprons	0	3	0
Seven Caps	0	3	0
Five handkerchiefs	0	5	0
Three handkerchiefs	0	5	0
Two napkins	0	1	6
Sundrys	0	1	0
Three pair of Gloves and two bonnets	0	10	0
Four sheets and two shifts	0	7	6
Bed and furniture	4	0	0
Two beds	0	10	0
Barrel wheel and Cart [?]	0	6	0
Two Cows	7	0	0
Mare	7	0	0
Saddle Bridle and whip	1	1	0
hoe and ax	0	8	0
[total this column]	36	12	3
Tub Barrel and wheel	0	3	0
Looking glass	0	0	6
Linnen yarn	0	18	0
Pot hooks and crock	0	3	0
Reel and Strainer	0	1	0
Three pails	0	3	6
Half a doz. plates & two basons	0	10	0

(Continued)

Table 12.2 (*Continued*)

Trenchers pans & Dishes	o	3	6
Mugs pepper box and glass	o	1	o
Pot, cups bottles shears &c	o	1	8
Two iron pott and hooks	o	9	6
Book	o	5	o
Tallow	o	4	o
Barrels and corn	o	7	o
Churn, bushel, and flax seed	o	6	o
Spools, mug dough trough	o	5	o
Hackel, flax, tow, and smoothing iron	o	13	o
Chains	o	2	o
Bels, horse gears auger, Noggin, and Dog	o	5	o
Bags	o	5	o
Iron and pott rack	o	3	o
Pocket book Specticles and box	o	o	9
pair of buckles and chest	o	15	o
[column total]	6	o	5
Brought over from the other side	36	12	3
Total	42	12	8

Source: Chester County Probate Inventories, No. 2201.

The Inventory of the Estate of Thomas Benedict late of Norwalk deceased taken this 28th day of June An. D. 1763

Table 12.3 The Inventory of the Estate of Thomas Benedict late of Norwalk deceased taken this 28th day of June An. D. 1763

Broad Cloth Coat 43/ Black Jacket 4/6 pair Shoes & buckles 1/6	2	9	o
Blue Coat 10/ hat 4/6 great Coat 6/ Light Col^d Jacket 2/9	1	3	3
Blk breeches & buckles 3/ piece of Deer leather 1/6 Wig 3/	o	7	6
Mittens 9d Leather Breeches 6/ old bible 2/ Old books 2/9	o	11	6
Hone 1/8 razor 6d Sheep Sheers 1/3 2 Good Augers 2/6 1 D. 1/	o	6	11
Hand saw 2/ old Iron 1/6 hammer 6d gouge 6d Chizzel 3d	o	4	9

(*Continued*)

Table 12.3   (*Continued*)

Collar and gears 3/6 Seed pail 2/ Narrow Ax 2/ Spade 1/3	0	8	9
Half Bushel 3/0 Corn fan 3/[?] wheat Riddle 1/3 old oat Cradle 1/3	0	8	9
Sheep Skin 6d 5¾ bushels wheat at 5/ = 28/9 1½ bus. Barley at 3/	1	13	9
Old Casks in Chamber 3/6 2 bushels Corn 5/6 bushel Oats 1/6	0	10	6
Wedges for Sythe 1/ Ox plough & Irons 9/6 Horse plough & Irons 5/6	0	16	6
Large Chain 7/ Same Small 4/6 old Ox Cart & Irons 45/ Ox yoke 3/	2	19	6
½ lb Lead 3d pair horse tracers 3/ 7¾ lb New Cheese a/3 ½ peck Peas 1/6	0	6	0
20 yards Tow Cloth 33/ Two Wollen Shirts 8/ 2 Linnon Same 2/0	2	3	0
2 pair Linnen Breeches 2/ 2 pair Stock[in]gs 1/6 13 yards Ruseel 32/6	1	16	0
25 lb Wool [at] 1/10 45/10 pair Cards 9d old Churn 9d old Reel 9d	2	9	11
Old Cask in the Cellar Soap hough 3/ Square table 7/6 bread tray 9d Candle box 1/	0	12	3
Salt box 9d Milk pail 2/ great Jugg 2/ Same small 1/9 brass kettle 18/	1	4	6
Tankard 3/ Iron Kettle 2/ knot Dish 3/6 Same small 3d bowl 6d	0	9	0
Tray 6d Salt Mortar 6d old Stand 1/ hand Irons 10/6 Iron pot 1/3 Earthenware 1/6 Steely[ar]d 2/9	0	18	0
knives & fork 2/ Sugar box 4d Bottle Wood 6d Pewter platter NBason &c 10/	0	12	10
2 great Chairs 10/ Desk 35/ Books at Tho, Betts 7/6 3 flan[ne]ll sheets 10/	3	2	6
pair Good Sheets 12/ Same 6/ Same 8/ table Cloth 1/6 Same 9d	1	8	3
4 Towels 1/3 4 pillow Cases 3/0 Checked blanket 4/6 new Blanket 5/0	0	13	9
Bedsted 8/0 Case bottles 8/ bed 20/ Chest with draws 3/ Sieve 6d	2	9	6
5 old Blankets & Cushing 3/ Chaff bed 4/6 bolster 1/9 2 old under Beds 6d	0	9	9
2 Corn bags 2/ wheel 2/ frying pan 1/ wood dish 3d	0	5	3

(*Continued*)

Table 12.3 (Continued)

2 pillows & bolster 5/ Glass & Candlestick 9d 5 small Chairs 2/ Tramell 4/6	0	12	3
Tramell 3/6 Peal and Tongs 4/6 Brom 4d Iron kettle 1/6 Iron pot 5/6	0	15	4
Barril with pork in it 32/ 2 tubs & fat 2/9 flour & cask 3/3	1	18	0
2 hay forks 1/ 2 hay rakes 6d old broad ax 9d old shov[ell] 9d	0	3	0
bay Mare £5 : 10 pair Oxen £12 old Brown Cow 63/ Same 80/	24	13	0
Red Cow 86/ year old Steer 23/ Same heifer 20/ calf 13/	7	2	0
The dwelling house & well £30 the Barn £15	45	0	0
About Six Acres adjoining the house and Barn	66	0	0
5 Acres South of the aforesaid Piece & adjoining	47	10	0
The Sedge at the old Fort	15	0	0
Calf Pasture Island £2 Peach Island 10/	2	10	0
Total	343	6	8

Source: Thomas Benedict Probate Packet, 1763, Fairfield Probate District, Probate Records, v. 13, p. 56 Connecticut (microfilm, LDS Family History Library Reel 4276, from originals in the Connecticut State Library, Hartford).

Slaves in the Inventory of Thomas Beach, Clarendon Parish, Jamaica, May 1776

> *Thomas Beach owned over 250 slaves at the time of his death, most of them engaged in sugar production. His total personal estate was valued at a little over £28,000, of which over £20,000 was in slaves. In the original, appraisers listed every slave by name, but below, parts of the inventory have been summarized.*

Table 12.4 Slaves in the Inventory of Thomas Beach, Clarendon Parish, Jamaica, May 1776

Carpenters			
Michael a mulatto	140	o	o
Dick same	140	o	o
Johnson	180	o	o
Frank	150	o	o
Quashee	150	o	o
Tom Bull	150	o	o
Harry	150	o	o
John	130	o	o
Coopers			
Trojan	140	o	o
Ned	150	o	o
Billy a mulatto	150	o	o
Valentine	140	o	o
Masons			
York	160	o	o
Quashee	160	o	o
Black Smiths			
Pompey very old	30	o	o
Cudjoe	40	o	o
Frank	110	o	o
Sawyers			
Tom	160	o	o
Peter	140	o	o
Fortune	140	o	o
Sunday	150	o	o
Penn Keepers			
Peter	20	o	o
Guy	20	o	o
Hesigo	130	o	o
Hannibal	120	o	o
Wainmen			
Lance	160	o	o
Cudjoe	50	o	o
Quaso	140	o	o
Beavis	120	o	o
Dick Mason	130	o	o
Sugar Boilers			
Billy	140	o	o
Quaco	140	o	o

(*Continued*)

Table 12.4 (*Continued*)

Distillers			
Jamaica	120	o	o
Captain	120	o	o
Scotland	140	o	o
Sampson	120	o	o
Doctress			
Soona old	40	o	o
Butcher			
Dorman	140	o	o
Drivers			
Quamina very old	10	o	o
James	200	o	o
Doctor	150	o	o
Quaw	160	o	o
Field Men etc.			
Mundingo Cudjoe	60	o	o
Robin	110	o	o
Adoo	140	o	o
Plato	130	o	o
Coachman Harry	150	o	o
Philander (in gaol for transportation)	20	o	o
38 more (named)	3350	o	o
Watchmen			
Sapio old	20	o	o
Chelsea	130	o	o
8 more (named)	610	o	o
Field Women			
Driver Gabba	50	o	o
Marechy	40	o	o
Chloe	60	o	o
Nanny	100	o	o
Betty	80	o	o
52 others (named)	4185	o	o
Men Boys			
Cato	70	o	o
Saphos John	60	o	o
10 others (named)	750	o	o
Women Girls			
Quasheba	80	o	o
Abbas Fanny	80	o	o
9 others (named)	625	o	o

(*Continued*)

Table 12.4   (*Continued*)

Boys about 12 Years Old and under			
Frank	60	0	0
Camillas Quaw	50	0	0
Dianas Sammy	20	0	0
30 others	1245	5	0
Girls About 12 Years old & under			
Amelias Benneba	50	0	0
Jubas Rosannah	40	0	0
Bellas Assa	20	0	0
22 others (named)	770	0	0
Invalids			
15 (named)	101	10	0
The Undermentioned Negroes did Formerly reside in Spanish Town			
Men			
Anthony a cook	110	0	0
Billy a waiting man	120	0	0
Cudjoe a coachman	140	0	0
Mingo a postillion	130	0	0
Women			
Amelia a cook	120	0	0
Hannah cooks assistant	100	0	0
Camilla a seamstress	140	0	0
Abba a washer	140	0	0
Lemon a washer	100	0	0
Boys and Girls			
4 Boys (named)	190	0	0
5 Girls (named)	290	0	0
Total	20,046	15	0 (total from original)

Source: Thomas Beach Inventory, 1B/11/3/57/116-122 (1776), Jamaican Archives, Spanishtown, Jamaica. Trevor Burnard supplied me with this source.

Study: Jackson Turner Main, *Society and Economy in Colonial Connecticut* (Princeton, NJ: Princeton University Press, 1985), on inventories to measure wealth; Paul G. E. Clemens, "The Consumer Culture of the Middle Atlantic, 1760–1820," *William and Mary Quarterly*, 3rd ser., LXII (2005), 577–624, on inventories and household consumption; Toby Ditz, *Property and Kinship: Inheritance in Early Connecticut, 1750–1820* (Princeton, NJ: Princeton University Press, 1986), on wills and family.

Further exploration: Thomas Benedict's inventory contains two "tramells." What did the appraisers mean by these listings? One way to approach this question is to check the *Oxford English Dictionary*. The dictionary provides definitions of each word over centuries of English history, and can be accessed online if your library has a subscription. The word "tramell" takes you to definition of "trammel." (The online version makes tracing variant spellings easier.) The *OED* provides four possible eighteenth-century definitions: (1) a fishing net; (2) horse hobble; (3) device used to hold pots above a cooking fire; and (4) plaits of a woman's hair. Can you suggest the most likely meaning of the item in Benedict's inventory from the items with which it is grouped?

4. Household Consumer Goods of the Comfortable and Prosperous

Most households had a range of locally crafted and imported consumer goods, as the probate inventories included in this reader indicate. Tall case clocks were generally of local manufacture, at least in the Middle Atlantic and New England, and usually found, until after the American Revolution, only in the houses of the most prosperous farmers and planters. Pewter goods were far more common. They could be locally made or imported. Most householders had pewter dinnerware as well as coffee and teapots, even if they also had less expensive (and more decorative and fashionable) earthenware. Pewterware was durable, and in addition to its utilitarian value, pewter could serve as a financial reserve (at about a penny per pound) for the household.

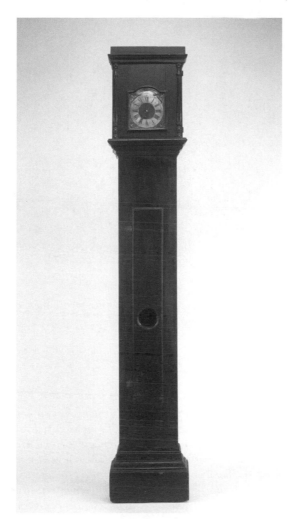

Figure 12.3   Tall case clock, ca. 1740, by Seth Yongs, Hartford, Connecticut.
Maple, pine case. 30-hour, brass, steel, and iron. 86.5 x 15 x 7.39.
Source: Courtesy of Historic Deerfield.

Figure 12.4   London pewter teapots, made by Edward Ubley, ca. 1720–35.
Source: The Colonial Williamsburg Foundation.

5. Colonial Taverns

Taverns were central to the everyday of life of virtually every town, village, and highway in colonial America. They were sites of conviviality, drinking, gaming, and politics. They provided rooms for travelers and stables for horses. Many were owned by women, but most customers were men. They ranged from elegant stone structures to much smaller wooden hovels. All served prodigious quantities of alcohol – the drink of choice for every age and for women as well as men.

In the first entry below, Sarah Kemble Knight describes being forced, while on a journey in 1704 from Boston to New Haven, to stay overnight at a tavern. Knight was a 38-year-old widow at the time, and a shopkeeper and private tutor – a woman of independent means. Her journal was first published in the mid-nineteenth century, and has been reprinted numerous times. The second entry comes from James Birket, a West Indian merchant. In 1750–1 he traveled from Antigua to New Hampshire, and then overland to Philadelphia. His account contains numerous cryptic references to the accommodations he found along the way. The image is a modern architectural drawing of the Old Stone Tavern in Cumberland County, New Jersey, a sparsely settled region of the colony. The tavern dates from approximately 1730 and also served periodically as a court house.

Sarah Kemble Knight's Account of a Night at a Tavern, 1704

Being come to mr. Havens', I was very civilly Received, and courteously entertained, in a clean comfortable House; and the Good woman was very active in helping off my Riding clothes, and then ask't what I would eat. I told her I had some Chocolett, if shee would prepare it; which with the help of some Milk, and a little clean brass Kettle, she soon effected to my satisfaction. I then betook to my Apartment, wch was a little Room parted from the Kitchen by a single bord partition; where, after I had noted the Occurrances of the past day, I went to bed, which, tho' pretty hard, Yet neet and handsome. But I could get no sleep, because of the Clamor of some of the Town tope-ers in next Room, Who were entred into a strong debate concerning ye Signifycation of the name of their Country, (viz.) *Narraganset*. One said it was named so by ye Indians, because there grew a Brier there, of a prodigious Highth and bigness, the like hardly ever known, called by the Indians Narragansett; And quotes an Indian of so Barberous a name for his Author, that I could not write it. His Antagonist Replyed no – It was from a Spring it had its name, wch hee well knew where it was, was extreem cold in summer, and as Hott as could be imagined in the winter, which was much resorted too by the natives, and by them called Narragansett, (Hot and Cold,) and that was the originall of their place name – with a thousand Impertinances not worth notice, wch He utter'd with such a Rorcing voice and Thundering blows with the fist of wickedness on the Table, that it peirced my very head. I heartily fretted, and wish't 'um tongue tyed; but wth as little succes as a friend of mine once, who was (as shee said) kept a whole night awake, on a Jorny, by a country Left. and a Sergent, Insigne and a Deacon, contriving how to bring a triangle into a Square. They kept calling for tother Gill, wch while they were swallowing, was some Intermission; But presently, like Oyle to fire, encreased the flame. I set my Candle on a Chest by the bed side, and setting up, fell to my old way of composing my Resentments, in the following manner:

> I ask thy Aid, O Potent Rum!
> To Charm these wrangling Topers Dum.
> Thou hast their Giddy Brains possest –
> The man confounded w^{th}the Beast –
> And I, poor I, can get no rest.
> Intoxicate them with thy fumes:
> O still their Tongues till morning comes!

And I know not but my wishes took effect; for the dispute soon ended w^{th} 'tother Dram; and so Good night!

Source: *The Journal of Madame Knight* (Boston, 1920), pp. 16–19.

James Birket's Cursory Remarks about his Tavern Accommodations, 1750

[September 18]
Set out for Rhode Island. Our first Stage was 19 miles to A house Kept by one Robins where we dined upon Roast^d Partridges Fat bacon & Irish Potatoes now plentifully Produced in that Part of the world & tollerably good. In the Afternoon we travelled 19 miles more to One Mother Stacks, who I thought really very Slack in her Attendance for twas with great Intreaty and fair words that we obtained a Candle altho twas So dark when we lighted that we could Scarce See Another & What was worse She had nothing in the world for Supper However upon Rummaging the Chace box we found in our own Store a Couple of Roasted Fowles Some white biscuit, Lemons, Rum, Sugar &C So that out of our own Store we made a Handsome Supper & Liquor to it but could not do So well for Lodging our Beds being very Indifferent –

[October 12, having entered the colony of New York]
... from Marrowneck to Kingsbridge is 12 Miles here we dined with Some other Travelers at One Stephensons a Quaker who keeps one of the Best Eating houses we met with, we had a Bass fish taken out of the river by the door before our Eyes & some very good oysters &C This is one of the best built houses for a Tavern I have yet seen in America large and lofty And a Noble Prospect down towards the Sound...

Source: *Some Cursory Remarks Made by James Birket in his Voyage to North America, 1750–1751* (New Haven, 1916), pp. 25, 39.

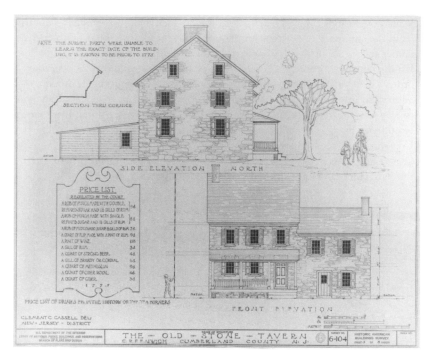

Figure 12.5   Old stone tavern, Cumberland County, New Jersey, mid-eighteenth century.
Source: Historic American Buildings Survey, Library of Congress.

Study: Sharon Salinger, *Taverns and Drinking in Early America* (Baltimore, MD: Johns Hopkins University Press, 2002).

Discussion Questions

1   What can you suggest about the life of laborers in the Middle Atlantic from the inventory of Archibald Curry and the examination of Daniel Tice? How did they get by from year to year?

2   What does the inventory of Sarah McWilliams and Tice's mention of Hannah Huster tell us about women on their own in the region? Can you explain the choices that McWilliams made in her will?

3   What picture do you get putting the Brinton home together with the household possessions of a man like Thomas Benedict? How would you group the goods owned by Benedict? What goods were used for production? Which to supply comfort? Would you define him as prosperous?

4   What conclusions can you reach about the distinctive nature of sugar plantations
    from the summary of a Jamaican planter's slaveholdings? What do the slave
    names tell us about the slave system in the British West Indies?
5   Do the consumer goods pictured in this chapter suggest luxury or everyday
    utility? Can you reach this conclusion simply by observing them? What
    additional information can you gain from the inventories that will allow you
    to evaluate the visual images of the material objects? What other information
    would you like to have to refine your analysis?
6   Consider the two diary excerpts about taverns. What do they suggest about
    gender and class divides in colonial America? How does tavern life fit into
    the pattern of colonial culture described in chapter 15?

Chapter 13   Family and Gender Relations

1. Grand Jury Presentation of Martin Rierden, 1736

In June 1736 the Chester County, Pennsylvania, grand jury "presented" Martin Rierden, a laborer, for fornication with Margaret Kain (a single woman, and as she notes below, a servant) after she gave birth to a male child. Grand juries in colonial America, either of their own knowledge, or after hearing evidence from a county sheriff or local constable, presented people for disturbances of the peace, crimes of violence, crimes involving property, and moral offenses. Grand juries commonly presented couples (or single women) for fornication (sex between unmarried people) when the sex resulted in the birth of a child. In the case below, Margaret Kain gave evidence about the paternity of her child. She listed goods and money that Martin had given her after the birth of their child, and then gave the deposition below.

When I was in labour of Martin Rerton, his Child, by the oppinion of the Mid-wife & her assistante, I was in a dangerous Condition, upon which Martin went and brought a Doct.ʳ to Deliver me, who gave me some stuff and in or about 3 or 4 hours after was Safe Delivered, & Martin Made a Sadle to the Doct.ʳ for his fee.

[F]u[r]ther when I was about 3 or 4 months gon with Child to Martin he brought me a Botle of Stuff from a Doct.ʳ in order to Make Me Miss-carrie, the words I replied to him was, that it was a Sin to get yᵉ Child, But a greater

Sin to put it back he Said it was no Sin being it had not Quickned, & to Save both our Credits, and I having a great regard for him, I told him I took it, but did not, but Cast it away, I told him I might as well go in the bed & kill one of My Masters Childer that Lay with me, and when he found it did me no good, he said he woud bring me Some Saven, & that would do it, & I woud not have it, all that is above said I can give my oath to ye truth of it before the Court if required, without any Malice.

Note. Martin pled not guilty, but does not appear to have stood trial before a jury. In February 1739 the Quarter Sessions Court fined him 10 pounds and he had to give [recognizance] bond for future good behavior.

Source: Presentation of Martin Rierdon, June 11, 1736; Recognizance of Martin Rierdon, Depositions of Margaret Kaim and Margaret Hubbard, August 21, 1739, Chester County Quarter Sessions Court; February 28, 1739, Docket Book. Chester County Archives and Records Services, West Chester, Pennsylvania.

Study: Cornelia Hughes Dayton, "Talking the Trade: Abortion and Gender Relations in an Eighteenth-Century New England Village," *William and Mary Quarterly*, 3rd ser., XLVIII (January 1991), 19–49.

2. From the Letterbook of Eliza Lucas Pinckney, 1742

Eliza Lucas Pinckney (1722–93) is known both for her letterbook, one of the most revealing sources left by an eighteenth-century woman, and for her successful experiments to grow indigo, a plant Europeans acquired from India and used to make blue dye for textiles. Pinckney was born in the West Indies and educated briefly in Great Britain. When she was 15, her father, a British army officer, moved the family to a plantation in South Carolina in the vicinity of Charleston, and within a year, when her father was forced to return to the Caribbean by the outbreak of war, she found herself in charge of one of his plantations. She began her letterbook in 1739, and started experimenting with indigo the next year, when war made the marketing of Carolina's staple crop, rice, difficult. In 1744 she married Carolina attorney Charles Pinckney and moved to Charleston. Of her husband, she wrote, "and next to my God, to make it my Study to please him." Charles died of malaria in 1758, and she outlived him by more than three decades, living through the violently factious revolutionary war in the Carolinas.

*   The two extracts below speak to the religious and familial concerns that shaped the life of Pinckney as a plantation mistress in South Carolina.*

D[ea]r. Miss B[artlett] [April 1742]

... Why, my dear Miss B, will you so often repeat your desire to know how I trite away my time in our retirement in my fathers absence. Could it afford you advantage or pleasure I should not have hesitated, but as you can expect neither from it I would have been excused; however, to show you my readiness in obeying your commands, here it is.

In general then I rise at five o'Clock in the morning, read till Seven, then take a walk in the garden or field, see that the Servants are at their respective business, then to breakfast. The first hour after breakfast is spent at my musick, the next is constantly employed in recolecting something I have learned least for want of practise it should be quite lost, such as French and short hand. After that I devote the rest of the time till I dress for dinner to our little Polly and two black girls who I teach to read, and if I have my paps's approbation (my Mamas I have got) I intend [them] for school mistres's for the rest of the Negroe children – another scheme you see. But to proceed, the first hour after dinner as the first after breakfast at musick, the rest of the afternoon in Needle work till candle light, and from that time to bed time read or write. 'Tis the fashion here to carry our work abroad with us so that having company, without they are great strangers, is no interruption to that affair; but I have particular matters for particular days, which is an interruption to mine. Mondays my musick Master is here. Tuesdays my friend Mrs. Chardon (about 3 mile distant) and I are constantly engaged to each other, she at our house one Tuesday I at hers the next and this is one of the happiest days I spend at Woppoe. Thursday the whole day except what the necessary affairs of the family take up is spent in writing, either on the business of the plantations, or letters to my friends. Every other Fryday, if no company, we go a vizeting so that I go abroad once a week and no oftener...

... O! I had like to forgot the last thing I have done a great while. I have planted a large figg orchard with design to dry and export them. I have reckoned my expence and the prophets to arise from these figgs, but was I to tell you how great an Estate I am to make this way, and how 'tis to be laid out you would think me far gone in romance. Your good Uncle I know has long thought I have a fertile brain at schemeing. I only confirm him in his opinion; but I own I love the vegitable world extremly. I think it an innocent and useful amusement. Pray tell him, if he laughs much at my project, I never intend to have my hand in a silver mine and he will understand as well as you what I mean.

[To George Lucas]

I have been thinking, My Dear brother, how necessary it is for young people such as we are to lay down betimes a plan for our conduct in life in order to living not only agreeably in this early season of it, but with cheerfulness in maturity, comfort in old age, and with happiness to Eternity; and I can find but one scheme to attain all these desireable ends and that is the Xtian scheme. To live agreeably to the dictates of reason and religion, to keep a strick gaurd over not only our actions but our very thoughts before they ripen into action, to be active in every good word and work must produce a peace and calmness of mind beyond expression. To be consious we have an almighty friend to bless our Endeavours and to assist us in all difficulties, to be consious We have to the utmost of our power and ability endeavoured to please him, and shall finally injoy Him for ever, who is infinite perfection it self, gives rapture beyond all the boasted injoyments of the world – allowing them their utmost extent and fulness of joy.

Let us then, my dear Brother, set out right and keep the sacred page always in view. You have entered into the Army and are not yet sixteen years of age. Consider then to how many dangers you are exposed, (I dont now mean those of the field) but those that proceed from youth, and youthful company, pleasure, and disipation. You are a Soldier, and Victory and conquest must fire your mind. Remember then the greatest conquest is a Victory over your own irregular passions. Consider this is the time for improvment in Virtue as well as in every thing else, and tis a dangerous weakness to put it off till age and infirmities incapacitates us to put our good designs in practise. But old age, you will say, is a long way off from you and me. True, and perhaps we shall never reach it. 'Tis then an additional reason why we should make use of the present and remember no time is ours but the present – and that so fleeting that we can hardly be said to exist.

Excuse my fears, my much loved brother, and believe they are excited by the tenderest regard for your wellfare, and then I will inform you I am in some pain (notwithstanding your natural good sence, for the force of Example is great) least you should be infected with the fashonable but shameful vice too common among the young and gay of your sex. I mean pretending a disbelief of and ridiculeing of religion; to do which, they must first Enslave their reason. And then where is the rule of life? However it requires some degree of fortitude to oppose numbers, but cherish this most necessary virtue; tis so to all mankind, particularly to a soldier. Stand firm and unshaken then in what is right in spite of infidelity and ridicule. And you cant be at a loss to know what is right when The Devine goodness had furnished you with reason, which is his natural revelation, and his written word supernaturally revealed and delivered to mankind by his son Jesus Christ.

Source: The letterbook is in the collections of the South Carolina Historical Society. The extracts here are taken from Pinckney family, *Pinckney Family Papers, 1708–1878*. (37/38) South Carolina Historical Society.

Study: Kathleen M. Brown, *Good Wives, Nasty Wenches, and Anxious Patriarchs: Gender, Race, and Power in Colonial Virginia* (Chapel Hill: University of North Carolina Press for the Omohundro Institute of Early American History and Culture, 1996).

3. Politics of Gender Relations in Pennsylvania, 1730s–1760s

While legal divorce was virtually impossible to obtain in colonial Pennsylvania, "self-divorce" was common – people simply left their spouses and often announced the fact in the newspaper. Publication of "divorce" announcements made it clear to creditors that a man was no longer responsible for his wife's debts, but women occasionally published their own announcements, or, as in the entry below, responded to their husband's statement. It is not impossible that the April 1/35 entry is a spoof.

April 17, 1735: We hear from Chester County, that last Week at a Vendue [public estate sale] held there, a Man being unreasonably abusive to his Wife upon some trifling Occasion, the Women form'd themselves into a Court, and order'd him to be apprehended by their Officers and brought to Tryal: Being found guilty he was condemn'd to be duck'd 3 times in a neighboring Pond, and to have one half cut off, of his Hair and Beard (which it seems he wore at full length) and the Sentence was accordingly executed, to the great Diversion of the Spectators.

January 14, 1762: WHEREAS Mary, the Wife of John Dicks, in Chester Town, Chester County, eloped from her said Husband on the 18th of this instant December, and took with her sundry valuable Shop Goods; this is therefore to forewarn all Persons from trusting her on his Account, for he will pay no Debts of her contracting after the said 18th of December instant. JOHN DICKS.

January 21, 1762: THESE are to certify to all whom it may concern, That on the 17th Day of December, 1761, my Husband John Dicks did beat and abuse me his Wife very much, and threatened to shoot me divers Times; and on the 18th I went to my Brother and Sisters, about one Mile and Half from Chester, and acquainted them of the Affair; my Brother and I returned to Chester immediately, when he, in his desperate Humour, shut the Door, and would not suffer me to enter my own House. And I do further certify, that I never eloped from him, nor carried off my Goods, only the Clothes on my Back, though he received of my Portion to the Amount of £300; and I have been obliged of late to bind him to the Peace, being in Danger of my Life. And I do also further certify, that he hath mortgaged his House and lands, and am afraid that I and my Children will come to Want. MARY DICKS [Chester County].

Source: *Pennsylvania Gazette* (dates as indicated).

Study: Clare A. Lyons, *Sex Among the Rabble: An Intimate History of Gender and Power in the Age of Revolution, Philadelphia, 1730–1830* (Chapel Hill: University of North Carolina Press for the Omohundro Institute of Early American History and Culture, 2006).

4. Scenes from the Life of a Great Tobacco Planter in Eighteenth-Century Virginia

William Byrd of Westover (1674–1744) is perhaps the best known of all early eighteenth-century Virginia tobacco planters and slaveowners. His father had established the family securely during the seventeenth century as one of the wealthiest and most powerful in Virginia, and the son, the author of the letters and diary entries below, had been educated in England, where he acquired both legal skills and education in the classics. Byrd came into his inheritance in 1704 with the death of his father, returned to Virginia, and became a member in 1708 of the colony's Council of State – a distinction that marked him as one of the Virginia's ruling oligarchy. He would subsequently return to England as Virginia colonial agent. In 1728 Byrd surveyed the Virginia–North Carolina border, and his description of the trip, published in the nineteenth century as History of the Dividing Line, *is one of the classics of colonial literature.*

Below are three types of documents. The first is an idealized painting from the early nineteenth century of a Virginia plantation. Next is a letter from Byrd to an English friend and patron. The third is a set of entries from one of several secret diaries Byrd kept in shorthand and clearly did not intend others to read.

Figure 13.1   The Plantation. Painting in oil on wood by an anonymous artist, American, ca. 1825.

Source: The Metropolitan Museum of Art, Gift of Edgar William and Bernice Chrysler Garbisch, 1963 (63.201.3). Image © The Metropolitan Museum of Art.

William Byrd to Charles, Earl of Orrey (Great Britain), Virginia, July 5, 1726

MY LORD, —

Soon after my arrival I had the honour to write to Your Ldsp to acquaint you that we had happily escaped all the Dangers of the Sea, and were safely landed at my own House. There was nothing frightfull in the whole Voyage but a suddain Puff that carried away our Topmast, which in the falling gave a very bad crack, but we received no other Damage, neither were our Women terrified at It. The beautifullest Bloom of our Spring when we came Ashore, gave Mrs. Byrd a good impression of the Country. But since that the Weather is grown Warm, and some days have been troublesome eno' to make Her wish herself back in England. She now begins to be seasoned to the Heat, and to think more favourably of our Clymate. She comforts herself with the thought that a warm Sun is necessary to ripen our fine Fruit, and so pays herself with the Pleasure of one Sense, for the Inconvenience that attends the others. I must own to Yr Ldship that we have about three months that impatient People call warm, but the Colonel would think them cool enough for a pair of Blankets, and perhaps a comfortable Counterpain into the Bargain. Yet there are not 10 days in the whole summer that Yr Ldsp would compain of, and they happen when the Breazes fail us and it is a dead Calme. But then the other nine Months are most charmingly delightfull, with a fine Air and a Serene Sky that keeps us in Good Health and Good Humour. Spleen and vapours are as absolute Rarities here as a Winter's Sun, or a Publick Spirit in England. A Man may eat Beef, be as lazy as Captain Hardy, or even marry in this Clymate, without having the least Inclination to hang himself. It would cure all Mr. Hutchinson's distempers if the Ministry would transport him hither unless they sent Lady G–[?] along with him. Your Ldsp will allow it to be a fair Commendation of a Country that it reconciles a Man to himself, and makes him suffer the weight of his misfortunes with the same tranquility that he bears with his own Frailtys. After your September is over, I shall wish your Ldsp a little of our Sunshine to disperse that Fogg and Smoake with which your Atmosphere is loaded: Tis miraculous that any Lungs can breath in an Air compounded of so many different Vapours and Exhalations like that of dirty London. For my part mine were never of a texture to bear it in winter without great convulsions, so that nothing could make me amends for that uneasiness but the pleasure of being near your Lordship. Besides the advantage of a pure Air, we abound in all kinds of Provisions without expence (I mean we who have Plantations). I have a large Family of my own, and my Doors are open to Every Body, yet I have no Bills to pay, and half-a-Crown will rest undisturbed in my Pocket for many Moons together. Like one of the Patriarchs, I have my Flocks and my Herds, my Bond-men and Bond-women, and every Soart of Trade amongst my own Servants, so that I live in a kind of Independence on every one but Providence. However this Soart of Life is without expence, yet it is attended with a great deal of trouble. I must take care to keep all my people to their Duty, to set all the Springs in motion and to make every one draw his equal Share to carry the Machine forward. But then 'tis an amusement in this silent Country and a continual exercise of our Patience and Economy.

Another thing My Lord that recommends this Country very much we sit securely under our Vines and our Fig Trees without any Danger to our Property. We have neither publick Robbers nor private, which Your Ldsp will think very strange, when we have often needy Governors, and pilfering Convicts sent amongst us. The first of these it is suspected have some-times an inclination to plunder, but want the pow'r, and tho' they may be Tyrants in their Nature, yet they are Tyrants without Guards, which makes them as harmless as a Scold would be without a Tongue. Neither can they do much Injustice by being partial in judgment, because in the Supreme Court the Council have each an equal Vote with them. Thus both the Teeth and the Claws of the Lion are secured, and He can neither bite nor tear us, except we turn him loose upon Ourselves. I wish this was the Case with all his

Majesty's good Subjects, and I dare say Your Ldsp has the goodness to wish so too. Then we have no such Trades carried on amongst us, as that of Horsebreakers, [Housebreakers?] Highway-men, or Beggers. We can rest securely in our Beds with all our Doors and Windows open, and yet find every thing exactly in place the next Morning. We can travel all over the Country by Night and by Day, unguarded and unarmed, and never meet with any Person so rude as to bid us Stand. We have no Vagrant Mendicants to seize and deafen us wherever we go, as in your Island of Beggers. Thus My Lord we are very happy in our Canaans if we could but forget the Onions and Fleshpots of Egypt. There are so many Temptations in England to inflame the Appetite and charm the Senses, that we are content to run all Risques to enjoy them. They always had I must own too strong an Influence upon me, as Your Ldsp will belive when they could keep me so long from the more solid pleasures of Innocence and Retirement. I doubt not but My Lord Boyle has learnt at Paris to perform all his Exercises in perfection and is become an absolute Master of the French Language. I wish every Secretary of State could write it as perfectly as his Ldsp does, that their Performances might not be subjected to the Correction of Mr. De La Fay. I am sure that Lord Boyle will in every respect Answer the affectionate care your Lordship has taken of him, and I suppose It will not be long before I shall have the pleasure to hear that he is happily married, for it now seems wholy to depend upon Him, to furnish Heirs to the Noble Family of his Name. I most heartily long to hear from Your Lordship, and shall rejoice at every happy Accident that befalls you, for I am as much as any Man alive, My Lord, yr etc, W. By[rd]

Source: *Virginia Magazine of History and Biography*, XXIV (1916), 26–8.

William Byrd of Westover's Diary, 1710, 1712

[July 29, 1710]. 29. I rose at 5 o'clock and read a chapter in Hebrew and a little Greek in Thucydides. I said my prayers and ate milk for breakfast. It rained this morning till 10 o'clock. I went to the store to put up some things to send to Williamsburg and gave John some rope for the press. About 1 o'clock Captain Broadwater came over in my sloop and dined with us. I ate some stewed pigeon. In the afternoon the Captain agreed to depart from his charter and take £10 per ton. I persuaded him to take my sloop with him and do some necessary things to her. I loaded my small sloop with 15 hogsheads for Captain Harvey. In the evening we took a walk about the plantation. I neglected to say my prayers but had good health, good thoughts, and good humor, thank God Almighty.

30. I rose at 5 o'clock and wrote a letter to Major Burwell about his boat which Captain Broadwater's people had brought round and sent Tom with it. I read two chapters in Hebrew and some Greek in Thucydides. I said my prayers and ate boiled milk for breakfast. I danced my dance. I read a sermon in Dr. Tillotson and then took a little [nap]. I ate fish for dinner. In the afternoon my wife and I had a little quarrel which I reconciled with a flourish. Then she read a sermon in Dr. Tillotson to me. It is to be observed that the flourish was performed on the billiard table. I read a little Latin. In the evening we took a walk about the plantation. I neglected to say my prayers but had good health, good thoughts, and good humor, thanks be to God. This month there were many people sick of fever and pain in their heads; perhaps this might be caused by the cold weather which we had this month, which was indeed the coldest that ever was known in July in this country. Several of my people have been sick, but none died, thank God.

31. I rose at 5 o'clock and read two chapters in Hebrew and some Greek in Thucydides. I said my prayers and ate boiled milk for breakfast. I danced my dance. My daughter was taken sick of a fever this morning and I gave her a vomit which worked very well and brought away great curds out of her stomach and made her well again. My people were all well again, thank God. I went to the store and unpacked some things. About 12 o'clock Captain Burbydge and Captain Broadwater came over. The first went away to Colonel Randolph's; the other stayed to dine with us. I ate hashed mutton for dinner. In the afternoon Dick Randolph came from Williamsburg and brought me the bad news that much of my wine was run out. God's will be done. In the evening Mrs. Harrison and her daughter came over. However I took a little walk. I said a short prayer and had good health, good thoughts, and good humor, thanks be to God Almighty.

[March 1, 1712]
1. I rose about 7 o'clock and read two chapters in Hebrew and some Greek in Lucian. I said my prayers and ate boiled milk for breakfast. I danced my dance. I settled some accounts and wrote a letter to England, and then read some Latin till dinner and then I ate some roast beef. Old Moll at the quarters and jenny were very sick, for which I caused them to be bled and to take the oil. In the afternoon I set some things in order in my closet and then read some Latin till the evening and then took a walk about the plantation and went to visit the sick people and they complained they were all [. . .]. My wife and Mrs. Dunn came and walked with me till night and then I read some news. About 8 o'clock came Mr. G–r–1 and I learned by him that all was well above. I said my prayers and had good health, good thoughts, and good humor, thank God Almighty.

2. I rose about 7 o'clock and read a chapter in Hebrew but no Greek because Mr. G–r–l was here and I wished to talk with him. I ate boiled milk for breakfast and danced my dance. I reprimanded him for drawing so many notes on me. However I told him if he would let me know his debts I would pay them provided he would let a mulatto of mine that is his apprentice come to work at Falling Creek the last two years of his service, which he agreed. I had a terrible quarrel with my wife concerning jenny that I took away from her when she was beating her with the tongs. She lifted up her hands to strike me but forbore to do it. She gave me abundance of bad words and endeavored to strangle herself, but I believe in jest only. However after acting a mad woman a long time she was passive again. I ate some roast beef for dinner. In the afternoon Mr. G–r–l went away and I took a walk about the plantation. At night we drank some cider by way of reconciliation and I read nothing. I said my prayers and had good health, good thoughts, and good humor, thank God Almighty. I sent Tom to Williamsburg with some fish to the Governor and my sister Custis. My daughter was indisposed with a small fever.

Source: Louis B. Wright and Marion Tinling, *The Secret Diary of William Byrd of Westover, 1709–1712* (1941), pp. 210–11, 494–5.

Study: Rhys Isaac, *Landon Carter's Uneasy Kingdom: Revolution and Rebellion on a Virginia Plantation* (New York: Oxford University Press, 2004).

Discussion Questions

1 What notions of gender relations are expressed in each of the documents above? Where do you see indications that religion shaped understandings of appropriate gender relations? That wealth (and class) mattered in gender relations? Do you find any common themes that run through all the documents despite the differences in class and region?

2 How does Margaret Kain explain herself to the grand jury? Can you combine her account with that of Daniel Tice in the last chapter to suggest more about what it was like to be poor in the middle of eighteenth century in rural Pennsylvania?

3 In what ways was the life of Eliza Lucas Pinckney different from that of the other women mentioned in these documents? What values defined her life? Did these differ as well from those of less well-off women?

4 In what ways is the plantation painting an embodiment of the values and lifestyle described in William Byrd's letters and diary? Does Byrd's letter contradict or reinforce his private thoughts as expressed in his diary? How would you compare his sense of family, and manhood, to the values of Eliza Lucas Pinckney?

5   Do the two stories told in the three newspaper accounts from Pennsylvania
    suggest a more assertive and autonomous role for women in colonial society
    than the other documents? Do you see elements of more "traditional" roles
    and values in these accounts as well?
6   If you found yourself living in the eighteenth century, would you prefer to live
    as Mary Dicks or Eliza Lucas Pinckney? Why?

Chapter 14   Religion

1. The Anglican Clergy of Maryland Appeal to the Bishop of London about the State of the Church in Maryland, 1696

Maryland, founded by a Catholic proprietor, had granted religious freedom to all Christians throughout the seventeenth century, and, in particular, had sizeable communities of Catholics and Quakers who worshiped freely and had full political rights in a nominally Anglican colony. When the English government made Maryland a royal colony in 1696, the Anglican clergy sought the aid of Virginia's royal governor Francis Nicholson in establishing their church as the dominant religious persuasion in the colony. This appeal to their bishop in London would be followed several years later by the dispatch to Maryland of an emissary (Thomas Bray) of the Anglican Society for the Propagation of the Gospel (SPG). Non-Protestants would lose political rights under the royal government but could still be employed by the proprietary interest (which retained significant land rights in the colony), and many Catholics continued to play key roles in commercial affairs and public life in Maryland.

When His Excellency, Governor Nicholson, came into the Country in the year 1694, there were but 3 Clergymen in Episcopal Orders, besides 5 or 6 popish priests, who had perverted divers idle people from the Protestant Religion. There was also a sort of wandering pretenders to preaching that came from New England and other places; which deluded not only the Protestant Dissenters from our Church but many of the Churchmen themselves, by their extemporary prayers and preachments, for which they were admitted by the people and got money of them.

The 3 Episcopal Clergymen, having made a hard shift to live here some time after they came hither, did afterwards marry and maintain their families out of the plantations they had with their cures.

And tho' the better and most responsible persons of the neighbouring Plantations that owned themselves to be of the Communion of the Church of England subscribed their names to some small Contributions for their officiating amongst them, that those Clergymen could not get the half and sometimes not the fourth part of their subscriptions, notwithstanding they endeavoured to acquit themselves to the best of their powers, in a constant and conscientious discharge of their ministerial function. . . .

Tobacco being the one and only staple commodity of the Country, is that out of which our small incomes are paid, the manner of which is thus: Every planter, for himself and his male children and White Servant-Man, as also for his Negro Slaves (both male and female), after their age of 16 years, is assessed 40^{lb} Tobacco [per] poll [for the support of the clergy]. . . . And we have lately received very certain advice from London that those of our Quakers that went to England in the last Maryland and Virginia fleet have petitioned the Lords of the Committee of Trade and Foreign Plantations [the advisory body to the king in Parliament on the American colonies] to have the 40^{lb} per Poll taken off as a burden upon their estate and (as we suppose they might have pretended) upeon their consciences too. . . . Should they obtain their petitions only for themselves, the incomes of some of the best Parishes, in respect of the Tobacco raised by the 40^{lb} per Poll would be so impaired that there would not be left a tolerable subsistence for a single Clergyman and his horse, and one horse, at least, we must all of us, of necessity, keep ready by us, not only to ride to Church on Sundays, but to ride all over our Parishes to Christenings, Weddings, visiting the sick, and burials on the week days, when or wherever we are sent for.

Could the Quakers clear themselves of the 40^{lb} per poll the Papists might all pretend to do so too, because they have Priests of their own to provide for; and could both these parties effect their designs, the Clergy and Church of England would be left in a very naked and poor condition here, besides that we might expect many that have their religion still to choose; would turn either Papists or Quakers, and refuse to pay too, for many of them look upon the Sacraments as needless impositions, and go neither to the Papists' Mass nor the Quakers' meetings, and seldom or ever to Church.

Now we become most humble petitioners to your Lordship, that if there should be occasion (as we have reason to fear there is) your Lordship would be pleased to espouse our Cause, and intercede with His Most Gracious Majesty that we may not be wholly discouraged from staying in these parts of the English Empire, and preaching the Gospel here, as well as the Papists and Presbyterians and Quakers do after their manner, and our just hopes, and that we shall not be thought much worse by great good and wise persons, for the Quakers' insinuations against us behind our backs, which we doubt not have been as maliciously as cunningly contrived. . . .

May it please your Lordship, as far removed as the Quakers and Papists seem to be in their different sentiments about religion, they are jointly bent against our Church, and daily endeavour to draw people to their parties, by suggesting to them that Lord Baltimore will govern here again; than which nothing can be more pleasing news to libertines and loose persons, who call seldom or never be gotten to come to Church at all; and should my Lord rule as formerly, the insolence of the Romish Priests (who are somewhat curbed by his Excellency's great care and vigilance) would soon be intolerable in these parts, that are so remote from England.

Besides there being great numbers of Irish Papists brought continually into this province, and many Irish Priests being suspected to be coming incog[nito] amongst us (as having no better place of refuge in the King's Dominions) upon their being banished from Ireland, there is great reason to fear there will be as much discouragement and danger coming upon all his Majesty's good Protestant subjects here as upon the English Clergy.

This expectation of the Lord Baltimore's being restored to the Government of Maryland animates the Priests and Jesuits to begin already to inveigle several ignorant people to turn to their religion. To which end they do (contrary to the Act of Parliament to deter them from perverting any of His Majesty's Protestant subjects to popery) introduce themselves into the Company of the sick, when they have no Ministers, that his Excellency hath been lately forced to issue out his proclamation against their so doing, to restrain them. . . .

Source: William Stevens Perry, ed., *Historical Collections Relating to the American Colonial Church* (New York: AMS Press, 1969), IV, 8–12. Perry's work was first published in 1878.

Study: Patricia U. Bonomi, *Under the Cope of Heaven: Religion, Society, and Politics in Colonial America* (New York: Oxford University Press, 1986).

2. Benjamin Franklin Offers his Opinion of the Great Revivalist, George Whitefield

Benjamin Franklin (1706–90) was a printer, Pennsylvania politician, colonial agent, businessman, inventor, and undoubtedly the best known American in Europe and America in the eighteenth century. He wrote his autobiography, which he addressed to his son, William, in 1771, while in England, and added material to it in the 1780s. It remained unpublished until after his death, and not until 1818 would a relatively complete edition appear. Most nineteenth-century editions "modernized" the text; more recent editions have returned to Franklin's own punctuation, capitalization, and spelling.

One of the many well-known parts of the autobiography is Franklin's story of George Whitefield's preaching in Philadelphia. Whitefield (1714–70) studied for the ministry at Oxford, and having experienced the "New Birth" and been ordained a deacon in the Anglican Church, he traveled in 1738 to the new colony of Georgia to preach. On his return to Great Britain, he was ordained a priest, but his preaching and his writings, which placed emphasis on the emotional impulses of his audiences, offended many Anglicans. When he returned to America in the fall of 1739, he was already well known as an evangelical capable of drawing crowds in the hundreds, even thousands, to revivals that took place outside, rather than in, the confines of churches of particular denominations. Whitefield would make several return trips to America.

Franklin remained skeptical of organized religion throughout his life, but he went to hear Whitefield in 1740 essentially to figure out "what all the fuss was about."

In 1739, arrived among us from England the Reverend Mr. Whitefield, who had made himself remarkable there as an itinerant preacher. He was at first permitted to preach in some of our churches; but the clergy, taking a dislike to him, soon refused him their pulpits, and he was obliged to preach in the fields. The multitudes of all sects and denominations that attended his sermons were enormous, and it was matter of speculation to me, who was one of the number, to observe the extraordinary influence of his oratory on his hearers, and how much they admired & respected him, notwithstanding his common abuse of them, by assuring them, they were naturally *half beasts and half devils*. It was wonderful to see the change soon made in the manners of our inhabitants; from being thoughtless or indifferent about Religion, it seemed as if all the world were growing religious, so that one could not walk through the town in an evening without hearing psalms sung in different families of every street.

And it being found inconvenient to assemble in the open air, subject to its inclemencies, the building of a house to meet in was no sooner proposed, and persons appointed to receive contributions, than sufficient Sums were soon received to procure the ground, and erect the building, which was one hundred feet long and seventy broad; and the work was carried on with such spirit as to be finished in a much shorter time than could have been expected. Both house and ground were vested in trustees, expressly for the use of *any preacher of any religious persuasion* who might desire to say something to the people of Philadelphia; the design in building not being to accommodate any particular Sect, but the inhabitants in general; so that even if the Mufti of Constantinople were to send a missionary to preach Mahometanism to us, he would find a pulpit at his service....

The last time I saw Mr. Whitefield, was in London.... He had a loud and clear voice, and articulated his words and sentences so perfectly, that he might be heard and understood at a great distance; especially as his auditors observed the most perfect silence. He preached one evening from the top of the Court-House steps, which are in the middle of Market Street, and on the west side of Second Street, which crosses it at right angles. Both streets were filled with his hearers to a considerable distance. Being among the hindmost in Market Street, I had the curiosity to learn how far he could be heard, by retiring backwards down the street towards the river; and I found his voice distinct till I came near Front Street, when some noise in that street obscured it. Imagining then a semicircle, of which my distance should be the radius, and that it were filled with auditors, to each of whom I allowed two square feet, I computed that he might well be heard by more than thirty-thousand. This reconciled me to the newspaper accounts of his having preached to twenty-five thousand people in the fields, and to the history of generals haranguing whole armies, of which I had sometimes doubted.

By hearing him often I came to distinguish easily between sermons newly composed, and those which he had often preached in the course of his travels. His delivery of the latter was so improved by frequent repetitions, that every accent, every emphasis, every modulation of voice, was so perfectly well turned and well placed, that, without being interested in the subject, one could not help being pleased with the discourse; a pleasure of much the same kind with that received from an excellent piece of Music. This is an advantage itinerant preachers have over those who are stationary, as the latter cannot well improve their delivery of a sermon by so many rehearsals.

Source: Jared Sparks, *The Life of Benjamin Franklin, containing the Autobiography, with Notes and a Continuation* (1844), pp. 136–7, 139–40.

Study: Louis Masur, The *Autobiography of Benjamin Franklin: With Related Documents* (Boston: Bedford/St. Martin's, 2003).

3. Dr. Alexander Hamilton Comments on the Revivalist James Davenport, 1743

James Davenport was an itinerant minister in New England during the Great Awakening. Originally traveling with George Whitefield, he soon branched out on his own, but his erratic behavior and unorthodox religious views made

him notorious, even among other evangelical preachers. Critics of the
Awakening pointed to Davenport as evidence of the dangers of itinerant
preaching, although his actual role in the revivals of the mid-eighteenth
century was far less than that of preachers such as Whitefield, Gilbert Tennent,
and Samuel Davies. The incident described below occurred in 1743 in
New London, Connecticut, and is described by Dr. Alexander Hamilton, a
touring Scottish physician.

Sunday, August 26 . . . I went home att 6 o'clock, and Deacon Green's son came to see me. He entertained me with the history of the behaviour of one Davenport, a fanatick preacher there who told his flock in one of his enthusiastic rhapsodies that in order to be saved they ought to burn all their idols. They began this conflagration with a pile of books in the public street, among which were Tillotson's Sermons, Beveridge's Thoughts, Drillincourt on Death, Sherlock and many other excellent authors, and sung psalms and hymns over the pile while it was a burning. They did not stop here, but the women made up a lofty pile of hoop petticoats, silk gowns, short cloaks, cambrick caps, red heeld shoes, fans, necklaces, gloves and other such aparrell, and what was merry enough, Davenport's own idol with which he topped the pile, was a pair of old, wore out, plush breaches. But this bone fire was happily prevented by one more moderate than the rest, who found means to perswade them that making such a sacrifice was not necessary for their salvation, and so every one carried of[f] their idols again, which was lucky for Davenport who, had fire been put to the pile, would have been obliged to strutt about bare-arsed, for the devil another pair of breeches had he but these same old plush ones which were going to be offered up as an expiatory sacrifise. Mr. Green took his leave of me att 10 o'clock, and I went to bed.

Source: Carl Bridenbaugh, ed., *Gentleman's Progress: The Itinerarium of Dr. Alexander Hamilton, 1744* (Chapel Hill: University of North Carolina Press for the Institute of Early American History and Culture, 1948), p. 161.

Study: David S. Lovejoy, *Religious Enthusiasm in the New World: Heresy to Revolution* (Cambridge, MA: Harvard University Press, 1985).

4. James Ireland's Battle with Satan, Virginia, ca. 1760s

James Ireland (1748–1806) was born in Scotland into a pious Presbyterian
family. His father provided him a good education, which is probably why
when he traveled to Virginia in his late teens and moved to the Shenandoah

*Valley backcountry of Virginia, he was made headmaster of a school. The
young people of the community were given, he noted, to "balls, dancing, and
chanting," and "when in companies together nothing was heard...but
obscene language, cursing, and swearing, drinking and frolicking, horse racing
and other vices." Ireland initially fit in comfortably, gaining a reputation as a
skilled dancer, but he was soon caught up in the religious revival, led by the
Baptists, that was sweeping the area. The appeal of the Baptists was not
merely that they denounced the "debauchery" of the easy life on the Virginia
frontier but that they coupled their attack on sin with an offer of membership
in an orderly, disciplined, and loving community. In the extract below, written
well after Ireland's experiences in the late 1760s, and published after his death,
Ireland describes his spiritual struggles when a friend tries to entice him back
to a life of dancing.*

...The news of my awakening impressions, had diffused itself through
every part of the settlement and its vicinity. It became the topic in all
companies that "James Ireland was going to be mighty good now, for he
is going to get converted."

My acquaintance had not seen me for some short period, previous to my
soul's distresses. There was a dance appointed to be held the Monday
following, at a wealthy neighbour's house. My countryman in company
with others, hearing the remarks they were making about me, and being
tolerably dissipated in language at times, swore they need not believe
anything about it, for there could not be a dance in the settlement without
my being there, and if they would leave it to him, he would convert me, and
that to the dance, on Monday; and they would see me lead the ball that day.
The deep impressions upon my soul had a very considerable influence upon
my exterior appearance of body; that wild vivacity that flashed in my eyes,
and natural cheerfulness that appeared in my countenance was entirely
gone; my eyes appeared solemn and heavy, my flesh began to pine away,
my ruddy checks and countenance had vanished, and all that remained was
a solemn gloomy paleness, whilst my head was often hanging down like
a bulrush, under the internal pressure of my guilty state. This my friend,
who had bound himself under an oath that he would convert me to the ball,
had never yet seen. Determined however to prosecute his purpose, which
I had also been informed of, disposed me to expect a visit from him, in
which he did not deceive me. He came to my school house; being there
myself, I heard the noise of a creature's feet some little distance from me,
which disposed me to look about, and soon I descryed the rider to be my
friend, coming to see me. Being fully persuaded he would use all the

influence he was master of, to persuade me to his wishes, I was seized with a momentary panic, which disposed me to lift up my heart to the Lord, and implore him not to suffer any reasonings he could use to have the least influence upon my mind, as also that the Lord would direct some word or other, that might be for his benefit.

When I viewed him riding up, I never beheld such a display of pride in any man, before or since, as I beheld in him at that juncture, arising from his deportment, attitude and jesture; he rode a lofty elegant horse, and exhibited all the affectation possible, whilst his countenance appeared to me as bold and daring as Satan himself, and with a commanding authority called upon me, if I were there to come out, which I accordingly did, with a fearful and timorous heart. But O! How quickly can God level pride to the ground, if He does but once touch the heart, as was soon manifested in him. In a few minutes did the person, who, no doubt, made sure, as he came to visit me, of making an easy conquest of me, find that the race is not to the swift nor the battle to the strong. For no sooner did he behold my disconsolate looks, emaciated countenance and solemn aspect, than he instantly appeared, as if he was riveted to the beast he rode on; his passions were so powerfully impressed, that I conceived he would have fainted and dropped from his horse.

For some short space of time, he was past utterance, and did nothing but stare at me with wild amazement. As soon as he could articulate a little his eyes fixed upon me, and his first address was this; "In the name of the Lord, what is the matter with you?" To which I replied, if he would light, hitch his horse, and come into the house, I would tell him. I stepped into the house before him, begging of the Lord to direct my speech unto him; his surprise and consternation still attending him, he repeated his former expression; "In the name of the Lord what is the matter with you?" I instantly took him by the hand, and with a tender heart, and tears streaming from my eyes, spoke to him as follows. "My dear friend I possess a soul that will be either happy or miserable in the world to come; and God has been pleased to give me a view of the worth of my soul, as also of the guilty and condemned state it lies in by reason of sin; and I plainly see that if my soul is not converted, regenerated and born again, I will be damned." Holding my hand fast in his, and looking at me, with all the eagerness of desire, he burst out into the following words, "O! You will not leave me nor forsake me now." To which I answered that I would not, upon condition he would renounce his former wicked ways, as I had done, and seek God through Jesus Christ, for pardon and salvation to our poor souls. To which he replied, with streaming eyes, from that moment forward, through the strength of the Lord Jesus Christ, he would.

Source: James Ireland, *The Life of the Reverend James Ireland, who was, for many years, pastor of the Baptist Church at Buck Marsh, Waterlick and Happy Creek, in Frederick and Shenandoah Counties, Virginia* (Winchester, VA: J. Foster, 1819), book 2, chapter 4, pp. 82–6. The quote in the headnote is from book 1, chapter 6, pp. 49–50.

Study: Rhys Isaac, *The Transformation of Virginia, 1740–1790* (New York: W. W. Norton, 1982).

Further exploration: Charles Evans edited a multi-volume series known as *Early American Imprints*. The series, based initially on the holdings of the American Antiquarian Society, included a full bibliographical listing, organized chronologically, to every work published in America through 1800. A second series extended the citations to 1819. Each work cited was reproduced on a microform card that allowed scholars to consult every published early American work at any library that had the cards and appropriate readers. These works are now available online from any library that subscribes to the electronic resource. Research libraries now have, in effect, collections that before could only be consulted by visiting rare book rooms at many different libraries.

Discussion Questions

1   What sense do you get from these documents about tensions among religions in the colonies?
2   What was the appeal of the religious revivals that occurred in the colonies in the mid-eighteenth century and are described (from different perspectives) in the selections from Franklin, Hamilton, and Ireland?
3   What explains the appeal of revivalist ministers such as Whitefield? Why might he have appealed particularly to women?
4   How would you compare Ireland's religious feelings with those of Eliza Lucas Pinckney (in chapter 13)?

Chapter 15   Culture

1. Cadwallader Colden [Coldengham, New York] to Mr. Peter Collinson [London, England], on Botany in America, November 13, 1742

In addition to his career in New York politics, Cadwallader Colden (1688–1776) corresponded widely on scientific topics, especially the plants and animals of America, with other gentlemen of the Enlightenment, such as John Bartram in Pennsylvania, Alexander Garden in South Carolina, and Peter Collinson in London, to whom he sent specimens. This work allowed them to see themselves as members of an Atlantic community of learned men, participants in the Enlightenment, as well as giving them a chance to assert the qualities and distinctiveness of America.

In this letter Colden speculates about the role of young women in collecting and analyzing specimens, and his daughter, Jane Colden (1724–66), before her marriage, would produce a catalog of over 300 plants of the New York region. Jane's catalog would employ the method of Carolus Linnaeus to identify plants "scientifically," and include the first identification of at least two new plants, but while her father would share his delight at her work with his correspondents, the catalog would not be published until the twentieth century (and resides today in the British Museum).

I have your very kind letter of the 3rd of September. If I have had the good fortune to gain your esteem in any degree & thereby a share in your Friendship I shall think my self well rewarded for any thing I have don & when I consider the trouble you take & the concern you have for the litle reputation I can hope to obtain I may flatter my self that I have gain'd no small share in both....

The Observation you made in your former [letter] that we have in America many different Species of Plants & Animals from those found in Europe or other parts of the World tho' under the same climate is certainly true & I think we may likewise add that we have different species of Men This naturally enough leads to the Question you put whether they be the effects of a different Creation But Dear Sir I dare not pretend to give any answer in a matter so high & out of my reach. It is a subject fit to be treated only by first rate Philosophers & Divines I should be glad to know your Sentiments on it...

We are very poor in Knowlege & very needy of assistance. Few in America have any taste of Botany & still fewer if any of these have ability to form & keep a Botanical Garden without which it is impracticable to give compleat Characters of Plants. In short I may positively assert that not one in America has both the power & the will for such a performance. Such a work is necessary it will be a lasting benefite to mankind it has all the motives to it which can incite a good man to any performance attended with trouble.... I shall not presume to give my thoughts on any particular of the Method to be observ'd in this work [of classifying the plants of America] because I have but a very Superficial Knowlege in Botany I shall only say that I wish it to be in English, tho' I know that it is more difficult to do it in this language than in Latin. To incourage you in this I inclose a Description in English of two American plants not as patterns but to convince you what may be don if I who have so little skill in Botany have been able to make them tollerable.... But to return to the reasons I have for desiring your work in English 1 We have nothing in Botany tollerably well don in English so far as I have seen 2 it will thereby be more usefull in America where the learned languages are little understood 3 It may set many who do not understand latin the Ladies especially on amusing themselves with this study & thereby procure more assistance in bringing this knowlege to perfection The Ladies are at least as well fitted for this Study as the men by their natural curosity & the accuracy & quickness of their Sensations It would give them means of imploying many idle hours both usefully & agreably As I cannot doubt that Mrs. Collinson has the same taste of pleasures with you I am fond to believe that she will with pleasure save you some trouble in such a work as I propose.

Source: *Collections of the New York Historical Society for the Year 1918* (New York, 1919), pp. 277–82.

Study: Susan Scott Parrish, *American Curiosity: Cultures of Natural History in the Colonial British Atlantic World* (Chapel Hill: University of North Carolina Press for the Omohundro Institute of Early American History and Culture, 2006).

2. Books and Reading in Eighteenth-Century America

In the mid-eighteenth century, most American property owners could sign their own name (a crude index of literacy) and more than half of all households contained books. Typically, however, the only book in the household was a Bible, and if there was more than one book, the other books were probably sermons, hymnals, Testaments, or copies of the Book of Common Prayer. Lawyers, ministers, merchants, wealthy farmers and planters, and crown officials often had much larger personal libraries, and in cities such as New York and Philadelphia booksellers advertised the latest London editions. Such books undoubtedly passed through the hands of many readers. Below are three documents that sample the taste for reading in the colonies: a listing of books from the inventory of a colonial governor; advertisements from the book catalog of a Philadelphia import firm; and private reflections on the reading of a fashionable English novel.

A Selection of Books from the Probate Inventory of Alured Popple, Governor of Bermuda, 1745

Alured Popple (1699–1744) came from a well-placed family of merchants and government officials. His grandfather and father had both served as secretary to the Board of Trade and he served as governor of Bermuda in the mid-eighteenth century. Most of the probate inventory of his possessions is taken up with a list of his books, but the document also notes that he owned an organ, a microscope, a damaged telescope, and a camera obscura at his death, as well as the standard household goods one might expect to find among the genteel.

The complete titles of several of the works have been supplied in brackets following the inventory entry. The numbers following the book title are the value in pounds, shillings, and pence of the item as determined by the appraisers ("x" has replaced values that cannot be determined from the original).

Table 15.1   A Selection of Books from the Probate Inventory of Alured Popple, Governor of Bermuda, 1745

A Bible	1	o	o
Atlas Maritimus and Commercialis, London 1728	2	5	o

[Atlas maritimus & commercialis; or a general view of the world, so far as relates to trade and navigation: ... Together with a large account of the commerce carried on by sea. To which are added sailing directions for all known coasts and islands on the globe; with a set of sea-charts ... The use of the projection justified by Dr. Halley. To which are subjoin'd two large hemispheres ... containing all the stars ... 2 parts. Part of the first part attributed to Daniel Defoe; the second by Nathaniel Cutler. The atlas attributed to John Harris, John Senex, and Henry Wilson.]

Bermuda Laws from 1690 to 1713/4	o	5	o
Millers *Gardeners Dictionary* London 1733	o	15	o
Dalton's *Justice* Savoy 1727	1	o	o

[The country justice: containing the practice, duty and power of the justices of the peace, as well in as out of their sessions.... By Michael Dalton ... And ... and appendix; being, a compleat summary of all the acts of Parliament ... By William Nelson ... Published London in the Savoy.]

Locke's *Works* 3 Vols. London 1714	1	10	o
Mrs Katherine Philips *Poems* Lond: 1667	o	3	o
Tournefort's *Voyage into the Levant* 2 Vol. 1718	o	16	o
Crouches *Compleat View of the British Customs* London 1726	o	2	o
Moxon's *Tutor to Astronomy and Geography* Lond: 1699 [?]	x	x	x
Desaugliers *Treatise of Fortification* Lond 1711	o	1	8

[Continuation of title: containing the ancient and modern method of the construction and defense of places. And the manner of carrying on sieges, ... Written ... by Mr. [Jacques] Ozanam, ... Illustrated with 46 curious copper plates. Done in English, and amended in several places, by J. T. Desaguliers.]

Donnes *Declaration that Self Homicides is not so natural Sin that it may never be otherways* Lond: 1648	o	1	o
Chamberlen's *Midwifery* London 1718	o	3	6
Bysshe's *Art of English Poetry* 2 Vols. Lond: 1714	o	5	o
The Art of Secret Information by Falconer Lond: 1685	o	o	8

[Cryptomenysis patefacta: or the art of secret information disclosed without a key. Containing, plain and demonstrative rules, for decyphering all manner of secret writing. With exact methods, for resolving secret intimations by signs or gestures, or in speech. As also an inquiry into the secret ways of conveying written messages: and the several mysterious proposals for secret information, mentioned by Trithemius, &c. By J[ohn] F[alconer]]

(*Continued*)

Table 15.1   (*Continued*)

The Tears of the Indians London 1656   o   o   8
[The tears of the Indians; being an historical and true account of the cruel massacres and slaughters of above twenty millions of innocent people; committed by the Spaniards in the islands of Hispaniloa, Cuba, Jamaica, &c. As also, in the conquest of Mexico, Peru, & other places of the West-Indies, to the total destruction of those countries. Written in Spanish by Casaus {Bartolomé de las Casas], an eye-witness of those things; and made English by J[ohn] P[hillips]].

A Complet History of Magick, Sorcery & Witchcraft 2 Vol.   o   3   1
     Lond. 1716

Bosman's *Description of the Coast of Guinea* Lond 1705   o   3   x

The History of the Buccaniers of America Lond. 1699   o   3   o
[A history of the bucaniers of America; from their original down to this time; written in several languages, and now collected into one volume. Containing 1. The exploits and adventures of Le Grand, Lolonois, Roche Brasiliano, Bat the Portuguese, Sir Henry Morgan &c. Written in Dutch by Jo. Esquemeling one of the bucaniers, and thence translated into Spanish. II. The dangerous voyage and bold attempts of Capt. Barth. Sharp, Watlin, Sawkins, Coxon, and others, in the South Sea. Written by Basil Ringrose, Gent., who was a companion therein, and examin'd with the original journal. III. A journal of a voyage into the South Sea by the freebooters of America from 1684, to 1689, Written in Fremch by the Sieur Raveneau de Lussan: never before in English. IV. A relation of a voyage of the Sieur de Montaubon, capt. of the freebooters in Guinea in the year 1695, &c. The whole newly translated into English, and illustrated with 25 copper plates. By A[lexandre] O[livier] Exquemelin.]

A Critical Essay concern'g Marriage Lond: 1724   o   2   4

The Growth of Deism and other Tracts Lond: 1709   o   2   8

The Alcoran of Mahomet Lond: 1649   o   1   8
[The Alcoran of Mohomet, translated out of Arabique into French; by the sieur Du Ryer, Lord of Malezair, and resident for the King of France, at Alexandria. And newly Englished, for the satisfaction of all that desire to look into the Turkish vanities.]

Source: Bermuda Government Probate Registry, Book of Wills (RG 1001/8), volume 8 (1744–72), folio 19ff, Bermuda Archives, from Microfilm Reel 1699976.

Study: Henry Farnham May, *The Enlightenment in America* (New York: Oxford University Press, 1976).

A Bookseller's Catalog, Philadelphia, 1762

> *In the South, wealthy tobacco and rice planters depended on the merchants to whom they shipped produce in London to supply them in return with the latest European books, but in places like Philadelphia and New York, from the mid-eighteenth century on, booksellers regularly advertised books for sale. Most of these advertisements appeared in local newspapers or in broadsides, but occasionally sellers published descriptive catalogs to help them attract customers. The entries below are taken from a 1762 catalog published by James Rivingston and Samuel Brown. The catalog was 88 pages long and contained over 780 annotated book titles, a long extract from a translation of Jean-Jacques Rousseau's* La nouvelle Héloïse, *and a title list of additional volumes.*

A Catalogue of Books Sold by Rivington and Brown...
Books of Entertainment, &c.
No. 1 THE CONNOISSEUR, a Collection of elegant Essays and Writings upon the Modern Manners, Customs, Virtues, and Vices of Mankind, written with infinite Vivacity, by Doctor Thornton and Mr. Colman. – *The Connoisseur* amongst a great Variety of Subjects, treats on the following:– An Account of a new Order of Females call'd *Demi Reps.* – Account of a Plague lately broke out, with the Effects of it amongst Members of Parliament, Officers of the Army and Navy, Alderman, the Nobility, Maids of Honour; at Court, &c. &c. – Letter on Married People *Fondling* and *Toying* before Company, with the Behaviour of a Loving Couple at Dinner; – On Free-thinking. – Letters complaining of the Whisperers and Giglers amongst the Fair Sex, Instance of their rude Behaviour during a Visit; at Divine Service, &c. &c. – On Bets; particularly the Custom of staking one Man's Life against an other. – Letter, proving the City of *London* to be an University, and that Arts and Sciences are taught there in greater Perfection than at *Oxford* and *Cambridge* – Description of a Quak Doctor, and of a Company of Strolling Players. – Character of Lady *Belle Modeley*, and the Colonel her Husband, with the Education of their Son and Daughter, and the Consequences thereof. – On the Vanity of People making Appearance above their Circumstances, with the Pride and Poverty of a certain little French Man. – On Conscience, with the Terrible Exit of *Tom Dare Devil*, a Buck and an Atheist, together with his Life and Actions. On Boxing, with a Description of a very Famous Boxing Match between *Slack* and *Petit*. – Letter on Duelling, with Proposals for making Duels publick Diversions. – Letter on Snuff-taking. Letter on the Villas of Citizens and Tradesmen, with a Description of a *Sunday's* Visit to a Citizen at his Country House. – On Dress. – On Courtship. – On *Orator Henley*. – On the Turf, with a

sprightly Description of the Famous *Newmarket* Horse Races. – Study of the *English* Language Recommended. – An humerous Survey of the Audience at the Play, the Behaviour of Persons in the Boxes, Pitt, Gallery, of the Ladies of Pleasure, and of the fine gentlemen on the Stage. – Two pretty Letters from a pretty Miss in Breeches, and from a Blood in Pettycoats. – On Frolicks. –On good Company. – Characters of a Gamester, Drunkard, Lounger, Wranglers, &c., &c. – Of keeping Secrets. – Of Matchmaking. – Of Drinking. – Of Love. – Of keeping Low Company. – Of the Knowledge of the *World*, &c. &c. – This most excellent Miscellany has passed thro' many Editions, is universally read, and has greatly contributed to reform the depraved Taste and Manners of the Age, &c. &c.

No. 3 The RAMBLER, by the Learned and Ingenious *Samuel Johnson*, containing some of the finest Essays in the *English* Language, amongst the rest, upon the following Subjects. – Affability. – Affection. – Affliction. – Ambition. – Amusement. – Anger. – Authors. – Beauty. – Bashfullness. – Benificence. – Business. – Censure. – Conversation. – Curiosity. – Education. – Fear. – Flattery. – Happiness. – Health. – Humor. – Knowledge. – The Ladies. – Learning. – Old Age. – Pevishness. – Pleasure. – Politeness. – Time. – Truth. – Virtue; interspersed with excellent *Novels*, *Tales*, &c. &c.

No. 5 *The* FEMALE SPECTATOR, written by Mrs. *Eliz. Haywood* to rectify those Errors, which small, as they may seem at first, may if indulged, grow up into greater, till they at last become Vices, and occasion all the Misfortunes of our Lives; this is a Book of very great Entertainment, containing amongst others, the following Subjects. – Fortune a Breaker of Friendship. – The Husband's Stratagem. –A widow's Reason for Marrying. – The Country Ladies Surprise. – the hard Fate of two Sisters. – A *Dutch* Woman's Story. – An Adventure of Gravesend. Second Marriages condemned. – The Coquette a She Fop. – Story of a Taylor in Love with Queen *Elizabeth*. – *Celemena's* Story. – *Strephon and Celia*, &c. &c.

No. 14 *The Devil upon Crutches,* with *Asmodeus's* Crutches, and Dialogues between two Chimneys of *Madrid*, an Humerous Satire upon the Follies of Mankind in General.

No. 780 *The Director: Or, Young Woman's best Companion,* being the plainest and cheapest of the Kind ever published. The Whole makes a Complete Family Cook and Physician. Containing above Three Hundred easy Receipts in Cookery, Pastry, Preserving, Candying, Pickling, Collaring, Physick, and Surgery To which are added, plain and easy Instructions for chusing *Beef, Mutton, Veal, Fish, Fowl*, and other Eatables. Directions for Carving, and to make Wines. Likewise Bills of Fare for every Month in the Year, with a complete Index to the Whole. A Book necessary for all Families; by Sarah Jackson, collected for the Use of her own Family, and printed at the Request of her Friends. The Third Edition, corrected and greatly improv'd by the Author: Particularly with an Addition of several new Cuts, which at one View shew regular and easy Forms of placing the different Sorts of Dishes from two to nine in a Course, either in the middling or genteelest Manner. With a Cut of 13 Dishes. Shewing how to set off a long Table in common Way, or after modern Taste: Not in any other Book extant. Also several Cuts representing the truffing of Fowls, &c. Dr. *Mead's* Account of a Person bit by a mad Dog, and his insalliable Cure. The Negro Caesar's Cure for Poison, and likewise for the Bite of a rattle-Snake.

No. 781 *The new Heloise*, or the Letter of two Lovers, living in a Village at the foot of the Alps; written by the Celebrated Mr. *Rousseau* of *Geneva*, who hath published the following Apology, by way of preface to that Work, in a dialogue between himself and his Friend. The following Extract from this Piece will serve to convey a just Idea of this much admired Novel...

Source: *A Catalogue of Books Sold by Rivington and Brown, Booksellers and Stationers from London, At their Stores, over Against the Golden Key, in Hanover-Square, New York: and Over against the London Coffee-House in Philadelphia ...* (1762).

Study: Hugh Amory and David D. Hall, eds., *The Colonial Book in the Atlantic World* (Cambridge and New York: Cambridge University Press for the American Antiquarian Society, 2000).

The Practice of Reading in Early America, from the Journal of Esther Edwards Burr on the Reading of Richardson's Pamela, *1755*

> *Esther Edwards Burr was in 1755 the daughter of a Congregationalist New England minister, Jonathan Edwards, and the wife of Aaron Burr, a Presbyterian minister and president of the College of New Jersey (now Princeton University). In 1752 Esther, then 20, had moved from her home in Northampton, Massachusetts, to marry Aaron, who lived in Newark, New Jersey. Within two years, shortly after the birth of her first child (Sally), she began keeping a journal of letters to her childhood Boston friend, Sarah Prince (also a minister's daughter). The women exchanged the journal entries periodically for several years.*
>
> *The following two journal entries record Esther's reaction to Samuel Richardson's novels,* Pamela *and* Clarissa, *published in the 1740s, and written in the form of letters by the heroines of each.*

(March 10, 1755) Monday P.M.
Phoo, folks always coming. Eve. I have borrowed Pamelia and am reading it now. I fancy I sha'nt like it so well as I did Clarissa, but prejudice must have

its weight. I remember you said that in your opinnion it did not equel her. Your judgment my dear has a very great influence on mine. Nay I would venture to report that such a Book surpast such an one, if you said so, if I had never laid my Eyes on 'em – but forall I intend not to be so complaisant but I will have a judgment of my own. Tis quite late. May guardian angels protect my dear friend this night.

(April 8, 1755) Teusday.
... To day I have [been] reading an account of Mr. *Bs*. going after the Coun[tess] of —. This appears very strange to me considering the [title] of the Book, which is, *Virtue rewarded* – I could but ju[st] stomach to allow it that title before, for he was a sad fello[w] to be sure, had one Child, bastard, and did his indevour to get many more as it seems by *Lady Davers*, and his own confession two – but I dont know – I have a poor judgme[n]t of my own. I wish you would be so good as to let me ha[ve] your thoughts on this affair, and I should be glad if it is not two much trouble on the whole History. I know you have made every usefull remark that could be made there is certainly many excellent observations and rules laid down [so] that I shall never regret my pains – you need not wonder if I write a little upon the scrawl for I have Sally in my Lap – In my humble opinion *Riches*, and *honour*, are set up two much – can Money reward virtue? And besides Mr. *Bs*. being a libertine he was a dreadfull high-spirited Man, impatient of contradiction as he says of himself – Pamela had a task of it, with all Mr. *Bs*. good qual[i]ties. She was as much affraid of him as of a Lyon – If the author had [le]ft it to me to have intitled the Books, I think I should hav[e] chose *Virtue tryed*, instead of *rewarded* – In that af[fai]r of the Contess he was vastly to blame, and would no dou[bt] have kept with her some part of his time at least, as his [wife?] if he had not been prevented just when he was.

Source: Carol F. Karlsen and Laurie Crumpacker, eds., *The Journal of Esther Edwards Burr, 1754–1757* (New Haven: Yale University Press, 1984), pp. 98, 107.

Study: Lucia McMahon and Deborah Schriver, *To Read My Heart: The Journal of Rachel Van Dyke, 1810–1811* (Philadelphia: University of Pennsylvania Press, 2000).

Further exploration: The *English Short Title Catalogue* is an on-line database available through the web page of many college libraries. The *Catalogue* contains bibliographic entries for books printed in England, in England's colonies, and in the English language from the beginning of print through 1800. References in colonial documents to books are often incomplete (for example, Dalton's *Justice*, rather than a full name and title), but the search engine of the *Catalogue* allows one to find full descriptions of a publication by entering only two or three words (or a date).

3. Observing the Transit of Venus from Newport, Rhode Island, June 5, 1769

The English astronomer Jeremiah Horrocks had predicted that the planet Venus would cross the Sun in early June of 1769 (and then not again until 1784). The transit was both a rare "curiosity" which would animate viewings throughout the colonies, and a chance for men (and women) who thought of themselves as enlightened scientists to gather data that was "useful" for astronomical calculations. The American Philosophical Society of Philadelphia (the colonial equivalent of the British Royal Society) would publish some of these observations in its first volume of Transactions, *and reports sent to Great Britain would be published by the Royal Society.*

Last Saturday, the third Instant, the Transit of Venus was observed in this Town.... The Day preceeding, and the Morning of the Day of the Transit, and during the whole Time of the Transit, numerous Altitudes of the Sun were taken, by an astronomical Sextant, most accurately constructed of 5 Feet Radius, furnished with Telescopic Sights, and Nonius divisions, to 5 seconds. The Sky was uncommonly clear and serene during the whole Observation. The Observation of the Transit was made through 2 Telescopes, a Reflector, and a Refractor. The Moment of the first external Contact was distinctly perceived through a Reflector, and given by One Observer; and the Moment of total Immersion was observed, and announced at the same Instant, by two Observers, one at the Reflecting, and the other at the Refracting Telescope. More Time is requisite for the numerous Calculations necessary to give the further Particulars and important Applications of this rare, curious and noble Phoenomenon. The Public are indebted to that eminent Benefactor and Promoter of Science and Literature, the Honourable ABRAHAM REDWOOD, Esq; for furnishing the Reflecting Telescope, and Sextant for this Observation.

Source: *The Pennsylvania Gazette*, June 15, 1769.

Study: Sara Gronim, "At the Sign of Newton's Head: Astronomy and Cosmology in British Colonial New York," *Pennsylvania History*, 66 (Supplement, 1966), 55–85.

4. Phillis Wheatley, *On Virtue*

Phillis Wheatley was born in Africa, perhaps among a Moslem people in the Senegal/Gambia region, kidnapped or sold into slavery, and bought at about age 7 in 1761 in Boston, Massachusetts, by John Wheatley as an attendant for his wife, Susannah. Susannah's daughter Mary taught Phillis to read the Bible, and within a few years she had mastered Latin and English texts, mostly poetry, and began writing her own poems. She traveled to London in the early 1770s, still a slave and accompanying her master, Nathaniel Wheatley, and there published, in 1773, Poems on Various Subjects, which included a certification from a group of notable white men that she could write and that the work was her own. She would be freed and return to Boston in 1774, marry in 1778 to a freeman, but live out her life in poverty. She died in 1784. The poem below takes as its theme "virtue," one of the key words in the religious and political discourse of the revolutionary era in North America. Most of her poetry reflects the Protestant culture she was exposed to in the Wheatley household. Scholars have occasionally criticized her poetry for having little to say against slavery (or, as in On Being Brought from Africa to America, *thanking God for her rescue from paganism), but such criticism, given her circumstances, seems deeply unfair.*

On Virtue

O Thou bright jewel in my aim I strive
To comprehend thee. Thine own words declare
Wisdom is higher than a fool can reach.
I cease to wonder, and no more attempt
Thine height t' explore, or fathom thy profound.
But, O my soul, sink not into despair,
Virtue is near thee, and with gentle hand
Would now embrace thee, hovers o'er thine head.
Fain would the heav'n-born soul with her converse,
Then seek, then court her for her promis'd bliss.

Auspicious queen, thine heav'nly pinions spread,
And lead celestial Chastity along;
Lo! now her sacred retinue descends,
Array'd in glory from the orbs above.
Attend me, Virtue, thro' my youthful years!
O leave me not to the false joys of time!
But guide my steps to endless life and bliss.
Greatness, or Goodness, say what I shall call thee,
To give me an higher appellation still,

Teach me a better strain, a nobler lay,
O thou, enthron'd with Cherubs in the realms of day!

Source: Phillis Wheatley, *Poems on Various Subjects, Religious and Moral* (Albany, NY: Barber & Southwick, 1793; reprinted from London edition), p. 12.

Study: Henry Louis Gates, Jr., *The Trials of Phillis Wheatley: America's First Black Poet and her Encounters with the Founding Fathers* (New York: Basic Books, 2003).

5. Musical Instruction

By the mid-eighteenth century, American provincial cities had musical instructors and dancing masters who in addition to teaching the better sort the arts required of European gentlemen and gentlewomen also transmitted, more generally, standards of European civility to the colonies. But smaller places developed their own vernacular musical and celebratory traditions, associated with religious services, tavern singing, and festive occasions. The first excerpt below is a New York newspaper advertisement. The second comes from a popular British advice book for young women.

William Charles Hulet, Advertisement for Music Lessons, 1770

The Guitar, Taught by W. C. Hulet, Dancing-Master, who has opened his Public Dancing-School, at his House in Broad Street, near the Corner of Beaver-Street, at Three o'Clock in the Afternoon; and an Evening School for such Ladies and Gentlemen, who cannot attend in Day-time. Likewise Hours set apart for such as would chuse to be taught in private. He flatters himself, that the Performance of several of his Scholars, has convinced the judicious and impartial, of his Abilities as a Master.

He teaches the Minuet and Country Dances, by the Whole, by the Month, or Quarter; And likewise the Violin, German-Flute, and Use of the Small-Sword.

N.B. The great Advantage that many Gentlemen have over others (that have not lern'd the Hornpipe) in Country Dancing, has induced Mr. Hulet to pen a private School for such Gentlemen, who may chuse to attend.

Source: *New-York Gazette and the Weekly Mercury*, October 15, 1770.

Young Ladies Conduct, Advice on Musical Instruction, 1722

MUSICK, as it is an Entertainment Innocent and Diverting, so it is a *Science* that within these few Years, hath arrived at great Perfection; so it is every

Day improving in the Kingdom: The *Harpsicord, Spinnet, Lute* and *Base Violin,* are Instruments most agreeable to the Ladies: There are some others that really are unbecoming the Fair Sex; as the *Flute, Violin* and *Hautboy;* the last of which is too Manlike, and would look indecent in a Woman's Mouth; and the *Flute* is very improper, as taking away too much of the Juices, which are otherwise more necessarily employ'd, to promote the Appetite, and assist Digestion. Musick is certainly a very great Accomplishment to the Ladies; it refines the Taste, polishes the Mind; and is an Entertainment, without other Views, that preserves them from the Rust of idleness, that most pernicious Enemy of Virtue.

Source: John Essex, *The Young Ladies Conduct: or, Rules for Education, under Several Heads; with Instructions upon Dress, both before and after Marriage. And Advice for Young Wives* (London, 1722), pp. 84–5.

Study: Cynthia Adams Hoover, "Music and Theater in the Lives of Eighteenth-Century Americans," in Cary Carson, Ronald Hoffman, and Peter J. Albert, eds., *Of Consuming Interests: The Style of Life in the Eighteenth Century* (Charlottesville: University of Virginia Press, 1994), pp. 307–53.

Discussion Questions

1　What does Colden's letter to Collinson suggest about the way wealthier colonists thought about their relationship to Great Britain? In what ways was an interest in botany "cultural capital" in Colden's efforts to be taken seriously by his British correspondent? How do you explain his willingness to involve women (including his daughter) in the world of scientific inquiry?

2　Review the range of reading material in the three selections concerning books. What do they suggest about the relationship of reading to class and gender? Does Esther Edwards Burr's reading also serve as "cultural capital" for her (and with whom)?

3　Select a work from Popple's inventory and explain what its interest might have been to Popple. Select one as well from the Philadelphia bookseller's catalog and explain what its interest might have been to a Philadelphian with enough money to afford such a book.

4　Why might colonists have been eager to participate in the observation of the transit of Venus? What does this newspaper story suggest about the breadth of scientific curiosity in colonial America?

5　How would you explain Phillis Wheatley's emphasis in her poetry on religious and moral themes? How do you think whites in Britain and America responded to the poetry of a black colonial?

Chapter 16   The Great War for Empire

1. Seven Years War Begins: George Washington to John Augustine Washington, 1754

George Washington wrote in 1754 to his half brother, John Augustine Washington, about coming under (French) fire for the first time in his life. Virginia's royal governor had sent George to the Ohio River Valley country to scare the French fur traders out of an area that the Virginians consider their own, and to force the Indian peoples of the region to switch their allegiance to the Virginians. This ambush of the French encampment effectively began the Seven Years War in the colonies.

[Camp in the Great Meadows, Pa., 31 May 1754]

Dear John,

Since my last we have arrived at this place, where 3 days agoe we had an engagemt wth the French that is, betwccn a party of theirs & Ours; Most of our men were out upon other detachments, so that I had scarcely 40 men under my Command, and about 10, or a doz. Indians, nevertheless we obtained a most signal Victory. The Battle lasted abt 10, or 15 minutes, sharp firing on both sides, when the French gave ground & run, but to no great purpose; there were 12 killed, among which was Monsr De Jumonville the Commandr, & taken 21 prisoners with whom are Monsieurs La Force, Druillong, together with 2 Cadets. I have sent them to his Honr the Governor at Winchester conducted by Lieut. West & a guard of 20 men. We had but one man killed,

2 or 3 wounded and a great many more within an Inch of being shoo; among the wounded on our side was Lieut. Waggoner, but no danger will ensue.

We expect every Hour to be attacked by a superior Force, but shall if they stay one day longer be prepared for them; We have already got Intrenchments & are about a Pallisado'd Fort, which will I hope be finished today. The Mingo's have struck the French & I hope will give a good blow before they have done, I expect 40 odd of them here to night, wch with our Fort and some reinforcements from Colo. Fry, will enable us to exert our Noble Courage with Spirit. I am Yr Affe Bror

   Geo. Washington

I fortunately escaped without a wound, tho' the right Wing where I stood was exposed to & received all the Enemy's fire and was the part where the man was killed & the rest wounded. I can with truth assure you, I heard Bulletts whistle and believe me there was something charming in the sound.

Note. George II, the British monarch during the Seven Years War, who read this letter after it was published in August 1754 in the *London Magazine*, reputedly observed, "He would not say so, if he had been used to hear many."

Source: W. W. Abbot, ed., *The Papers of George Washington, Colonial Series* (Charlottesville, VA: University Press of Virginia, 1983), I, 118–119.

Study: Edward G. Lengel, *General George Washington: A Military Life* (New York: Random House, 2005).

2. Description of the Battle of Ticonderoga, July 1758

William Pitt's appointment as Britain's war leader helped change British fortunes in the Seven Years War. Pitt spent enormous amounts of money subsidizing British allies on the continent and campaigns by British and colonial forces in America. The initial campaign, however, taken under the authority of his ministry, James Abercromby's assault on the forces of the Marquis de Montcalm at Ticonderoga in New York, was a disaster, as Abercromby's men attempted a frontal assault on the French positions. David Perry participated in the battle, and years later, recounted his experiences in the "French War" and the American Revolution. The excerpt comes from his 1822 memoir.

This year, in August, I was sixteen years old; at which age the young lads of that day were called into training-bands. In the spring of 1758, I was warned to training and there were recruiting officers on the parade ground, to enlist men for the next campaign. I enlisted into Capt. Job Winslow's company of Col. Prebble's regiment, to serve eight months. – People said I would not "pass muster," as I was small of my age; but there was no difficulty about that. When the company was full, we marched first to Worcester, staid there a few days, and then marched to Old Hadley. We remained there about a week. From this place we crossed the river to Northampton, where we drew five days' provisions – left the place in the afternoon, and encamped a few miles out of town, in the woods for the night. In that day there were no human habitations from Northampton, to within ten miles of Albany.... We had no other road than marked trees to direct our course–no bridges on which to cross streams; some of which we waded; others we passed on trees felled by our men; and for five successive nights we lay on the ground. We arrived at Greenbush, and, after a few days' tarry marched up the North River to a place called Setackuk, where the Indians had driven off, captured, or destroyed the inhabitants. We here took a number of horses to draw cannon to Lake George, but not having horses enough, some of the cannon were drawn by men.... When we arrived at the Lake, the army, consisting of British and Americans, amounted to about 20,000 men.... We encamped there until boats and provisions enough we collected to carry us across the Lake, with cannon, etc., to attack Ticonderoga....

Major Rodgers, with his Rangers was the first to land. He was joined by Lord Howe and his party, and we proceeded but a short distance into the woods, before we were met by the enemy, and a brisk fire ensued. It was the first engagement I had ever seen, and the whistling of balls, and roar of musketry terrified me not a little. At length our regiment formed among the trees, behind which the men kept stepping from their ranks for shelter. Col. Prebble, who I well remember, was a harsh man, swore he would knock the first man down who should step out of his ranks, which greatly surprised me, to think that I must stand still to be shot at. Pretty soon, however, they brought some wounded Frenchmen; and when I came to see the blood run so freely, it put new life into me. The battle proved a sore one for us. Lord Howe and a number of other good men, were killed.

The army moved on that day to within a short distance of the enemy, and encamped for the night. In the morning, we had orders to move forward again, in a column three deep, in order to storm the enemy's breast-works, known in this country by the name of "the Old French Lines." Our orders were to "run to the breast-work, and get in if we could." But their lines were full, and they killed our men so fast, that we could not gain it. We got behind trees, logs and stumps, and covered ourselves as we could from the enemy's fire. The ground was strewed, with the dead and dying. It happened that I got behind a white-oak stump, which was so small that I had to lay on my side, and stretch myself; the balls striking the ground within a hand's breadth of me every moment, and I could hear the men screaming, and see them dying all around me. I lay there some time. A man could not stand erect, without being hit, any more than he could stand out in a shower, without having drops of rain fall upon him; for the balls came by handsfull. It was a clear day–a little air stirring. Once in a while the enemy would cease firing a minute or two, to have the smoke clear away, so that they might take better aim. In one of these intervals I sprang from my perilous situation and gained a stand which I thought would be more secure, behind a large pine log, where several of my comrades had already taken shelter, but the balls came here as thick as ever. One of the men raised his head a little above the log, and a ball struck him in the center of the forehead and tore up his scalp clear back into the crown... We lay there till near sunset and, not receiving orders from any officer, the men crept off, leaving all the dead and most of the wounded...

We got away the wounded of our company; but left a great many crying for help, which we unable to afford them I suppose, that as soon as we left the ground, the enemy let loose his Indians upon them: for none of those that we left behind were ever heard of afterwards. We started back to our boats without any orders, and pushed out on the Lake for the night. We left between 6 and 7,000 in killed and wounded on the field of battle, which I believe is a greater number than ever was lost on our side, in one day in all the battles that have been fought in America.

Source: David Perry, "Recollections of an Old Soldier: The Life of Captain David Perry, A Soldier of the French and Revolutionary Wars... Written by Himself" (Windsor, VT, 1822), pp. 8–13.

Study: Fred Anderson, *Crucible of War: The Seven Years' War and the Fate of the Empire in British North America, 1754–1766* (New York: Vintage Books, 2000).

3. Pontiac's Rebellion: Captain George Etherington to Major Henry Gladwin, Michilimackinac, June 12, 1763

Pontiac's Rebellion broke out in the aftermath of the Seven Years War. Native Americans were angered by the trading terms imposed by the British, and realized that the British victory over the French only made their own lands more vulnerable to settlement. Historians speculate that as warfare and diplomacy came to dominate Native American life, women's role in the consensual governance of tribal affairs was undercut, but here we see the part they played in a successful assault on a British outpost in the Ohio River Valley.

Sir

Notwithstanding what I wrote you in my last that all the Savages were arrived, and that every thing seemed in perfect Tranquility, yet on the 2nd Instant the Chipawas who live in a plain near this Fort Assembled to play ball as they had done almost every day since their arrival, they played from Morning till Noon then throwing their Ball close to the Gate & observing Lieut.[s] Leslie & me a few Paces out of it, they came behind us, seized, & carried us into the Woods.

In the mean time the rest rush'd into the Fort, where they found their Squaws whom they had previously planted there with their Hatchets hid under their Blankets, which they took & in an Inst. kill'd Lieut. Gamet & fifteen Rank & File, a Trader named Tracy, they wounded two & took the rest of the Garrison Prisoners five of which they have since killd. They made Prisoners of all the English Traders and robb'd them of every thing they had, but they offered no violence to any of the Persons or Properties of the French Men.

When this Massacre was over Messrs Langlade & Farli the Interpreter came down to the place where Lieut.[s] Leslie and me were Prisoners, & on their giving themselves a Security to return us when Demanded they obtained leave for us to go to the Fort under a Guard of Savages, which gave time by the Assistance of the Gentlemen above mentioned to send for the Ottawas who came down on the first Notice, and were very much displeased at what the Chipawas had done.

Since the arrival of the Ottawas they have done every thing in their power to Serve us and with what Prisoners the Chipawas have given them and what they have bought, I have now with me Lieut. Leslie and Eleven private & the other four of the Garrison who are yet living remain in the hands of the Chipawas. . . .

The Chipawas who are Superior in number to the Ottawas have declared in Council to them, that if they do not remove out of the Fort that they will cut off all Communication to this Post, by which mean's all the Convoy's of Merchants from Montreal, La Bay, St Joseph's and the upper Posts would perish. but if the News of your Posts being attacked (which they say was the reason they took up the Hatchet here) be false, & you can send up a Strong Reinforcement with Provisions & accompanied by some of your Savages I believe the Post may be Reestablished again . . .

Source: From photographic reproductions in the Library of Congress of records in the British Museum, Additional Manuscript 21655, folio 212 C, as transcribed in Sylvester E. Stevens and Donald Kent, *The Papers of Col. Henry Bouquet*, series 21655 (Harrisburg: Pennsylvania Historical Commission, 1943), pp. 205–6.

Study: Gregory Evans Dowd, *War under Heaven: Pontiac, the Indian Nations, and the British Empire* (Baltimore: Johns Hopkins University Press, 2002).

4. Frontier Life during Warfare: Captain Lewis Ourry (Fort Bedford) to Colonel Henry Bouquet (Fort Pitt), August 27, 1763

After the end of the Seven Years War, Pontiac, an Ottawa leader, formed alliances with other Native peoples to drive the British troops and colonial settlers out of Great Lakes and Ohio River Valley region. In the spring and summer of 1763, the Native American alliance struck at a string of British frontier forts. The letter below, from Colonel Lewis Ourry, who was in command at Ford Bedford, to Colonel Henry Bouquet, who had successfully marched to the aid of a besieged Fort Pitt, is particularly valuable for the picture it paints of life on this military frontier.

Sir,

I must begin by that which is uppermost, the Joy I share with you at the Defeat of the Savages that attempted to prevent your Convoy's getting to Fort Pitt; and the great pleasure I feel, with the rest of our Friends at your arrival there unhurt, at the same time that I simpathise with you, for the Loss of our Brethren left on the Field, and for the wounded. . . .

I have forwarded & provided Carriage for as many Women & Children as were willing to go below this Post [Fort Bedford], and indeed for a few more than were inclined. And have notified to those that chuse to Stay, that it may be on their own Bottoms, No Provisions being allowed at this Post for Women. . . .

The 19th Col[onel] Stephen arrived here with 98 Vollunteers, besides Ten Captains, Field amongst them, Some of his Parties have been very Successfull in Virginia & Maryland, in overtaking & routing Several Gangs of Savages, killing and Scalping Some Indians, and Stripping them of much Booty, Scalps, Prisoners, & Horses. . . .

Before Noon [the 20th] the Town was like a Fair. The mottled Crew of Women, Children, Drivers, Sorebacks, & Side Saddles, that flocked in, furnished, thro' the Dust that they kicked up, a diverting Scene, to those that had nothing to do with them, but to me it was far otherwise, tho' I had not much trouble with them that Day, the Sending of the Dumb Creatures to Pasture being my first Care . . . The Same Afternoon Col[onel] Stephen decamped.

The next Day being the Sabbath, was a Day for rest; nevertheless I was harrassed with many Petitions & Intreaties; and my Floor was Sprinkled partly with Mothers Tears, & partly with Children's P-ss – Distressfull Scene!

That Monday was a Day of Toil – draughting the Horses & appointing the Drivers – Matching Stubborn Women, with illnatur'ed Waggoners and impudent Strumpets with knavish Horse Masters, but finally I Started the Carravan, and the Spit-fires lay that Night at the Snake Spring.

The next morning early I sent an Officer and Party of Provincials to join & escort them to Littleton where they arrived Safe, the 24th in the forenoon, and proceeded without halting there.

Source: British Museum, Additional Manuscript 21642, folio 468, A.L.S., as transcribed in Sylvester Stevens et al., eds., *The Papers of Henry Bouquet*, 6 vols. (Harrisburg: Pennsylvania Historical and Museum Commission, 1951–94), vol. 6, ed. Louis M. Waddell, pp. 371–3.

Study: Holly A. Mayer, "From Forts to Families: Following the Army into Western Pennsylvania, 1758–1766," *The Pennsylvania Magazine of History and Biography*, cxxx (January 2006), 5–43.

Discussion Questions

1 Reading the four documents, what generalizations can you make about the nature of warfare in North America in the mid-eighteenth century?
2 Do Washington's comments suggest he was foolhardy, brave, or lucky? What do they suggest about his potential for future military leadership? How would you characterize the British actions in the battle at Ticonderoga – foolhardy, brave, or stupid?
3 Native American peoples played a major role in the Seven Years War. How successfully had they adapted to European ways of fighting? How successfully had Europeans and Americans adapted to Native American ways of fighting?
4 What does Ourry's military correspondence tell us about the way war affected women on the frontier?

Bibliography

This bibliography is meant to be suggestive rather than exhaustive, and except for the first two categories is limited to three representative books for each topic covered in this reader.

Document Collections

Robert Allison, *The Interesting Narrative of the Life of Olaudah Equiano* (1995).

Edward G. Gray, *Colonial America: A History in Documents* (2003).

Allen Greer, *The Jesuit Relations: Natives and Missionaries in Seventeenth-Century North America* (2000).

Evan Haefeli, and Kevin Sweeny, eds., *Captive Histories: English, French and Native Narratives of the 1704 Deerfield Raid* (2006).

Karen Ordahl Kupperman, ed., *Captain John Smith: A Select Edition of his Writings* (1988).

Jill Lepore, *Encounters in the New World: A History in Documents* (2000).

Billy G. Smith and Richard Wojtowicz, eds., *Blacks who Stole Themselves: Advertisements for Runaways in the Pennsylvania Gazette, 1728–1790* (1989).

Surveys

W. J. Eccles, *Canadian Frontier, 1534–1760* (1983).

David Hackett Fischer, *Albion's Seed: Four British Folkways in America* (1989).

Peter Charles Hoffer, *The Brave New World: A History of Early America* (2000).

Part I: Beginnings

English and African Background

Christopher Hill, *The World Turned Upside Down: Radical Ideas during the English Revolution* (1972).

Peter Laslett, *The World We Have Lost: England Before the Industrial Age* (1984).

John Thornton, *Africa and Africans in the Making of the Atlantic World, 1400–1800* (1998).

Images of the New World

Stephen Greenblatt, *Marvelous Possessions: The Wonder of the New World* (1991).

Peter Hulton, *America 1585: The Complete Drawings of John White* (1984).

Gordon Sayre, *Les Sauvages Americains: Representations of Native Americans in French and English Colonial Literature* (1997).

Native American Lives

Inga Clendinnen, *Ambivalent Conquests: Maya and Spaniard in Yucatan, 1517–1570* (1987).

Karen Ordahl Kupperman, *Indians & English: Facing Off in Early America* (2000).

Daniel K. Richter, *Facing East from Indian Company: A Native History of Early America* (2001).

Borderlands

James Brooks: *Captives and Cousins: Slavery, Kinship and Community in the Southwest Borderlands* (2002).

Steven Hackel, *Children of Coyote, Missionaries of Saint Francis: Indian–Spanish Relations in Colonial California, 1769–1850* (2005).

Bruce G. Trigger, *Natives and Newcomers: Canada's "Heroic Age" Reconsidered* (1985).

Founding Colonies

Charles McLain Andrews, *The Colonial Period of American History*, 4 vols. (1934–8).

Donna Merwick, *The Shame and the Sorrow: Dutch–Amerindian Encounters in New Netherlands* (2006).

Gary B. Nash, *Quakes and Politics: Pennsylvania, 1681–1726* (1968).

Northern Colonies: The Middle Colonies, New England, and British Canada

William Cronon, *Changes in the Land: Indians, Colonists, and the Ecology of New England* (1983).
James Deetz, *In Small Things Forgotten: The Archeology of Early American Life* (1996).
Philip J. Greven, Jr., *Four Generations: Population, Land, Family in Colonial Andover, Massachusetts* (1970).

Southern Colonies: Chesapeake, Carolinas, and the Caribbean

Kathleen M. Brown, *Good Wives, Nasty Wenches, and Anxious Patriarchs: Gender, Race and Power in Colonial Virginia* (1996).
Sidney W. Mintz, *Sweetness and Power: The Place of Sugar in Modern History* (1985).
Edmund Morgan, *American Slavery, American Freedom: The Ordeal of Colonial Virginia* (1975).

Part II: The Eighteenth Century

Politics

Richard Bushman, *The Varieties of Political Experience in Eighteenth-Century America* (2004).
Stanley Katz, *Newcastle's New York: Anglo-American Politics, 1732–1753* (1968).
Charles S. Sydnor, *Gentlemen Freeholders: Political Practices in Washington's Virginia* (1952), republished as *American Revolutionaries in the Making*.

Economy

Bernard Bailyn, *The New England Merchants in the Seventeenth Century* (1955).
Richard Dunn, *Sugar and Slaves: The Rise of the Planter Class in the English West Indies, 1624–1713* (1972).
John J. McCusker and Russell R. Menard, *The Economy of British America, 1607–1789* (1985).

Empire

David Armitage, *The Ideological Origins of the British Empire* (2000).
Linda Colley, *Britons: Forging the Nation, 1707–1837* (1992).
E. J. Marshall, ed., *The Oxford History of the British Empire*, vol. 2: *The Eighteenth Century* (1998).

Slavery

Philip D. Curtin, *The Atlantic Slave Trade: A Census* (1969).

Winthrop D. Jordan, *White Over Black: American Attitudes Toward the Negro, 1550–1812* (1968).

Philip Morgan, *Slave Counterpoint: Black Culture in the Eighteenth-Century Chesapeake and Lowcountry* (1998).

Everyday Life

Lois G. Carr, Lorena Walsh, and Russell R. Menard, *Robert Cole's World: Agriculture and Society in Early Maryland* (1991).

David Freeman Hawke, *Everyday Life in Early America* (1988).

Rhys Isaac, *The Transformation of Virginia, 1740–1790* (1982).

Family and Gender Relations

Sharon Block, *Rape and Sexual Power in Early America* (2006).

Kristen Fischer, *Suspect Relations: Sex, Race and Resistance in Colonial North Carolina* (2002).

Laurel Thatcher Ulrich, *Good Wives: Image and Reality in the Lives of Women in Northern New England, 1650–1750* (1982).

Religion

Patricia U. Bonomi, *Under the Cope of Heaven: Religion, Society and Politics in Colonial America* (1986).

Jon Butler, *Awash in a Sea of Faith: Christianizing the American People* (1990).

David D. Hall, *Worlds of Wonder, Days of Judgment: Popular Religious Belief in Early New England* (1989).

Culture

Hugh Amory and David D. Hall, eds., *The Colonial Book in the Atlantic World* (2000).

Margaretta Lovell, *Art in a Season of Revolution: Painters, Artisans, and Patrons in Early America* (2005).

Susan Scott Parrish, *American Curiosity: Cultures of Natural History in the Colonial British Atlantic World* (2006).

The Great War for Empire

Fred Anderson, *Crucible of War: The Seven Years' War and the Fate of Empire in British North America, 1754–1766* (2000).

Colin Calloway, *The Scratch of a Pen: 1763 and the Transformation of America* (2006).

Richard White, *The Middle Ground: Indians, Empires, and Republics in the Great Lakes Region, 1650–1815* (1991).

Index